D1240194

Accounting For Horror

Accounting For Horror

Post-Genocide Debates in Rwanda

Nigel Eltringham

Pluto Press

LONDON

First published 2004 by
Pluto Press
345 Archway Road, London N6 5AA

www.plutobooks.com

British Library Cataloguing in Publication Data
A catalogue record for this book is available from the British Library

ISBN 978 0 7453 2000 7 paperback

Library of Congress Cataloging in Publication Data
    Accounting for horror : post-genocide debates in Rwanda / Nigel
Eltringham.
        p. cm.
Includes bibliographical references.
    ISBN 0–7453–2001–5 — ISBN 0–7453–2000–7 (pbk.)
    1. Genocide—Rwanda. 2. Rwanda—History—Civil War,
1994—Atrocities. 3. Rwanda—Ethnic relations. 4. Tutsi (African
people)—Crimes against—Rwanda. I. Title.
    DT450.435 .E47 2004
    967.57104'31—dc22
                                                          2003018192

10   9   8   7   6   5   4   3   2   1

Designed and produced for Pluto Press by
Chase Publishing Services, Fortescue, Sidmouth, EX10 9QG, England
Typeset from disk by Stanford DTP Services, Northampton, England
Printed on demand in the EU by
CPI Antony Rowe, Chippenham and Eastbourne, England

To the memory of
Olive Jepson

Contents

Acknowledgements

The completion of this book was made possible by a scholarship from the Harold Hyam Wingate Foundation and a post-doctoral fellowship from the Economic and Social Research Council (UK).

I owe a debt of gratitude to a number of people for their generosity: Olive Jepson; my parents Jill and Peter; Sally and Peter Dodgson; and Tim and Judith Eltringham.

For encouragement, thanks go to Peter Gandy; Andrew and Audrey Hughes; and Nile and Nushin Green-Arbabzadah.

I am very grateful to a number of people for their hospitality: Dave and Anne Osterwind in Rwanda; Sue, Fritz, Esther and Myriam Zysset in Switzerland; Yves Capdeboscq in France; and Martin and Bekki Clark in the UK.

Thanks go to René Lemarchand, Saskia van Hoyweghen, Richard Fardon, Mauro de Lorenzo, Lissa Malkki, James Fairhead, Nayanika Mookherjee, Yvonne Kyriakides, Damian Walter, Sam Cyuma, Tom Kennedy, Linda Melvern, Ian Linden and Mukulika Banerjee for providing insightful comments on draft chapters. Special thanks go to Roger van Zwanenberg, Julie Stoll and Robert Webb at Pluto Press. Thanks also go to Isobel Nash for transcribing interviews. The ongoing encouragement, advice and overall support of Johan Pottier has been invaluable from the outset.

Thanks go to the numerous Rwandese in Rwanda and Europe (whose request for anonymity has been respected) who gave their time and trust to discuss what can only ever be a painful subject. I am especially mindful of those who have since been killed.

The completion of the book would not have been possible without the selfless support and encouragement of my wife Anna to whom I am forever indebted for many things.

Any errors are entirely my own.

London 2003

Abbreviations

AFDL	Alliance des forces démocratiques pour la libération du Congo-Zaire
AI	Amnesty International
AMASASU	Alliance des militaires agacés par les séculaires actes sournois des unaristes
APROSOMA	Association pour la Promotion Sociale de la Masse
AR	African Rights
ARDHO	Association Rwandaise pour la Défense des Droits de l'Homme
BBTG	Broad-Based Transitional Government
CDC	Comité de Concertation de Partis Politique Démocratiques
CDR	Coalition pour la Défense de la République (Coalition for the Defence of the Republic)
CLADHO	Collectif des Ligues et Associations de Défense des Droits de l'Homme
CNN	Cable News Network
DRC	Democratic Republic of Congo (formerly Zaïre)
FAR	Forces Armées Rwandaises (Rwandan armed forces prior to July 1994)
FAZ	Forces Armées Zaïroises
FDC	Forces Démocratiques du Changement
FIDH	Fédération Internationale des Ligues des Droits de l'Homme
FPD	Forum Paix et Démocratie
FRODEBU	Front Démocratique du Burundi
HRW	Human Rights Watch
ICG	International Crisis Group
ICTR	International Criminal Tribunal for Rwanda
ICTY	International Criminal Tribunal for the Former Yugoslavia
IDP	Internally Displaced Person
IRC	International Red Cross
IRIN	Integrated Regional Information Network for Central and Eastern Africa (United Nations: Office for the Co-ordination of Humanitarian Affairs)

MDR	Mouvement Démocratique Républicain
MDR-Parmehutu	Mouvement Démocratique Républicain – Parti du Mouvement de l'Émancipation Hutu
MNF	Multinational Intervention Force
MRND	Mouvement Révolutionnaire National pour le Développement
MRND(D)	Mouvement Républicain National pour le Développement et la Démocratie
MSF	Médecins sans Frontières
MSM	Mouvement Social Muhutu
NGO	Non-Governmental Organisation
NRA	National Resistance Army (Uganda)
ORINFOR	Office Rwandais de l'Information
PDC	Parti Démocratique Chrétien
PHR	Physicians for Human Rights
PL	Parti Libéral
PSD	Parti Social-Démocrate
RADER	Rassemblement Démocratique Rwandais
RANU	Rwandan Alliance for National Unity
RPA	Rwandan Patriotic Army
RPF	Rwandan Patriotic Front
RTLM	Radio Télévision Libre des Milles Collines
UN	United Nations
UNAMIR	United Nations Assistance Mission in Rwanda
UNAR	Union Nationale Rwandaise
UNCE	UN Commission of Experts (1994)
UNDPKO	United Nations Department of Peacekeeping Operations
UNGA	United Nations General Assembly
UNGC	United Nations Convention on the Prevention and Punishment of the Crime of Genocide (1948)
UNHCHR	United Nations High Commission for Human Rights
UNHCR	The United Nations High Commission for Refugees
UNSC	United Nations Security Council
UNSG	United Nations Secretary-General
UPRONA	Parti de l'Unité et du Progrès National (Burundi)
USCR	United States Committee for Refugees

Preface

Appreciating scale. I am looking into a room. On the floor, 'looking' directly at me, are countless, tightly packed terracotta figures (between 8 and 25 cm tall). Each figure is hand-crafted, each is different. This is the installation 'Field for the British Isles' by British artist Antony Gormley. Is this a way to appreciate the human scale of the Rwandan genocide? No, for what appears infinite, what cannot be taken in wholly, amounts to only 40,000 figures. In 1994, in four and a half months (a hundred days), at least twelve times as many ethnic Tutsi (500,000–800,000) were murdered in Rwanda.

How does one 'account' for such an event? 'Account' both in the sense of 'to account for' (to provide adequate explanation) and 'account' as in 'provide a processual narrative'. To an extent, 'devastation of such proportions' destroys our 'ability to imagine it' (Bartov 1998: 798). We are required to reduce it 'to a more manageable size and more conventional nature, so that the mind can take it in rather than totally blot it out' (ibid. 799). The question remains, however, whether in making things 'manageable' and achieving some sense of order we inadvertently (re)deploy the same ways of 'worldimagining' upon which perpetrators of genocide rely. Our attempts to 'account' must be tempered by a recognition that genocide itself 'disorders explicitly for a ... *reordering* purpose' (Apter 1997: 5; emphasis added).

Between 1995 and 1998, I worked for an NGO in Rwanda engaged in various 'conciliatory' projects. This experience required that I generate my own 'account' of the 1994 genocide, its causes and aftermath. Constant themes in Rwandese 'accounting' laid the basis for further research, and those themes provide the subjects of the following chapters. This book is not, therefore, simply a reflection on Rwandan accounts, but an exploration of how my own accounting merges and diverges with that of Rwandese, whose own accounts merge and diverge with each other and with those of non-Rwandan 'commentators' (journalists, academics, lawyers and human rights advocates).

The book draws on interviews conducted in Rwanda in 1998. Two groups were interviewed: officials of the Rwandan government (including ministers, ministerial officials and presidential advisers);

and representatives of 'civil society', including officials from various domestic NGOs, from the Roman Catholic Church, various Protestant denominations and the Rwandan press. Where those interviewed are referred to as 'returnee', this indicates that the respondent had returned to Rwanda after the 1994 genocide.

In 1999, interviews were conducted among Rwandese resident in Europe. The majority of these were 'in exile' (unable or unwilling to return to Rwanda). Those interviewed included former government ministers, former officials of Rwandan NGOs and former Rwandan journalists. It must be emphasised that none of the Rwandese interviewed in Europe are accused of inciting or participating in the 1994 genocide. A number of Rwandese not 'in exile' but who were either resident in Europe or in transit were also interviewed.

The majority of those interviewed requested anonymity. On one hand, this deprives the reader of being able to situate actors. And yet, it is unlikely that the use of 'proper names' would capture the multidimensional nature of actor identity any better than generic terms ('Rwandan academic' or 'Rwandan NGO worker').

To some readers, a concentration on the debates (the 'mere' words) of an élite class may be considered too narrow: what about 'ordinary' Rwandese? This book takes as its starting point the recognition that the 1994 genocide was a 'deliberate choice of a modern élite to foster hatred and fear to keep itself in power' (HRW & FIDH 1999: 1). The genocide was set in motion, continued and obfuscated by 'speech acts': verbal activity that constitutes action (Chilton 1997: 175). One must recognise that 'The violence is in the words before being in the acts' (Chrétien et al. 1995: 307). This book is based on the simple recognition that:

> Words can kill – or at least motivate a person to kill. It is through language that the primal impulses, the likes and dislikes, the hatreds and enmities, the stereotypes and degrading and dehu-manising characterisations of those who are not desirable or are rivals for political or economic power or status, are transmitted ... words are the carriers of deeds. (Hirsch 1995: 97)

The 'words that killed' were uttered by a visible set of actors: journalists, leaders of political parties, government officials and those who claimed to represent 'civil society'. It is appropriate, therefore, to place the focus on the manner in which the successor class (and its exile shadow) try to account for the horror of 1994, because if 'verbal communication is essential to the initiation and conduct of conflict, so it is essential to its prevention, resolution and conclusion' (Chilton 1997: 188). One must appreciate that 'There is the conflict itself, and there is the meta-conflict – the conflict about the nature of the conflict' and that it is among a visible political class (not 'ordinary' Rwandese) that this meta-conflict is played out (Horowitz 1991: 2).

Focusing on an élite also takes its lead from the contemporary political class inside Rwanda. This class places responsibility for 1994 on its predecessor, often citing the Swahili proverb, 'When elephants fight the grass gets hurt.' The contemporary political class in Rwanda clearly considers élite conduct critical.

In a sense, competing élite groups are never as homogeneous as the elephant metaphor implies. Likewise, this image of a monolithic duel (dual) conflict may obscure shared assumptions and practices deployed by both parties. There may also be continuity between the past conflict and current 'accounting', regarding the use of 'Certain modes of thought, logics, themes, styles of expression' (Peet & Watts 1993: 16) and 'analogies, historical references, clichés, appeals to collective fears, or senses of guilt' (Hajer 1995: 63; see Storey 2000).

The character of 'debates' considered here is heterogeneous and shifting. There are moments of clear opposition and of shared substance, and moments where dialogue suddenly becomes monologue as certain assertions are greeted with silence. And yet, throughout it all one detects shared assumptions, practices and epistemologies. Beyond substantive dissension there is consensus regarding not only what is worthy of debate, but how assertions should be made in order to be mutually evaluated.

The intention of this book is not to be 'corrective', gleefully pointing out the 'errors' of those who 'account'. No one, especially myself, speaks or writes from a final position, from an 'Archimedean point'. We should be wary of final accounts 'that purport to set the record straight' (Clifford 1986: 18). After all, 'There is no whole picture that can be "filled in", since the perception and filling of a gap lead to the awareness of other gaps' (ibid.). The Rwandan genocide 'will always defy all but partial and contradictory understanding' (C. Taylor 1999: 185).

At a general level, this book is self-consciously partial, choosing not to deal with (except in passing) three issues discussed by Rwandese but considered in detail elsewhere: international complicity and failure (see Melvern 2000; Power 2002); the role of religious institutions (see Van Hoyweghen 1996; Longman 1998; Eltringham 2000), and socio-economic development (see Uvin 1998).

Genocide is an absolutist exercise, one that seeks 'to achieve complete clarity' (Appadurai 1998: 915). Our response is absolute: condemnation. Our continuing position is absolute: the condemnation of impunity. But, we must also condemn the absolutes on which genocide perpetrators rely: the absolutist schema of social distinction that they project on to society and the absolutist version of history to which they appeal.

Ultimately, this book is a reflection on the nature and continuity of absolutist ways of envisaging society. It is based on a recognition that seeking and/or imposing absolute clarity is both the cause of *and* a response to genocide. As such, this introduction has resisted reducing the theme of the book to a single assertion. Instead, it takes as its starting point an observation by a Tutsi *rescapé*, which demonstrates the challenge for all who try to account for what is a 'tangled skein of order and disorder' (C. Taylor 1999: 29).

The oracle of Delphi in ancient Greece – so goes the anecdote – had a knot that had defied all the cunning and abilities of everybody of that time. No one had ever managed to undo the knot as whoever tried the test always ended up giving up because of the complexities in the knot. Then one day King Alexander the Great was presented with the knot and challenged to undo it in the shortest time. Alexander took the knot, turned it around, and started undoing it. As for everybody before, the more he untied it, the more complicated it became. Finally, impatient with unsuccessful attempts, Alexander opted for the easiest way out: he took his sword and cut the knot through, thus solving the puzzle in the most expedient manner.

This is a good representation of how the human mind works: whenever faced with a very complex and complicated case, it looks for ways of simplification. For instance, whenever people look at the Rwandan tragedy, they always ask you to narrow down the problem into a simple equation, easy to grasp in one hearing. Failure to do so is often taken either as hiding something or simply complicating a matter that in itself should be easy to understand. The truth, however, is always like the elephant in the blind men's story. Asked to identify what an elephant is, the blind men come up with different answers depending on what part of the elephant they had touched. The one who touched the side thought the elephant was a big wall, the one who touched the leg took it for a big tree, the one who touched the tusk thought an elephant was just a dry branch, while the one who touched the large trunk said it was a long, soft hose. But the truth was just there in the middle – as big as an elephant!

Many have looked and still look at the Rwandan tragedy as the result of ethnic hatred, others as the consequence of bad politics and power struggle; some take it for the direct outcome of colonial and neo-imperialist manipulations, while others take it to be the outlet of socio-economic frustrations, and so on. Blind men with a big elephant in the middle to identify! And the truth again is there in the middle – as big as all those elements put together. (Rwandan Protestant Church worker, personal communication, Kigali, March 1998)

1
'Ethnicity':
The Permeant Debate

In his report of 11 August 1993, Bacre Waly Ndiaye (UNHCHR Special Rapporteur for Extrajudicial, Summary or Arbitrary Executions) stated:

> The cases of intercommunal violence brought to the Special Rapporteur's attention indicate very clearly that the victims of the attacks, Tutsis in the overwhelming majority of cases, have been targeted solely because of their membership of a certain ethnic group, and for no other objective reason. Article II, paragraphs (a) and (b), [of the Genocide Convention] might therefore be considered to apply to these cases ... The violations of the right to life, as described in this report, could fall within the purview of article III of the convention. (UN 1993 paras 78–80; see HRW et al. 1993: 49–50)

Noting the involvement of state officials in the killings and the role of *Radio Rwanda* (the official state radio), Ndiaye finished the section entitled 'The Genocide Question' with a warning to all engaged in inciting violence by reproducing (without comment) Article IV of the UN Convention on the Prevention and Punishment of the Crime of Genocide (UNGC): 'Persons committing genocide or any of the other acts ... shall be punished, whether they are constitutionally responsible rulers, public officials or private individuals.'

Eight months later, between 7 April and mid-July 1994, *at least* 507,000 Tutsi (HRW & FIDH 1999: 15), around 77 per cent of the population registered as 'Tutsi', were murdered in state co-ordinated massacres committed by militia, the *gendarmerie* and elements of the army, often with the participation of the local population.[1]

On 6 April 1994, the Rwandan President (Juvénal Habyarimana) was returning to Kigali from a summit in Dar es Salaam when his aircraft was shot down around 8:23 p.m. This event had signalled the start of the genocide. As *de facto* custodians of the term 'genocide' the UN was slow to designate the events in Rwanda accordingly (see Melvern 2000: 152ff). On 7 April, the UNSC strongly condemned 'acts of violence' (UN 1994a). On 20 April, in a report to the UNSC, the UNSG spoke of 'a torrent of widespread killings' and observed that 'the violence appears to have both political and ethnic dimensions' whose victims 'could possibly number tens of thousands' (UN 1994b). The report, however, stated that the killings had been started by 'unruly members of the Presidential Guard' and implied that the real issue was fighting between the RPF and FAR, that a cease-fire between these two sides would end the violence. A UNSC resolution on 21 April, stated that it was 'appalled at the ensuing large-scale violence in Rwanda, which has resulted in the death of thousands of innocent civilians', but continued to associate the 'resolution of the Rwandan crisis' (the 'mindless violence and carnage which are engulfing Rwanda') with a cease-fire between the RPF and FAR (UN 1994c). In a letter to the UNSC on 29 April, the UNSG stated that 'as many as 200,000 people may have died during the last three weeks' and recognised that the fighting between the RPF and FAR was distinct from 'massacres of innocent civilians on a massive scale' caused by 'deep-rooted ethnic hatreds', although he still maintained that the massacres were due to 'uncontrolled military personnel' and the 'breakdown of law and order' (UN 1994d).

Only on 30 April, did a statement by the President of the UNSC recognise that the 'slaughter of innocent civilians [has] continued unabated *in a systematic manner* in Rwanda' (UN 1994e; emphasis added) and stated that 'the killing of members of an ethnic group with the intention of destroying such a group in whole or in part constitutes a crime punishable under international law'. The statement did not, however, contain the word 'genocide' nor refer to the convention (the UNGC) from which the clause had been extracted. Likewise, a UNSC resolution on 17 May recalled that 'the killing of members of an ethnic group with the intention of destroying such a group, in whole or in part, constitutes a crime punishable under international law' (UN 1994f) but failed to name the crime and its convention.

In his report of 19 May, the UN High Commissioner for Human Rights stated that the number of deaths so far 'may exceed 500,000' and insisted that 'All relevant international human rights instruments to which Rwanda is party, including the [UNGC] must be fully respected' (UN 1994g para 33). On 25 May, the resolution of a special session of the UNHCHR, referred to the 'systematic slaughter and massacres' in Rwanda and stated that 'the killing of members of an ethnic group, with the intention of destroying such a group in whole or in part, constitutes the crime of genocide'; that the commission believed that 'genocidal acts may have occurred in Rwanda'; and that the UNHCHR's Special Rapporteur (René Degni-Ségui) should gather information on possible violations of human rights, 'including acts of genocide' (UN 1994h).

In his report of 31 May, the UNSG stated that on 'the basis of the evidence that has emerged, there can be little doubt that the events in Rwanda constituted genocide 'since there have been large-scale killings of communities and families belonging to a particular ethnic group' (UN 1994i para 36). Despite this, in its resolution of 8 June, the UNSC stated that reports indicated that '*acts of genocide* have occurred in Rwanda' (UN 1994j; emphasis added). On 28 June, however, Degni-Ségui's report quoted verbatim Article II of the UNGC (UN 1994k paras 44–5) and concluded that 'The conditions laid down by the 1948 Convention are thus met' and that 'the term "genocide" should henceforth be used as regards the Tutsi' (ibid. para 48). Degni-Ségui called on the UN to 'Condemn the genocide perpetrated in Rwanda' and to establish an *ad hoc* international tribunal or extend the mandate of the ICTY (ibid. paras 70; 75). This position was reiterated by the UN Commission of Experts (UNCE, established by the UNSC in July 1994), who concluded in their interim report (1 October 1994) that the Tutsi had been victims of a genocide (UN 1994o paras 44; 124; 148) and that those responsible should be tried before an international criminal tribunal (ibid. paras 133–42). Subsequently, both the statute of the International Criminal Tribunal for Rwanda (ICTR) (Article II, UN 1994q) and Rwanda's domestic law (1996) regarding genocide[2] define the crime according to the UNGC.

GENOCIDE: LEGAL AND LAY MEANINGS

From its inception, the UNGC has been subjected to criticism, described as 'a purely political ploy' (Bauer 1998: 33) and 'a rhetorical rather than a juridical device' (Novick 2001: 101). Everything from the definition of target groups, the scope of acts deemed genocidal, who can be considered 'a perpetrator' and how to locate intent have been treated to exhaustive examination (Fein 1993: 8; see Freeman 1991: 185).[3] Although this, primarily, sociological literature often directs its critique towards the UNGC, one senses that the real gulf is between universal legal definitions and the context-specificity of social science. Clifford Geertz, for example, talks of the 'skeletonisa-tion' and 'sterilisation' of fact in legal processes (or at least in Western *jurisprudence*), that legal processes are 'a distinctive manner of imagining the real', which produce 'close-edited diagrams of reality' (see de Sousa Santos 1987: 297). Geertz concludes that 'whatever it is the law is after, it is not the whole story' (1983: 170–3). Likewise, Yehuda Bauer denies the possibility of the 'objective stance' claimed by the law, arguing that 'the very decision to deal with some facts rather than others is in itself subjective' (1987: 209). The imperative of legal processes is 'just give us the facts' and not subjective, multiple interpretations of events (Wilson 1997: 146).

The role of social science, therefore, should be to 'restore to accounts of political violence both the surrounding social relations and an associated range of subjective meanings' (Wilson 1997: 135). As will become clear, however, the 'natural science' pretensions of social science have themselves provided both genocide perpetrators and subsequent judicial responses with 'grammars of truth' – essentialist ways of imagining social reality (Linke 1997: 562).

Michael Freeman warns social scientists that their critique of the deracinating perspective of law must be done with an awareness of the 'epistemological limits to social scientific (as to all) understanding and [that they] should write with a full awareness of the morally tainted history of scientific discourse' (1991: 195). Freeman is alluding to the role played by supposedly neutral, 'objective discourse' emanating from social science, which has *facilitated* genocide, above all the imperative to categorise social reality by 'manufacturing difference' (Hinton 1998: 14). This categorical drive of social science has provided genocide perpetrators with 'vocabularies of motive' (Alvarez 2001: 2) and 'grammars of truth' (Linke 1997: 562; see Prunier 1995: 37 n. 90). One need only recall the 'research' of German anthropologists Otmar von Verschuer, Otto Reche and Hans Gunther and their contribution to classifying 'race' in Nazi Germany, or that Josef Mengele's first degree was in anthropology (see Schafft 2002).

At the same time as recognising the danger that 'academic and scientific discourses may dehumanise the human', Freeman argues that despite its horror 'genocide is social behaviour, and it would surely be a greater moral error for social science to evade rather than to confront it' (Freeman 1991: 187–8). This confrontation must, however, recognise the false-dichotomy often drawn between the descriptive imperative of legal thinking and the 'explanatory' claims of social science. Social scientists, as much as jurists, encounter tension between their desire to provide context-specific description/ explanation and to generalise for the purposes of comparison (see

Holy 1987). Both trade precision for universality. Both are challenged to integrate the local with the global, the literal with the figurative and the objective with the subjective.

The difficulty of reconciling the literal/objective with the figurative/subjective is most pronounced in how groups targeted in genocide are defined. There is a tension between the desire to grapple the initiative from perpetrators by formulating our own independent ways of defining the targeted group and the inevitable (if unpalatable) recognition that because perpetrators define their victims we must give perpetrator definitions temporary credence. Even if we decide not to do this (for obvious reasons), we may still fall back on essentialising categories that share the same epistemological assumptions as the categories used by perpetrators: that society can (and should) be understood according to 'objective manageable schema'.

DEFINING TARGETS

[The perpetrator's] essential idea ... one which they have passed on to international opinion over the years (and even during the weeks of the genocide) is that they were engaged in an ethnic conflict of long-standing. (Chrétien et al. 1995: 127)

Influencing *all* post-genocide statements made by Rwandese is the manner in which the application of the UNGC to Rwanda has modified and/or solidified perceptions of ethnic identity. Rwandese must respond to this new, external register. Historical narratives remain the main recourse by which actors conceptualise social distinction in Rwanda (see Chapter 6), the belief that in describing ethnicity's past 'reality' is to describe its current '*actualité*'. The application of the UNGC and its use of the term 'ethnical' (left undefined) has introduced a further referent to be negotiated. The focus here is not day-to-day life in Rwanda and the role that 'ethnicity' may or may not play therein. Rather, the concern is with the interplay between abstract notions of 'ethnicity' deployed by two *visible* groups: the perpetrators of the genocide and 'international commentators' (social scientists, lawyers, journalists, diplomats).

It is often stated that Hutu, Tutsi and Twa are not, 'in reality', ethnic groups because they do not conform to the 'conventional' definition of such entities: they do not speak different languages, practise different religions, eat different foods, reside in different territories. Although this is true empirically, the juxtaposition of 'real ethnic groups' vs Rwanda assumes that a valid, single definition exists for 'ethnic groups' elsewhere. If one dismisses the question of ethnicity in relation to Rwanda, one fails to explore the relationship between *the belief* that universally definable 'ethnic groups' exist (even if not in Rwanda) and the exploitation of this form of essentialist thought by those who perpetrated the 1994 genocide.

The UNGC itself contains no definition of the four groups it seeks to protect. The meanings of national, ethnical, racial or religious groups were, perhaps, 'left unexamined, since [they were] understood to be universal and therefore not in need of interpretation' (Wilson 1997: 150).[4] What, then, does an 'ethnic group' consist of?

It is important to ask what is the *function* of defining entities as 'ethnic'. Roger Fowler summarises our 'will to categorise' as follows: 'If we imagined the world as a vast collection of individual things and people, we would be overwhelmed by detail. We manage the world, make sense of it, by categorising phenomena, including people' (1991: 92; see Staub 1989: 59). A quality like 'ethnic' is, therefore, assigned 'according to the requirements of the classifiers' (Eriksen 1996: 8). Drawing social distinctions helps the individual to 'create order in an otherwise excruciatingly complicated social universe [by dividing] the social world into kinds of people [giving] the individual the impression that he or she understands society' (Eriksen 1993: 24). Without constructed maps of *perceived* social distinction, 'life is filled with uncertainty and anxiety' (Staub 1989: 15). We appear to abhor the amorphous.

The search for categorical certainty proceeds from an ever-present disposition, a taken-for-granted assumption (or 'habit of the mind') that social distinctions are *a priori*, natural, self-evident, necessary and *always* present (see Bourdieu 1977; Bourdieu & Passeron 1977). If, however, we are to escape what René Lemarchand calls the 'confinement of the apparently obvious' (1996: 6) we must recognise that such classifications are made/invented by us: 'They are our product ... abstractions away from the concrete reality of the world of persons' (Stanton 1989: 4). The value placed on the belief that society can and *must* be understood by 'manageable schema' is exacerbated in contexts of heightened uncertainty and doubt, contexts in which genocide provides a 'macabre form of certainty' (Appadurai 1998: 909; see Freeman 1991: 190).

As an analytical tool by which one 'understands society', the assumption of a universal 'ethnic quality' evokes Max Weber's concept of the 'ideal type' and his recognition that no conceptual tool can do justice to the infinite diversity of empirical phenomena. Analysts (principally social scientists) construct an 'ideal type' by extracting and accentuating from reality what are considered to be generic or 'essential' characteristics of phenomena, synthesising them into a single, universal, abstract, heuristic construct (Weber 1949: 90). An 'ideal type' is, however, a 'mental construct [that] cannot be found empirically anywhere in reality' (ibid. 90). The analyst must only determine whether, in a particular context, an ideal type 'approximates or diverges from reality' (ibid.). The ideal type is not an end to be 'discovered' in reality, but a *means* which facilitates *contingent* comparative study. Used correctly, the analyst will *never* discover the 'ideal type' in reality. In addition, the content of an ideal type is not stable. The characteristics an analyst considers 'essential' (for a group to be considered 'ethnic') is an idiosyncratic choice. Similarly, correspondence between the analyst's choice of 'relevant' characteristics and the self-perception(s) of actors themselves is unlikely. These two perceptions are 'fundamentally different things', because identity 'exists in the minds of individuals and assumes in their minds the most multifarious nuances of form and content, clarity and meaning' (ibid. 96).

All concerned navigate the social world by means of isolating 'ethnic identity' at this level of 'ideal type'. The analytical tool of 'ethnicity' is not concerned with 'the many', but with 'the one', extrapolating to individuals the purported characteristics of an imagined, archetypal 'everyman' or 'Adam-like' figure. As such, 'ethnicity' is a universalising concept, a means 'to pass from the particular to the general' (Radcliffe-Brown 1951: 15). When we assign the quality 'ethnic' to a particular group of persons, such definitions should remain contingent 'tokens of reality which we *assume* can be redeemed' (Fardon 1987: 168; emphasis added).

Problems arise, however, when we 'misplace concreteness' (Whitehead 1967: 58) and set out to 'prove' that our abstract concepts (our 'ideal types') really do *correspond* to reality, rather than being contingent approximations. The problem is not that we classify, but 'that we treat the classifications as if they had ultimate reality. We forget that it is we who made the classifications and we treat our abstractions as if they were concrete' (Stanton 1989: 4). There is a danger that the fragile line separating the figurative and literal understanding of these concepts will collapse. It is this precariousness that perpetrators of genocide exploit, transforming our 'tokens of reality' (ethnic groups) from being qualified concepts ('what *appears* to be') to being normative concepts ('what has *always* been' or 'what *ought* to be').

ETHNICITY AND CULTURE

While it is often suggested that social distinctions emerge from an innate human propensity to distinguish 'insiders' and 'outsiders' (Us and Them),[5] one can argue that it proceeds equally from the 'innate propensity' of external analysts to distinguish between 'them' and 'them'. It has become clear that many of the 'tribal/ethnic' entities 'identified' by anthropologists in Africa *had* no empirical expression outside the mind of the ethnographer (see Southall 1970; Kuper 1988). For example, 'Abstract loyalty to, and identification with entities such as "the Nuer" [Evans-Pritchard 1940] or "the Dinka" [Lienhardt 1961] were in many cases unthinkable to the agents themselves, whose main principles of organisation were kinship and locality' (Eriksen 1993: 88; see Ranger 1994[1983]: 248).

By what criteria, therefore, would an analyst demarcate a social group as 'ethnic'? Conventionally 'ethnic' groups are said to share a 'culture', as in 'An ethnic group is generally defined as a group whose members share a common language or culture' (ICTR 1998 para 513). What, however, is 'culture'? At its most basic, we can take it to mean *observable behaviour* determined by apparently 'shared' norms and values (in itself a problematic assertion [see Holy & Stuchlik 1983: 11; Argyrou 2002; Street 1993]). In the context of 'ethnic groups', however, anthropologists Edmund Leach (1954), Michael Moerman (1965) and Fredrik Barth (1969) established that there is no necessary correspondence between perceived social distinction and observable practices. So-called 'ethnic' distinction has 'no imperative relationship with particular "objective" criteria' (Ardener 1989b: 111). Thus, 'ethnic boundaries are between whoever people think they are between' (Fardon 1987: 176).[6]

As we shall see below, this self-ascriptive construction of an 'imagined community' (B. Anderson 1983) was forestalled in Rwanda where a 'sanctioned identity' – inscribed on ID cards/birth certificates – determined one's 'ethnic' affiliation.

We should not, however, dispense with the concept of 'culture' without recognising that it began as part of the same classificatory apparatus that binds the concept of 'race' with European colonialism and ideas of social evolution. For the anthropologist Edward Tylor, 'culture' was 'that complex whole which includes knowledge, belief, art, morals, law, custom, and any other capabilities and habits acquired by man [sic] as a member of society' (1871: 1). This corresponds to 'culture' as shared norms, values and practices. Tylor's concept of culture was, however, intimately linked with a belief in social evolution. 'Culture' was the *benchmark* by which the relative progress of groups along an evolutionary chain could be assessed, 'with especial consideration of the civilisation of the lower tribes as related to the civilisation of the higher nations' (ibid.). Anthropology, therefore, was 'the science of culture', which lays down 'the lines of development along which the lowest prehistoric culture has gradually risen to the highest modern level ... placing each [culture] at its proper stage in a line of evolution' (Tylor 1893). The 'educated world' of Europe and North America set the standard by being at 'one end of the social series and savage tribes at the other, arranging the rest of mankind between these limits according as they correspond more closely to savage or to cultured life' (1871: 26). Anthropology measured progress along a line 'from grade to grade of actual savagery, barbarism, and civilisation' (1893).

Although we should avoid 'etymological fallacy', the association of 'culture' with social evolution remains pervasive. Under 'culture' my *Oxford English Dictionary* of 1987 does not refer to 'knowledge, belief, art, morals, law' and so on, but to 'improvement', 'intellectual development' and the 'particular form, stage, or type of intellectual development or civilisation'. A definition of 'ethnic group' that relies wholly on the criteria of 'culture' draws on a classificatory concept that shares epistemological roots with racism.

ETHNICITY: A SINGLE DEFINITION?

Perceived groups were/are assigned the 'ethnic quality' according to a set of archetypal 'characteristics'. In this way, the 'ethnic quality' is assigned according to a *polythetic* classification (see Needham 1975) as the analyst looks for multiple (hence *poly*) 'characteristics of ethnicity'. These may include (1) an existing 'name' for a group (an *ethnonym*); (2) members speak a different language or dialect; (3) members demonstrate distinct religious practices; (4) live in a particular geographic territory; (5) express commitment to particular 'values' or 'norms'; (6) dress in a particular way; (7) share a sense of fictive/metaphoric kinship, a sense of shared history, ancestors or provenance; (8) are economically specialised; (9) possess a characteristic physical appearance; (10) have particular forms of leadership; or (11) are perceived to be 'racially' or biologically different.

To get diverse groups to fit the 'ethnicity' box involves a sleight of hand on the part of the analyst-classifier. Few social groups considered 'ethnic' share *all* these traits, but are deemed 'ethnic' by virtue of having *some* of these characteristics. Ethnic group 'A' may display features one to five, while group 'B' may display characteristics six to eleven. Both groups can be construed as 'ethnic', but 'without sharing any of the defining features' (Fardon 1999: 67).

There are no hard and fast rules determining how many of these characteristics *must* be present or that are considered essential. The 'ethnic quality', therefore, is not assigned according to a *single* set of criteria (Fardon 1987: 171). Rather, as a polythetic concept, 'ethnicity' is used to facilitate broad comparison. To enjoy its pervasive reach, 'ethnicity' *must* be a polythetic concept, but is it an unjustifiable way of satisfying our desire to categorise the social world? What makes 'ethnicity' a viable abstract concept? Is it just an 'odd-job' word (Needham 1971: 5) which depends on drawing selective, tenuous links – on organising the world according to vague 'family resemblance'?

Anthropologists have always demonstrated 'classificatory zeal' even if it is often disguised as comparison (Holy & Stuchlik 1983: 15). At heart, the 'ethnic quality' was a means by which social scientists could play the game of comparison, in which 'highly divergent phenomena had to be objectivised and treated as if they were analogous with one another' (Fardon 1999: 67). Problems arise, however, when the desire to create a sense of similarity out of diversity is used without question (Parkin 1987: 55). Although ethnicity is a polythetic concept, it may be (mis)understood to indicate that all groups classed as 'ethnic' correspond to the same set of criteria. When applied to newly encountered contexts, this misunderstanding of the 'ethnic quality' reifies groups as being more distinct than they really are, exaggerating the clarity of social distinction.

We may argue that we need to redesign our analytical concepts and sacrifice the desire for universalising categories to the need for specificity. The moment, however, has passed. The concept of 'ethnicity' is out of its box and no longer under the control of the analyst. While the classification of 'ethnic groups' originated with the external analyst, it has been co-opted by the groups as people have chosen to represent themselves as being members of an 'ethnic

group' (see Fardon 1987: 173). The classifier's model has been internalised by the classified. The external imposition of clear labels for
groups of people has had a 'socially reifying effect on groups as ...
members start using them in their self-identification' (Eriksen 1993:
90).[7] Once social distinctions were externally objectified as 'ethnic',
'actors were able to pursue ethnic goals or adopt ethnic stratagems'
(Fardon 1987: 177; see R. Cohen 1978: 383). As Stanley Greenberg
observes, 'distinctive groups like the Sikhs in India, Ibo in Nigeria,
and Malays in Malaysia were barely conscious of their "sameness"
one hundred years ago' (1980: 14). Over time, actors have come to
regard themselves as members of an 'ethnic group' as defined by
anthropologists, colonial administrators and post-independence
governments (see Allen 1996: 252–4; James 1996: 185–6; Vail 1989).

Although we should not present actors as 'collaborating dupes or
naïve and gullible people, beguiled by clever colonial administrators and untrustworthy anthropologists' (Vail 1989: 3), there has
clearly been a process of 'ethnic learning', the process by which
'groups develop ethnic awareness as a result of others using ethnic
solidarities to compete' (C. Newbury 1988: 15). The analytical
construct of 'ethnicity' has become instrumental in its own right,
the 'conscious and imaginative construction and mobilisation of
difference' (Appadurai 1996: 14).[8] Local actors have also found it
useful to present themselves as 'ethnic' in order that non-local actors
view their predicaments as commensurable to other 'ethnic'
situations already 'understood' (see A. Cohen 1985: 99). Although
the polythetic understanding of an 'ethnicity' should act as a form
of 'translation' in new contexts as in 'You may understand this best
by thinking of it as, *in some respects*, like something you already
know about' (Fardon 1999: 65; emphasis added), the 'ethnic quality'
is often understood as if all entities deemed 'ethnic' are *identical*, as
in 'You've seen this before and this situation is exactly the same.'
Such reliance on pre-acquaintanceship inevitably accentuates
'common properties' to the detriment of context-specific ones (see
Filmer 1972: 212).

None of this implies that what have become known as 'ethnic
groups' emerged from a vacuum and are wholly the construct of
anthropology/colonialism. Social entities clearly existed prior to
being stamped with the ethnic label, but 'Pre-colonial notions of distinctions [and] their practical significance ... were defined differently.
We read ethnic intention into them with the benefit of hindsight'
(Fardon 1987: 178). As an example, Richard Fardon demonstrates

that what constituted 'the Chamba' prior to colonial rule is different from what constitutes 'the Chamba' today (a self-referential term used by quarter of a million people in Nigeria and Cameroon).[9]

The (re)construction of groups by the analyst is not a once-and-for-all action, but a dialectical process as the negotiation of the 'reality of ethnicity' is tossed back and forth from external theoretician to internal theoretician and back again (see Ardener 1989a: 67). The role of 'classifier' constantly changes hands. No sooner has the external analyst 'stabilised' reality than local actors adopt and modify the reworked external model and incorporate it into local understandings (ibid. 68). Again, the analyst must incorporate these changes into his or her model, and so the rolling process continues. The process by which the ephemeral nature of what ethnicity 'really is' continues today. Consequently, the external analyst can no longer resort to a 'pure', 'neutral' definition of 'ethnicity', for the concept has become intrinsic to the very social reality that is being analysed (Eriksen 1996: 9). The boundary between 'ethnicity' as an external, 'neutral' analytical concept and local understandings of social distinction has collapsed (ibid. 12).

So is 'ethnicity' a viable concept? Yes, because the *belief* in its salience is part of the situation with which we are engaged. We must look, however, to the manner in which actors define and deploy the *notion* of 'ethnic' distinction rather than fall back on our own independent, insulated, abstract concepts. In the context of Rwanda two questions arise. First, to what extent does ethnicity, a classificatory construct of social science, share the same epistemological assumptions as the construction of targets by genocide perpetrators in terms of 'self-evident' schematic understandings of society? If social science *and* legal processes require actors to fall within 'natural', 'self-evident' categories then so do perpetrators of genocide. Second, to what extent is it anachronistic to interpret the narrow, *racial* construction of social distinction in Rwanda according to contemporary *polythetic* understandings?

'ETHNICITY' IN RWANDA

The literature on the formation of ethnic identities in Rwanda is vast and riven with controversy. Furthermore, this 'history' is not a prologue to current debates, but is central to them (see Chapter 6). If, however, we are to appreciate the colonial distortion of social distinction in Rwanda, we require a sense of what the terms 'Hutu' and 'Tutsi' indicated (or were coming to indicate) immediately prior to colonisation.

At the beginning of the 1960s, the received understanding was that 'ethnic' groups in Rwanda were primordial and their stratification static. An extensive body of research in the 1970s and 1980s, however, proposed a far more complex picture. Two central insights emerged. First, diachronically (over time) social distinction denoted by the terms 'Hutu' and 'Tutsi' was evolving in both pre-colonial and early-colonial Rwanda. Second, synchronically (at a moment in time) the form these distinctions took was not uniform throughout the area that constitutes contemporary Rwanda. Both over time and at any moment in time the terms 'Hutu' and 'Tutsi' were polyvalent – there was no single meaning valid for the whole territory at any one time.

For the period prior to 1860, historians know virtually nothing about how the terms 'Hutu', 'Tutsi' and 'Twa' were used in social discourse (Pottier 2002: 13). We do know that the formation of pre-colonial Rwanda was driven by the expansion of a core central kingdom ruled by a *mwami* ('king') drawn from the *Bahindiro* Tutsi lineage of the *Nyiginya* clan (see D. Newbury 1998: 85ff). Although Catharine Newbury's research (1974; 1978; 1988) was carried out in an area which came under the control of the central kingdom only in the latter half of the nineteenth century (a period covered by reliable oral data), it suggests a model of how *Bahindiro* control had evolved within the central kingdom and continued to expand in the nineteenth century (especially under *mwami* Rwabugiri 1860–95 [see D. Newbury 1974]).

In areas into which the kingdom expanded, land distribution lay in the hands of hereditary patrilineages[10] and social identity was expressed in terms of corporate lineages and non-corporate social categories, translated as 'clans'.[11] The importance of lineages was gradually eroded as land distribution was centralised in the hands of chiefs appointed by the *mwami* (to whom they delivered tribute) and who entered into clientage relations with individuals.[12] The growth of the power of the central kingdom (inward centralisation – downward penetration – outward expansion) concentrated power in the hands of a minority who held (or came to hold) 'Tutsi' status as they used this authority to expand their control over key resources (land, cattle and people) while the majority (Hutu and Tutsi) were forced to accept clientage ties which became increasingly unequal. Thus:

while Tuutsi [*sic*] identity may be of long-standing, it would seem that Hutu identity [became] a strong identitive category cutting across clan and lineage divisions only when there had occurred social and political transformations which facilitated horizontal linkages beyond the limits of 'traditional' [lineage and clan] social groups. (C. Newbury 1978: 17)

These transformations (erosion of lineage power and extension of individual clientage) occurred at different times, at different rates, and with different intensity in different parts of the kingdom. By the end of the nineteenth century, however, the majority of the population ('Hutu' and 'Tutsi') had become part of an impoverished, dependent peasantry, exploited by clientage ties (Vidal 1974: 58–64).

My own reading of the divergent historical literature suggests six values of the term 'Tutsi', which implied (at different times and in different contexts) one or more of the following: a description of status (wealth in cattle); membership of certain 'high' lineages; the possession of authority derived from the *mwami*; 'social recognition' as a 'Tutsi' owing to wealth or in order to extend central control (by co-opting the lineage heads); those who owned cattle; and simply 'non-Hutu'. With the expansion and centralisation of the kingdom, it appears that the first four were conflated into an '*élite* Tutsi' identity.

Ultimately, it was 'wealth and power [that] conferred the Tutsi quality' (Kagabo & Mudandagizi 1974: 76). The paramount meaning of 'Tutsi' denoted proximity to the central court, 'proximity to power' (C. Newbury 1988: 51). In contrast, 'Hutu', which had initially indicated 'social son, client, or someone who does not possess cattle' (Jacob 1984: 590), 'came to be associated with and eventually defined by inferior status' (C. Newbury 1978: 21).

It was to the apex of this system, the court of the central kingdom, that colonial authorities came (German 1897–1916, Belgian 1916 onwards) and, observing the predominance of the Tutsi in that particular, *unrepresentative* context, wrongly extrapolated this predominance downwards through the whole administrative hierarchy and outwards to the entire territory. Thus 'The aristocrats of the Rwandan court [were taken] to be the models of the "Tutsi" in general' (Chrétien 1985: 137). Wishing to give the impression that they understood Rwandan society (Eriksen 1993: 24), colonial authorities imagined it according to a European 'feudal' model composed of *Seigneurs Tutsi* and *Serviteurs Hutu* (Chrétien 1985: 130; see De Lacger 1939a: 45). And yet, of the c50,000 Tutsi men in

Rwanda in 1900, only 2,500 (5 per cent) held any political authority, the rest being *'petits'* or *'non-élite* Tutsi' (Linden 1977: 18).

The Belgian authorities (with a significant input from Roman Catholic missionaries) intensified the existing *process* of hierarchisation with a form of indirect rule that devolved new forms of power and wealth accumulation to the chiefs, accelerating the crystallisation of social distinction that had begun under Rwabugiri. The ever-growing exactions emanating from the Belgian administration augmented the power and wealth of *'élite* Tutsi' chiefs by adding systematic *corvée* (forced, unpaid labour) to existing 'traditional' obligations.[13] *Uburetwa*, a form of exploitative land clientage (through which the population regained access to the land formerly held by the lineage) was modified and expanded.[14] Although *uburetwa* was restricted to those designated as 'Hutu', *petits Tutsi* were also heavily exploited (see Reyntjens 1985: 133–4).

With the increase in the power of the chiefs exploitative forms of *ubuhake* (a form of cattle clientage) were extended (see C. Newbury 1978: 22ff; Prunier 1995: 29ff). In 1936, Native Tribunals (headed by *'élite* Tutsi' chiefs) were introduced, further augmenting their power (see Lemarchand 1970a: 75–6). These changes 'placed increasing power in the hands of the chiefs and provided new opportunities for abuse of this power and the accumulation of wealth' (Jefremovas 1991: 80; see C. Newbury 1988: 128; 1978: 23ff). Between 1932 and 1957, education ('the portal which gave access to political power' [Linden 1977: 152]) was mostly restricted to *'élite* Tutsi' – who accounted for 75 per cent of students (Chrétien 1997: 14). In 1926, the Belgian authorities rationalised the complex chief system of the central kingdom *and* applied it to the whole territory, resulting in a 'more starkly authoritarian system, centred on the rule of a single and virtually omnipotent chief' (Lemarchand 1977: 78).[15] Whatever positions of authority Hutu and Twa had formerly held were largely removed in this policy of 'Tutsification'.[16] Abuses by the chiefs were overlooked and 'many Rwandans saw Belgian rule as the beginning of the "time of the whip"' (des Forges 1972: 274).[17] And yet, by the end of the 1950s, the average family income of Hutu and *petits Tutsi* (90–97 per cent of those designated as Tutsi) was virtually the same (Linden 1977: 226), with only c10,000 *'élite* Tutsi' (out of c300,000 of those designated 'Tutsi') being associated with the political class (Harroy 1984: 234; see Codere 1973: 20), a 'minority among their own people' (Prunier 1995: 28 n. 72).

All of these *practical* changes were determined by a racial, social evolutionary ideology: the 'Hamitic Hypothesis'.[18] The various (often contradictory) forms of the 'hypothesis' have been considered in detail elsewhere (Sanders 1969; W. Evans 1980; Taylor 1999: 58ff; Chrétien 1985: 130ff; Rekdal 1998: 21ff). The form in which it was applied to Rwanda maintained that a superior 'Caucasoid' race from north-eastern Africa (*faux nègres*) were responsible for *any* signs of 'civilisation' in East and Central Africa and represented a cultural evolutionary intermediary (Tylor 1871) between 'barbarism' and 'civilisation' (Chrétien 1985: 131). There was an opposition between the 'Negro as such' (the Bantu) and the 'Hamite'.[19]

From the distorted perspective of the central court, the Belgian authorities assumed that the kingdom was systematically divided into 'self-evident' categories of Hutu, Tutsi and Twa; that the Tutsi (a minority) ruled over a majority – implying superior martial skill and intelligence; that the Tutsi at the central court possessed a different physiology from that of Hutu; and that only Tutsi were pastoralists. As a whole, these elements 'indicated' Tutsi provenance *outside* Rwanda and thus a *racial* distinction associated with superior 'cultural' and moral characteristics:

1895 [Tutsi are] Hamitic Pastoralists [from] Ethiopia [who have subjugated a] tribe of Negro Bantus. (Count von Götzen [German Governor], quoted in Chrétien 1985: 135)

1902 The Batutsi ... are superb men, with fine and regular features, with something of the Aryan and the Semite. (Léon Classe [Vicar Apostolic from 1927], quoted in Chrétien 1985: 137)

1903 We can see Caucasian skulls and beautiful Greek profiles side-by-side with Semitic and even Jewish features, elegant golden-red beauties in the heart of Ruanda and Urundi. (Joannes van den Burgt, quoted in Prunier 1995: 7)

1917 [The Tutsi is] closer to the White man than the Negro ... he is a European under a black skin. (François Menard [Roman Catholic missionary], quoted in Gahama 1983: 275)

1925 Gifted with a vivacious intelligence, the Tutsi displays a refinement of feelings which is rare among primitive people. He is a natural born leader, capable of extreme self-control and of calculated goodwill. (Belgian Colonial Report, quoted in Prunier 1995: 6)

1931 The Batutsi were destined to reign ... over the inferior races that surround them. (Pierre Ryckmans [Belgian Governor General], quoted in Chrétien 1985: 138)

1933 [The Tutsi are] Abyssinian monophysites. (André Pagès [Roman Catholic missionary] 1933: 8)

1939 The physical type of the Mahutu is that common of blacks [with an] average size of 1.67m, very dark skin colour and curly hair, brachycephalous and prognathous, with a crushed nose and thick lips. [The Tutsi are] a ruling minority. Their supremacy is not disputed [for three reasons, political, economic and] racial, their superiority of physical type, a people of tall imposing appearance [which] to the simple and half-civilised ... generates prestige and influence. [The Tutsi] who are they and where do they come from? When we go from upper Egypt or the plateaux of Abyssinia to Rwanda, we recognise them as follows ... tall men, on average reaching 1.79m ... their limbs are long and lanky, with regular features, noble bearing, grave and haughty. ... They are the Caucasian type like the Semite of Asia. (Louis de Lacger [Roman Catholic missionary] 1939a: 42; 44; 49; see Sasserath 1948: 27–8)

Furthermore, the 'scholar-turned-administrator or the administrator-turned-scholar' (Ardener 1989a: 67) played a significant part in this process. These 'scholars' (Pagès 1933; De Lacger 1939a; 1939b) played the same 'comparative game' discussed above with the 'Hamitic Hypothesis' acting as a comparative tool by which 'useful' comparison could be made with groups elsewhere (not unlike the function of 'ethnicity'). De Lacger, for example, considered the Hutu to be the 'anthropological type' of the Bantu while the 'Hamitic' Tutsi were 'the brothers of the Nubians [southern Egypt and northern Sudan], the Galla [Ethiopia] and of the Danakil [Eritrea]' (1939a: 49).

The works of Alexis Kagame[20] (1952; 1954; 1958; 1959) demonstrate that the 'classified' incorporated these racial ideas into existing understandings of aristocratic 'Tutsi' rule. In *Inganji Karinga* (*Karinga – the Triumphant Dynastic Drum* 1959) Kagame insisted that 'the Tutsi' had Ethiopian/Hamitic origins (see C. Taylor 1999: 76). This 'reality of ethnicity' was tossed back and forth from external to internal theoretician and back again, with Kagame's *protégé* Jacques Maquet, speaking of the '*hétérogénéité raciale*' of Rwanda society (1950:

77–9) and accepting the classification found in Charles Seligman's *Races of Africa* (1930) (see 1961: 10–12).

The culmination of this process of *racialisation* was the census of 1933–34, in which every Rwandan was assigned an 'ethno-racial' label (15 per cent Tutsi, 84 per cent Hutu, 1 per cent Twa) and issued with an ID card upon which the label was inscribed. Although the issuing of cards was motivated primarily by administrative concerns, rather than to *ascribe* 'ethno-racial' identity *per se*, the outcome was the same (see Longman 2001: 352ff). While the criteria by which one's *ethnie* was determined remains a matter of controversy,[21] the census was the zenith of the racialisation of Rwandan society. The census was not, in itself, the main issue, but that the identities it imposed were understood as racial.

Following patrilineal custom, children would inherit the identity inscribed on their father's ID card (see Chrétien et al. 1995: 161). Until 1997, the French term *ethnie* and the Kinyarwanda term *ubwoko* appeared on the ID card.[22] For the colonial authorities both terms were 'synonyms for race in the biologically determinist sense' (C. Taylor 1999: 62). Here again we encounter the importance of classification. The Kinyarwanda word *ubwoko* can be translated as either 'clan', 'tribe' or 'racial group' (Chrétien et al. 1995: 333 n. 65). Marcel d'Hertfelt (1971: 3 n. 2), however, notes that prior to colonial rule the term *ubwoko*, translated as 'clan', was applicable only to the broad classification of items (a herd of cattle, plants or a species) but never for a corporate group. *Ubwoko* was/is a mono-dimensional 'identity'. In contrast, the terms *umuryaango* and *inzu* (which were/are used to denote major and minor lineages) indicate groups with internal, corporate integrity (see D. Newbury 1980: 392; C. Newbury 1988: 96–8).

Ubwoko, therefore, is a mono-dimensional classification and does not equate with a multidimensional, polythetic understanding of 'ethnicity'. In genocidal propaganda, the bulk of which was written or spoken in Kinyarwanda, the term *ubwoko* indicated simple mono-dimensional 'separateness', often expressed as biological immutability (see below) rather than the multidimensional markers associated with 'ethnicity'. Thus, 'the "ethnic groups" of Rwanda and Burundi, for want of being able to be characterised as such, were conceived of as "races"' (Chrétien 1985: 139).

It has been suggested that 'ethnicity' is simply a euphemism for distinctions previously understood as 'racial' (see Yinger 1994: 16–18; Fardon 1987: 171; R. Cohen 1978: 379). And yet, 'ethnicity' is not a simple synonym for 'race' (a mono-dimensional classification) because the contemporary globalised 'ethnic quality' is polythetic, inherently multidimensional. The later substitution of colonial 'race' (biocentric and mono-dimensional) with contemporary understandings of 'ethnicity' (multidimensional) tends to exaggerate contemporary social distinction as if 'the Tutsi' and 'the Hutu' are now distinguishable by more than an imposed racial construction.

In the contingent, comparative domain of anthropology, the ideal type of 'ethnic group' is, perhaps, acceptable, as long as it is understood as a '*token* of reality' and not 'something which defines identity exclusive of all other factors' (Ranger 1996: 327). In Rwanda, however, a person's *ethnie/ubwoko* was state-imposed and any sense of their figurative, contingent character was jettisoned. Were it not for ID cards, references in political discourse to 'ethnicity' may have remained abstract and negotiable. By means of ID cards, however, the figurative became the literal as every individual was imbued with the immutable characteristics of one of three archetypal 'everymen'.

It may be argued that Hutu, Tutsi and Twa could be differentiated by other polythetic characteristics such as diet, occupation and dialect (see Taylor 1999: 69ff; HRW & FIDH 1999: 34; Prunier 1995: 30). Such markers have on the whole disappeared and whatever prior salience they possessed (or continue to possess) was subsumed under a *racial* understanding of social distinction. Unlike behavioural markers, the superlative, officially sanctioned racial identity was immutable, and could not be effaced over time even if behavioural markers disappeared. Whatever had come before was now irrelevant. Ultimately, social distinction in colonial Rwanda was *racially* constructed and did not conform to the current multidimensional understanding of 'ethnicity'.

RACE 1959–94

The presence of the motif of 'race' can be traced from the eve of decolonisation to the 1994 genocide. On 24 March 1957, nine Hutu (educated at the *Grand Séminaire* at Kabgayi), published the Bahutu Manifesto (*Notes on the Social Aspect of the Racial Native Problem in Rwanda*). Although the document contained proposals for social, economic and political reform (the recognition of individual landed property, freedom of expression and extension of education to all Hutu) a truncated version demonstrates that racial immutability had become the *modus operandi* for defining social groups in political discourse. With a sleight of hand *race* as 'superiority' became *race* as 'foreign interloper', as the discourse of 'Bantus and Hamites' no longer justified indirect rule, but the ambitions of a new educated class. What 'was once legitimation now was condemnation' (Linden 1977: 270):

> The indigenous racial problem is undoubtedly internal ... Into political, social and economic problems a racial element has been added whose harshness seems to become more and more pronounced ... At the heart of the problem is double colonialism:[23] the Muhutu must suffer the domination of the hamite and the European ... What does the indigenous racial problem consist of? ... Some people ask whether it is a social conflict or a racial conflict? In reality and in people's minds, it is both ... it is a problem of a political monopoly of one race, the mututsi ... We must abandon the belief that Rwandan élites can only be found among the ranks of the hamites ... [And if only] white–black colonialism is ended, this would leave in place the even worse colonialism of hamite over the Muhutu ... a system which systematically favours the political and economic promotion of the hamite ... [We call for] the economic and political emancipation of Muhutu from the traditional leadership of the hamite. (My translation from Overdulve 1997: 98–111)

In his Lenten letter of February 1959, Mgr André Perraudin (Apostolic Vicar of Kabgayi) stated that 'In our Rwanda, differences and social disparities are mostly connected to racial differences, in the sense that, wealth on one hand and judicial and political power on the other, are really, in a great degree, in the hands of people of the same race [Tutsi]' (Perraudin 1959). Although Perraudin also stated that 'racial differences must dissolve into the higher unity of the communion of saints', his assertion that the 'racial' problem existed legitimised the analysis found in the manifesto.

The assertion found in the manifesto (and reiterated by Perraudin) regarding racial inequality was misleading. According to Jean-Paul Harroy (the last Belgian Vice-Governor General), out of a Tutsi population of 300,000 in 1956, only 10,000 were directly involved in what he describes as 'the growing conflict' because they 'benefited from feudal privileges' (1984: 234). These 10,000 correspond to the 5 per cent of Tutsi men who had held political authority in 1900 (Linden 1977: 18), a number that had probably grown with the expansion of the administration and the population. Even though only a minority of Tutsi possessed wealth or political power (the rest being *petits Tutsi*), the manifesto/Perraudin globalised this to the whole 'Tutsi *race*'. Consequently, when the 'Coup of Gitarama'[24] (28 January 1961) installed the Hutu party MDR-Parmehutu[25] in government, a party whose programme 'was indistinguishable from that set forth in the [Bahutu] Manifesto' (Lemarchand 1970a: 151), the UN Commission for Ruanda-Urundi reported that a 'racial dictatorship of one party has been set up in Rwanda' (quoted in Lemarchand 1970b: 920).

The racial motif appeared again in 1973. Although the conflict was primarily intra-ethnic (between northern and a southern Hutu élites) the inter-ethnic aspect was racial. In February, MDR-Parmehutu activists set out to 'verify' whether the official 10 per cent quota for Tutsi was being respected in schools with the intention of expelling 'surplus' students. In March, the same witch-hunt occurred among the professional classes (see Reyntjens 1985: 502–3). Special attention was paid to those categorised as *ibiymanyi* or 'hybrids' (those with mixed parentage) and *abaguze ubwoko* or 'cheaters', those who had 'illegally' changed their ethnic/racial identity.[26] Thus, the biocentric, mono-dimensional racial nature of 'ethnicity' remained preponderant.

Mono-dimensional racial distinction was central to genocidal propaganda. In December 1990, the pro-genocidal newspaper *Kangura* spoke of 'Tutsi, Twa or Hutu ... the races which live in Rwanda' (quoted in Chrétien et al. 1995: 50). By 15 February 1991, the International Commission of Jurists had already denounced this paper's 'veritable call to racial hatred' (ibid. 40). The ironic title *Batutsi Bwoko Bw'imana* ('Tutsi: Race of God') appeared on the cover of the December 1993 issue of *Kangura*, under which was a machete and the question 'What weapons can we use to defeat the *Inyenzi* [RPF/Tutsi] once and for all?' (see HRW & FIDH 1999: 74). The February 1994 edition of *La Médaille Nyiramacibiri* stated 'By the way, the Tutsi race could be extinguished' (quoted in Prunier 1995: 222), and in a broadcast on *Radio Télévision Libre des Mille Collines* (RTLM) on 2 July 1994, the presenter referred to the piles of dead bodies and asked rhetorically 'of which race are these people?' (quoted in Chrétien et al. 1995: 81).

Likewise, the racial 'Hamitic Hypothesis' featured in genocidal propaganda. In a now-infamous speech on 22 November 1992, Léon

Mugesera, vice-president of the Gisenyi *préfecture* section of the MRND(D)[27] stated:

> Recently I said to someone who had just boasted that he belonged to the PL [*Parti Libéral*] that 'the mistake we made in 1959, when I was still a child, was that we let you leave [Rwanda] unharmed'. I asked him if he had heard the recent story of the Falashas who had returned home to Israel from Ethiopia?[28] He answered that he knew nothing about it! I said to him: 'Can't you read or hear?' Let me tell you that your home is Ethiopia and that we shall send you by the river Nyabarongo so that you'll get there quickly. (My translation from a French translation by Thomas Kamanzi)

To his audience, reference to a member of the PL would have implied that his interlocutor was a Tutsi,[29] while mention of the Nyabarongo River refers to massacres of Tutsi in 1992 following which bodies had been dumped in the river. Likewise, an article in the February 1992 edition of *Kangura* stated:

> The Tutsi ethnic group is descended from the large family which we call 'Nilotic' or 'Hamite'. In that family there are several ethnic groups, the populations of Abyssinia, known as Ethiopia; Somalia and Djibouti as well as those in Northern Kenya [and the] Masi of Kenya and Tanzania. It is a family known for their propensity for war to the point that those countries of which they are members find themselves in a state of perpetual conflict. See what has happened in Somalia. You understand therefore what to expect in Rwanda. (Quoted in Chrétien et al. 1995: 111)

Likewise, the January/February 1992 edition of *Kangura Magazine* claimed that a genocide of the 'Bantu' had been planned and 'consciously orchestrated by the Hamites, thirsty for blood' (quoted in Chrétien et al. 1995: 169). Among the 'enemies' identified in a memorandum of 21 September 1992, issued by Colonel Déogratias Nsabimana, FAR Chief of Staff, were the 'Nilo-Hamitic people of the region' (HRW & FIDH 1999: 63). Elsewhere, the Tutsi were denounced as 'invaders' who had 'stolen the country' (*Kangura* January 1994; quoted in Chrétien et al. 1995: 118).

The distinction between 'Hutu' and 'Tutsi' was also likened to various forms of biological immutability comparable to race. In January 1991, *Kangura* compared 'ethnic identity' to gender (see

Chrétien et al. 1995: 96). In March 1993, *Kangura* stated 'Specialists in human genetics tell us that the small population of Tutsi [in Rwanda] is due to the fact that they only marry one another ... a cockroach cannot give birth to a butterfly. A cockroach gives birth to another cockroach' (ibid. 155), and in July 1993, 'The offspring of a snake is a snake' (ibid. 158).

The central theme was the immutability of two biologically/racially distinct groups, the fact that 'a Tutsi' could not become 'a Hutu' and *vice versa* (see Chrétien et al. 1995: 96; 98). The March–April 1992 edition of *Kangura Magazine* emphasised the racial homogeneity of the Tutsi, declaring: 'The Tutsi do not need to be the same colour, to have the same origin, the same rank in order to be united and agree with one another. Everywhere they are one' (ibid. 251). Given supposed immutability, the issue of *abaguze ubwoko* or 'ethnic/racial cheaters' appeared in genocidal propaganda. A writer in *Kangura* in March 1991 wrote: 'I do not hate the Tutsi, but I hate those who refuse to call themselves Tutsi ... Tutsi, don't try to hide yourselves' (ibid. 97; see 102–3; 311). In December 1990, *Kangura* spoke of 'wolves dressed in a Rwandan skin' (ibid. 219) and claimed that *ibiymanyi* (those of mixed parentage) were joining the RPF (ibid. 159). The February 1992 edition of *Kangura Magazine* asked 'How many children of mixed marriages hide their true Tutsi identity ... for strategic reasons' (ibid. 251).

For the perpetrators of the genocide, the imperative of 'unmasking Tutsi' demonstrates that distinction was not premised on behavioural markers or even physiology, but by internal, indelible, 'hidden' biological difference. This corresponds to Omer Bartov's concept of the 'elusive enemy':

> [The] elusive enemy ... as presented by the [Nazi] regime, meant that he might lurk anywhere ... as in all nightmares, this elusive enemy generated much greater anxiety than the easily identifiable one. The notion that the enemy is among us yet cannot be unmasked has always been the stuff of fear and paranoia and the cause of destructive imaginings and violent eruptions. (1998: 779–80)

An article in *Kangura* in December 1990 stated 'The enemy is always there, among us, and only waiting for the right moment to try and liquidate us' (Chrétien 1991: 116).

Given patrilineal descent, a child of a Tutsi woman married to a Hutu would officially inherit a 'Hutu' identity. Tutsi women, therefore, were portrayed as the 'subversive' point at which 'racial purity' was most under threat as they were able to 'undermine the categorical [racial] boundary between Hutu and Tutsi' (Taylor 1999: 177). Consequently, the 'Hutu Ten Commandments' (first published in *Kangura* in December 1990) talk of the 'trickery' of Tutsi women; declare that any Hutu man who marries a Tutsi woman or has one as a mistress is a 'traitor' and that no member of the FAR should marry a Tutsi (see Chrétien 1991: 119–20; Malkki 1995: 68–9).[30] Tutsi women were crudely portrayed as 'whores' in genocidal propaganda (see Chrétien et al. 1995: 274; 366) and brutally victimised during the genocide (see HRW & FIDH 1996).

The genocidal mentality demonstrated a clear 'abhorrence of taxonomic hybridity' (Appadurai 1998: 910). In the drive for racial clarity, foetuses were removed from Hutu women during the genocide where the father of the child was a Tutsi (see ICTR 1998 para 121). For the perpetrators, the very existence of 'hybrids' was a nonsensical aberration within the context of the racial clarity they wished to impose on society. Such a drive must be understood as an abhorrent *extension* of a normal predisposition to 'create order in an otherwise excruciatingly complicated social universe [by dividing] the social world into kinds of people' (Eriksen 1993: 24). As Geertz observes, we arrange 'things of this world, and human beings among them ... into categories, some hierarchic, some co-ordinate, but all clear-cut, in which matters out-of-category disturb the entire structure and must be either corrected or effaced' (1983: 180). For the perpetrators of the genocide, targets had to be clear-cut, there could be no 'out-of-category' exceptions (or 'category violation') and where empirical social reality was contrary to their logic it had to be effaced (see Hayden 1996: 784).

In order 'to cleanse grey areas and achieve complete clarity and purity' (Appadurai 1998: 915) genocide perpetrators must define their targets in a watertight manner. The physical act of 'cleansing' is preceded by and dependent on an abstract 'ideal type'. The strain of forcing empirical reality to correspond to such figurative constructions gives rise, paradoxically, to the fact that perpetrators do not trust the very image they project on to reality. The disjuncture between the figurative construct and the attempt to actualise it (to make it literal) breeds unease and paranoia in the minds of perpetrators and explains why the 'elusive enemy' generates greater anxiety than the easily identifiable one (Bartov 1998: 779–80).

The paranoiac idea of the 'elusive enemy' was clearly present in genocidal propaganda, especially in the concept of *ibyitso* (see Chapter 4). In radio broadcasts on 11 October and 2 November 1990, Habyarimana claimed that the RPF were disguising themselves as civilians (Article XIX, 1996: 27; 115; 121). In February 1992, *Kangura* announced that 'The enemy is able to cleverly conceal and infiltrate himself' (quoted in Chrétien et al. 1995: 154). Likewise, in March 1993 *Kangura* stated: 'In our language a Tutsi is called a cockroach because he takes advantage of the night, he conceals himself in order to achieve his objectives' (quoted in ibid. 156).

The very notion of elusive enemies 'is a crucial precondition for atrocity and genocide, since it postulates that the people one kills are never those one actually sees but merely what they represent, that is, what is hidden under their mask of innocence and normality' (Bartov 1998: 785).[31] Indeed, Arjun Appadurai (1998: 919) suggests that 'ethnic' violence, including genocide, provides a fleeting moment in which the figurative construct of an 'ethnic group' (a 'token of reality') is made 'graspable', that the act of killing makes literal, concrete victims that vindicate the figurative. In a sense, perpetrators need a real victim to prove the 'truth' of their constructs (see Taussig 2002). There is a reciprocal link between ethnic identity as a 'token of reality' and genocide, which produces 'tokens of ethnicity out of the bodies of real persons' (Appadurai 1998: 920).

The paranoiac fear of the 'elusive enemy' in Rwanda emerged from the fact that multidimensional markers of ethnicity were absent. And yet, the imposed 'racial' categories, whether inscribed on ID cards or perceived in physiological stereotype, provided no guarantees for the killers. Tutsi were murdered, having been identified in one of five ways: their name appeared on a pre-written list (see HRW & FIDH 1999: 114); their name and location read out on *RTLM* (see Article XIX 1996: 120); they were already known to their assailants (because of ID cards); they were identified as Tutsi because of ID cards in their possession; or, because they 'looked' Tutsi. For example, on 4 June 1994 *RTLM* encouraged killers to 'Look at a person, notice his height and physical appearance, if you only see his pretty little nose – smash it' (ibid. 193). There was, however, no inevitable correspondence between the ID card and ethno-racial identity.

First, the imposition of 'ethno-racial' identity (as found on an ID card) was not determined by physiognomy, but on the identity held by one's father. Added to this, in the paranoiac minds of the killers, was the presence of *abaguze ubwoko* or 'cheaters', those who had changed their 'ethno-racial' identity. For example, Timothy Longman (2001: 345ff) recounts the story of Claudette whose ID card (and those of her family) declared that she was Hutu. There was, however, a rumour that her grandfather was Tutsi, and thus – according to patrilineal descent – the whole family were *abaguze ubwoko*. As a consequence, Claudette's grandfather and father were killed, while Claudette and one of her sisters narrowly escaped death.

While having 'Tutsi' on your ID card guaranteed death, it was the lack of correspondence between identity and physiognomy that meant that where someone lacked an ID card but 'looked' Tutsi they may be killed, or if someone held a 'Hutu' ID card but looked 'sufficiently Tutsi' they would also be killed. For example, in May 1994 *RTLM* announced: 'Whoever does not have his identity card should be arrested and maybe lose his head there' (quoted in Article XIX 1996: 116). Thus, the Hutu relatives of Col. Tharcisse Renzaho (the *préfet* of Kigali active in the genocide and now on trial at the ICTR [see AR 2001]) were killed having been mistaken for Tutsi (HRW & FIDH 1999: 33; 199). Likewise, Christopher Taylor recounts the story of a young man who, although classified patrilineally as Tutsi, passed through every roadblock because he had 'typically' Hutu features. In contrast, another Rwandan was nearly killed because of his 'Tutsi-like' features despite the fact that his official identity was Hutu (C. Taylor 1999: 72). Lemarchand (1996: 8; referring to Cros 1992) recounts the testimony of another Hutu, who 'looked' Tutsi. His home was set on fire in 1959; his home was burned again in 1963, his livestock and crops destroyed and in 1973, despite his Hutu ID card, his fellow students tried to expel him from school. It is clear that given the obsession with the 'elusive enemy', the abhorrence of 'taxonomic hybridity' and the disjunction between construct and empirical reality, perpetrators did not consider ID cards or physiognomy to be infallible.

Contexts of genocide involve 'categories under stress, and ideas striving for the logic of self-evidence' (Appadurai 1998: 911). The obsession with 'unmasking' the *abaguze ubwoko* demonstrates that in order to impose 'categorical certainty' (see Linke 1997: 566) perpetrators require 'the brutal negation of social reality in order to reconstruct it' (Hayden 1996: 784). Such literal 'reconstruction' is preceded, however, by an abstract, figurative construct.

Reducing the focus to the continuity of a perception of racial immutability 1957–94, is not meant to imply that the genocide did not proceed from a composite of political and economic causes (see D. Newbury 1999; Pottier 2002: 20–3).[32] It is essential, however, to appreciate that operative social identity in Rwanda was based wholly on a 'hard', constructed, mono-dimensional *racial* distinction and not on a 'soft' multidimensional, behaviour-based *ethnicity*.

One can argue that 'Hutu' and 'Tutsi' are 'ethnic' identities by virtue of a single element of polythetic classification: perceived racial distinction. Tutsi, therefore, were 'ethnic' victims of a genocide in this sense or because they were targeted as a 'racial group' (both found in the UNGC). And yet, a misunderstanding of the polythetic quality of ethnicity, one that assumes that all 'ethnic groups' possess the same set of multiple behavioural markers, distorts the mono-dimensional, constructed racial distinction found in Rwanda. Such a misunderstanding of the contemporary 'ethnic quality' projects on to Rwanda a sense of group distinction far more concrete than is warranted, pandering to the assumption that there 'must be something more to it'. It is here that we encounter a tension between figurative, analytical notions of social distinction and the literal logic of perpetrators. Given that genocide proceeds from perpetrator definitions divorced from empirical reality, does an external recognition of genocide that relies on its own abstract conceptions negate perpetrator constructions or tend to share the same epistemological basis? As Michael Taussig writes:

> What distinguishes cultures of terror is that epistemological, ontological, and otherwise purely philosophical problem of reality-and-illusion, certainty-and-doubt, becomes infinitely more than a 'merely' philosophical problem. It becomes a high-powered tool for domination. (2002: 182)

DEFINING ETHNICITY:
THE INTERNATIONAL CRIMINAL TRIBUNAL FOR RWANDA

In the context of applying the UNGC to Rwanda, there appears to have been a failure not only to appreciate the distinction between contemporary, multidimensional conceptions of 'ethnicity' and mono-dimensional race, but that to search for ethnic distinction as an empirical reality (rather than a contingent 'token of reality') shares assumptions with perpetrator definitions. The manner in which the

ICTR initially tackled the question of 'ethnicity' serves as an example of these external misconceptions.

Jean-Paul Akayesu (former *bourgmestre* of Taba commune) was found guilty on 2 September 1998 of genocide, crimes against humanity (extermination, murder, rape) and was sentenced to life imprisonment. In the judgment, the Trial Chamber of the ICTR made the following statement:

> The Chamber notes that the Tutsi population does not have its own language or a distinct culture from the rest of the Rwandan population. However, the Chamber finds that there are a number of objective indicators of the group as a group with a distinct identity. Every Rwandan citizen was required before 1994 to carry an identity card which included an entry for ethnic group (*ubwoko* in Kinyarwanda and *ethnie* in French), the ethnic group being Hutu, Tutsi or Twa. (ICTR 1998 para 170)

The judgment also recognised that references to 'ethnic' groups were to be found in various domestic instruments[33] and notes that identity was patrilineal. At this point, the ICTR follows the argument above, that identity was determined by what was written on one's ID card (and birth certificate). Omitted from this statement, however, is reference to the 'logic' from which descended these 'objective' expressions of difference: *race*. Despite this, the judgment, at this point, is coherent: Tutsi are an 'ethnic' group by virtue of an ascribed identity found on ID cards. And yet, in paragraph 511 the judgment declares that what *really* defines Tutsi is that they constitute a 'permanent and stable' group, one in which membership is determined by birth.[34] Reference to permanency and stability not only contains implicit primordialism (a claim made in genocidal propaganda), but fails to ask by virtue of *what* were these groups 'permanent and stable' – imposed (not self-ascribed) racial distinction found on ID cards.

By paragraph 513 an 'ethnic group' is described as one 'generally defined as a group whose members share a common language or culture'. When one compares this with paragraph 170 ('the Tutsi population does not have its own language or a distinct culture from the rest of the Rwandan population'), then it appears that the ICTR does not consider the Tutsi an 'ethnic group' according to the (incorrect) 'general definition'. By paragraph 516 it is argued that the UNGC should be applicable to *any group* deemed 'permanent and stable', even if they do not correspond to the four groups explicitly protected. Reading between the lines, the introduction of the meta-criteria of 'permanence and stability' is a way of resolving the fact that the ICTR cannot get the Tutsi to fit the 'general definition' of ethnicity, even though the emphasis on ID cards (para. 170) as the basis for 'ethnic' identity had already resolved this issue. As William Schabas notes: 'the categorisation of Rwanda's Tutsi population clearly vexed the Tribunal. For the Tribunal, the word "ethnic" came closest, yet it was troublesome because the Tutsi could not be mean-ingfully distinguished, in terms of language and culture, from the majority Hutu population' (2000: 131).

Ultimately, the Trial Chamber concluded that the Tutsi were an ethnic group because of ID cards and because witnesses identified themselves according to ethnic labels (although the latter clearly proceeded from the former). Thus, Tutsi 'constitute a stable and permanent group and were identified as such by all' (ICTR 1998 para 702).

This confusion would have been avoided if the perpetrator con-struction of *race* had been placed centre stage, as one of the UNGC's designated groups; or as a component of ethnicity understood poly-thetically. Neither option would require a 'general definition' of what constitutes an 'ethnic group'. The 'general definition' of 'ethnicity' to which the ICTR refers ('a group whose members share a common language or culture') does *not* correspond to contemporary polythetic classification nor to the conclusions of Leach, Moerman and Barth. Neither does it correspond to the mono-dimensional *racial* distinction imposed by colonialism and expressed by the perpetra-tors of the genocide. And yet, the Trial Chamber remained intent on glossing *race* as 'permanency and stability'. The ICTR appears to have assumed that social distinctions existed *out-with the law* (as an empirical reality) rather than being constructed/stabilised (in their operative sense) *by the law* (ID cards, birth certificates).

Paragraph 514 reads: 'The conventional definition of racial group is based on the hereditary physical traits often identified with a geo-graphical region, irrespective of linguistic, cultural, national or religious factors.' Earlier (in para 170) it was noted that ethnic identity is conferred patrilineally. To suggest, even in passing, that racial groups are defined by 'hereditary physical traits' not only flies in the face of empirical evidence regarding phenotype (perhaps reflected in the very need for ID cards), but contradicts the assertion made earlier that identity was inherited patrilineally and not conferred by means of a physical examination; whether one 'looked Tutsi' or 'looked Hutu'. In other words, being assigned an identity was *not* dictated by one's 'physical traits', but the identity inscribed on your father's identity card. Furthermore, the correspondence of heredity with physical traits was something that even the killers do not appear to have trusted. The ICTR, therefore, not only failed to deal with 'ethnicity' in a coherent manner, but where it introduced the notion of *race*, treated it in a manner unrelated to the ascription of identity in Rwanda.

So why did the ICTR not avoid these problems and take a perpetrator-oriented approach and ask the simple question 'How did the perpetrators define their targets'? Did the ICTR fear, that by defining the Tutsi as a *race* (in accordance with how they were defined by perpetrators) they would be accused of endorsing this view? In the end, the ICTR did not really deal with how Tutsi were targeted: the perception of racial distinction. This was unfortunate given that *race*, unlike notions of ethnicity (understood behaviourally) has no empirical basis (hence, the 'elusive enemy'). By failing to underline this point, the ICTR missed the opportunity to reveal the wholly ideational nature of the genocidal mentality.

Concentrating on *racial* distinctions deployed by perpetrators need not have troubled the ICTR. As Thomas Hylland Eriksen notes:

[R]ace may assume sociological importance even if it has no 'objective' existence. Social scientists who study race relations ... need not themselves believe in the existence of race, since the object of study is the social and cultural relevance of the *notion* that race exists. (1993: 5; emphasis added)

Similarly, Annex V of UNESCO's *Declaration on Race and Race Prejudice* declares that it 'resists any suggestion that racial and ethnic groups exist in an objective sense, addressing the concept only within the context of denouncing theories about racial superiority' (1978; quoted in Schabas 2000: 122), while the final report of the UNCE (9 December 1994) states that 'to recognise that there exists discrimination on racial or ethnic grounds, it is not necessary to presume or posit the existence of race or ethnicity itself as a scientifically objective fact' (UN 1994s para 159).

In employing multidimensional understandings of ethnicity that elide reference to race (because this may be misconstrued as implying that racial distinction *actually* exists) the ICTR obscured the racial constructs deployed by the perpetrators. Such a move could inadvertently make social distinction in Rwanda appear more concrete than it actually was. By failing to demonstrate explicitly that claims to *objective* 'permanence and stability' (ID cards) proceeded solely from *subjective* racism, one may make perpetrator definitions appear concrete. And yet, the ICTR could have placed the emphasis on the *notion* of racial distinction without conceding that racial distinction existed objectively.

In the context of the UNGC, Tutsi were victims of genocide because they were constructed as a racial group or as an 'ethnic group' understood polythetically with *perceived* racial distinction as a characteristic. By refusing to take a perpetrator-oriented approach to defining Tutsi (asking 'how did perpetrators define their victims?'), the Akayesu judgment not only failed to get '<u>the</u> Tutsi' to match its 'general definition' of 'ethnic group' but introduced dubious criteria for defining 'race' unrelated to Rwanda.

These early problems have, to an extent, been resolved. There has been a clear evolution in how the ICTR conceptualises Tutsi. By the time of the judgment of Clément Kayishema (former *préfet* of Kibuye) and Obed Ruzindana (a Kibuye businessman) on 21 May 1999, a second chamber of the ICTR demonstrated a more astute position, emphasising the primacy of perpetrator definitions: 'An ethnic group is one whose members share a common language and culture; or, a group which distinguishes itself, as such (self-identification); *or, a group identified as such by others, including perpetrators of the crimes (identification by others)*' (ICTR 1999 para 98; emphasis added).

In the Kayishema and Ruzindana judgment, the ICTR concluded that the Tutsi were an ethnic group because 'Rwandans were required to carry identification cards which indicated the ethnicity of the bearer' (ICTR 1999 para 523) and that this designation was conferred patrilineally. Hence, people were killed because of their ascribed identity as found on *imposed* identity cards (determined by concepts of race) not on whether the perpetrators considered the holders to 'share a common language and culture' or displayed 'hereditary physical traits'.

The Akayesu judgment failed to acknowledge explicitly that it is perpetrators who define victims, that 'Perpetrators construct their victims as threats or obstacles by ideologies which may vary from the relatively realistic to the utterly fantastic' (Freeman 1991: 189). Targets of genocide are defined in 'the paranoid imagination of despots' (Fein 1993: 13) and 'by means of criteria which have nothing to do with the properties of the category' (Du Preez 1994: 49). It is futile (and distasteful) to try and search for a simple empirical correspondence between self-ascribed 'identity' and being targeted in genocide. Surely, it is only the perpetrator's definition of a target group that is relevant (Chalk & Jonassohn 1990: 10), given that perpetrators delimit a target group by whatever criteria *they* choose (see Drost 1959). As André Sibomana observes:

> Those who decided to commit genocide in Rwanda and organised and executed it did not go and ask Tutsi how they thought of themselves. They decided unilaterally that Tutsi no longer had the right to live just because they were Tutsi. (1999: 83)

People become victims of genocide because they are compelled to 'conform to a definition that they might not share, based on categories imposed on them by a larger community or political regime' (Bartov 1998: 772). The choice of targeted identity and defining its parameters is the prerogative of the perpetrator. The choice does not (obviously) lie with the targeted individual. There is little sense, therefore, in asking 'how did the victims think of themselves?' or 'how would abstract social science describe them?', but to ask 'did the perpetrators *construct* their targets as a "national, ethnical, racial or religious group" *irrespective* of empirical reality?'

The troubling aspect of the ICTR's approach (in the Akayesu case at least) is that it asked 'how would abstract social science describe the Tutsi?' To answer this question, it drew on 'general', supposedly 'objective' definitions of ethnicity. These definitions shared an assumption with perpetrator definitions regarding the utility of 'manageable schema' and demonstrate the same 'classificatory zeal'. Some external analysts remain committed to the principle that they *can* formulate an independent concept of targeted groups that they can 'call their own', one that exists in the 'rarefied ether of scientific objectivity' (Wilson 2001: 225).

Why? For the very same benefits that accrue to all who seek to draw self-evident social distinctions, including perpetrators of genocide, that it gives one the impression that one understands a society. In this sense, the external analyst may hold the same assumption as perpetrators of genocide, that our analytical 'tokens of reality' can be *fully* redeemed in reality. Both external analysts (the ICTR) and genocide perpetrators seek to essentialise the complex reality of society by reducing and simplifying 'complex phenomena into a more manageable, schematised form' (Hinton 2002: 12). Some external analysts appear to assume that they can only make a contribution if they hold in their hands an *independent* definition. As they try to construct *post facto*, independent schema that provide categorical clarity, they appear blinded to the fact that they are making the same epistemological assumptions as perpetrators. Propelled by a need to isolate objects *on their terms*, they fail to recognise that perpetrators demonstrate the same desire, to isolate (by whatever means) objects for destruction.

One way in which external analysts can proceed is to turn the tables on perpetrators, depriving them of the pseudo-objectivity that fuels their murderous projects, to refuse to propose 'general', 'objective' definitions of ethnicity and place the full focus on the groundless imaginings of perpetrators. In this way, the external analyst cuts off the perpetrator's supply of 'objective' oxygen. At the same time, it stops in its tracks the reification of social distinction in Rwanda. The genocide occurred because of a *perception* of racial difference. When ethnicity is understood as polythetic and when a *notion* of racial difference is one possible component of 'ethnicity' we can conclude that Tutsi killed in 1994 were defined either 'ethnically' or 'racially' according to the UNGC. The perpetrators, however, did not understand 'ethnicity' in a polythetic sense, but only according to mono-dimensional racism. *This must be communicated explicitly.*

One encounters a sense of frustration among Rwandese who welcome the designation of 1994 as genocide, but refute the unnecessary reification of 'ethnicity'. External analysts, however, appear determined to hold in their hands an independent, neutral 'objective' definition of a group lest people think they believe the perpetrator's model is accurate.

2

The Precursor Debate

The genocide of 1994 was not the first episode of systematic violence against Tutsi. As we shall see, it is the events of November 1959 that the current Rwandan government considers as the first episode of genocide against Tutsi in Rwanda.

Before moving on to look at that assertion in detail, a short sketch of the events of November 1959 is required. In February 1957, *mwami* Rudahigwa's council (*Conseil Supérieur*) called for a swift transfer of power to new 'indigenous' ministries staffed by Rwandese (Linden 1977: 249). The Hutu counter-élite, educated and supported by the Roman Catholic Church, interpreted this move as an attempt to institutionalise the apparatus of '*élite* Tutsi' hegemony (*mwami*, chiefs, sub-chiefs) in order that it could be transferred intact at independence. To prevent this the Bahutu Manifesto was published in March 1957 (see Chapter 1) which counteracted the anti-colonial, nationalist position of the *mwami* and his court with its racial representation of 'double colonialism' of the Belgians *and* 'Hamites'. In June 1957, Grégoire Kayibanda (a signatory of the manifesto) formed the *Mouvement Social Muhutu* (MSM), an all-Hutu party whose programme 'was indistinguishable from that set forth in the [Bahutu] Manifesto' (Lemarchand 1970a: 151). In September 1957, the *Pères Blancs* sent Kayibanda to Belgium for journalistic training and the MSM remained dormant. In November 1957, a second Hutu organisation was formed, the *Association pour la Promotion Sociale de la Masse* (Aprosoma), which negotiated with the *mwami* on the subject of Hutu representation in government (Linden 1977: 252). Although this approach was initially rejected, a ten-person commission (with equal Hutu and Tutsi representation) was formed to study '*le Problème Mututsi–Muhutu*'. In June 1958, the *Conseil Supérieur* considered the commission's findings and declared that no 'Hutu–Tutsi problem' existed and that ethnic identity should be removed from all official documents (ibid. 255). On his return in October 1958, Kayibanda began to organise MSM and promote its racial understanding of Rwandan society.

On 25 July 1959, *mwami* Rudahigwa died in Bujumbura. His son, Jean-Baptiste Ndahindurwa, was proclaimed *mwami*. On 15 August, pro-monarchy/anti-colonial/anti-missionary '*élite* Tutsi' created the *Union Nationale Rwandaise* (UNAR). Dedicated to a constitutional monarchy, this nationalist party maintained that the 'Hutu–Tutsi problem' was a creation of colonialism and demanded immediate independence from Belgium. Although under the nominal presidency of a half-Congolese Hutu (François Rukeba) the leadership was dominated by Tutsi chiefs (see Linden 1977: 263; Lemarchand 1970b: 902). Faced with a decidedly anti-colonial, nationalist party, the Belgians tried to counter-balance UNAR, by creating (on 14 September 1959) the *Rassemblement Démocratique Rwandais* (RADER) intended to be an inter-ethnic party around which élites associated with the colonial authorities could unite. Soon after, a joint letter from the Roman Catholic episcopacy denounced UNAR (illogically) as being under the influence of 'communists and islamisists' and resembling 'national socialism' (quoted in Linden 1977: 266). In response, UNAR pamphlets stated that Mgr Perraudin (Apostolic Vicar of Kabgayi) and the RADER leaders were 'enemies of the people' that must be 'made to disappear by all means' (quoted in ibid. 267). In October 1959, Kayibanda transformed the MSM into the *Parti du Mouvement de l'Émancipation Hutu* (Parmehutu). In early November, UNAR militants attacked two MSM/Parmehutu activists. These attacks were interpreted as an attempt by UNAR to destroy Parmehutu by assassinating its leaders (ibid. 267). From 3 November, Tutsi were attacked, their houses burned and *at least* 200 killed (see below). By 14 November, order had been restored by the Belgians (although clearly in favour of Parmehutu) and by the end of 1959 many of the Tutsi chiefs and sub-chiefs had been either killed or gone into exile (see Reyntjens 1994: 27).

As we shall see, Parmehutu (and its racial representation of Rwandan society) was not put into power by the 'social revolution of 1959', but by subsequent developments in 1960–61 (engineered by the Belgians). And yet, the post-independence regimes of Kayibanda and Habyarimana and genocidal propaganda interpreted the events of *November 1959* retrospectively as the 'decisive moment', the moment at which '<u>the</u> Hutu' had 'liberated' themselves from '<u>the</u> Tutsi', conveniently eliding not only the role played by the Belgian administration in putting Parmehutu in power, but also that less than 5 per cent of Tutsi had held authority in what was essentialised as the 'oppressive Tutsi hegemony'.

PRECURSORS OF 1994: RWANDAN GOVERNMENT

What was formerly described as the 'Hutu' or 'Social Revolution of 1959' has been described by the Rwandan government as 'The 1959 Genocide':

> The first genocidal massacres were in 1959, propagated by the Belgians in close collaboration with the Catholic Church. Genocide continued in 1963, 1967, and the last one in 1994. (Rwandan presidential adviser (RPF), returnee, Kigali, May 1998)

> The first acts of genocide were committed in 1959, 1960, 1961. (RPF party official, returnee, Kigali, June 1998)

> The 1994 genocide had been planned since 1959. A philosophy for thirty-five years which accepted that Hutu should kill Tutsi. (Official Rwandan government spokesperson (RPF), returnee, Kigali, June 1998)

> Genocide in Rwanda has its own history, it goes back a long time. Genocide started in 1959, then 1963, 1966, 1967, 1973, 1993, 1994. (Paul Kagame, quoted in Jere-Malanda 2000)

For the Rwandan government genocide is not restricted to the events of 1994. Rather, the post-independence period of 1959 onwards constituted an ongoing 'genocidal project'.

PRECURSORS OF 1994: RWANDAN EXILES

The statements above consider 1959 as the 'inaugural' year of genocide of Tutsi. Exiles did not deny that both massacres and serious human rights abuses were committed in 1959, but disputed the designation of those events as genocide:

> I know that there were some terrible events. People were killed. But, to call it genocide is inappropriate. There were deaths. That must be regretted. But it was not a genocide. For me, it was a revolution. (Former Rwandan minister, exile, Belgium, March 1999)

> Yes, it was a revolution in 1959, of course. Yes, Tutsi were killed in a genocide in 1994, but not in 1959. (Rwandan academic, exile, France, July 1999)

In the context of 1959, the exiles proposed 'extenuating circumstances' to suggest that the Rwandan government was 'comparing the incomparable' (Rwandan NGO worker, exile, Belgium, March 1999). The events of 1959 were a result of 'three kinds of pressure' (Rwandan journalist, exile, Switzerland, June 1999). First, the context of de-colonisation, in which the UN had recommended that Belgium grant Rwanda independence and install a democratic government. Second, the existence of a 'Hutu intelligentsia', supported by the Roman Catholic Church, whose objective was to remove political and socio-economic inequalities. Third, that the Roman Catholic Church considered the Tutsi monarchy to be an obstacle to extending church influence. The events of 1959, therefore, must be understood as a result of these three processes. Those killed in 1959 'were to do with independence, the creation of a republic. This was in fashion. There were a lot of factors. Therefore, it is difficult to say it was a genocide' (Rwandan academic, exile, Belgium, February 1999).

The main argument proffered by exiles to dispute that 1959 should be considered genocide was that the 'social revolution' was directed only against a Tutsi élite, in a context of 'democratisation', rather than an intention to eliminate all Tutsi:

One cannot speak of genocide because there was no intention to kill all Tutsi. (Rwandan journalist, exile, Switzerland, June 1999)

It was really those in power who were targeted. The violence was not generalised to all Tutsi. (Rwandan NGO worker, exile, Switzerland, May 1999)

In 1959 it was only the Tutsi élite that was targeted. Therefore, the idea that 1959 was a genocide doesn't hold. (Former Rwandan minister, exile, Switzerland, May 1999)

The 1959 revolution was aimed at those who were in power. (Rwandan NGO worker, exile, Belgium, March 1999)

The exiles also argued that because the Rwandan state was not under 'Hutu control' in 1959, but a UN Protectorate administered by Belgium, the killings of 1959 cannot be considered a genocide committed by a 'Hutu government' (as in 1994). For example, 'the Hutu were the majority, but they had no power. How can a dominated people plan and execute a genocide if they have no power?' (Rwandan journalist, exile, Switzerland, June 1999).

The exiles argued that the first killings in 1959 were of Hutu leaders: 'The killings of Tutsi began after the Tutsi had killed Hutu leaders' (Rwandan academic, exile, France, July 1999); 'It is true that in 1959 there were massacres, but they started after the assassination of Hutu leaders' (Rwandan journalist, exile, Switzerland, June 1999).

The exiles argued that 1959 was not genocide because of the small number of victims in comparison with 1994. For example: 'There were not many killed in 1959, Tutsi were only chased away' (Rwandan academic, exile, France, July 1999); 'Only 1,000 people were killed' (Rwandan NGO worker, exile, Belgium, March 1999); 'I thought a lot were killed, but in fact there were very few' (Rwandan academic, exile, France, July 1999).

Exiles asserted, that to argue that 1959 was not an episode of genocide in no way diminishes the reality of genocide in 1994. For example: 'Yes, of course 1959 was a revolution. Yes, Tutsi were killed in a genocide in 1994, but not in a genocide in 1959' (Rwandan academic, exile, France, July 1999). While the exiles conceded that there were moments of violence in 1959, they insisted that this was a 'revolution' based on a genuine demand for democracy and social justice, which took place in the context of de-colonisation and the end of divisive Belgian administration.

PRECURSORS OF 1994: REFLECTION

The Rwandan government may have good reason to consider 1959 an episode of genocide. The failure to judicially recognise episodes of genocide has been commonplace since the inception of the UNGC (1948). Helen Fein (1993: 6) notes that between 1960 and 1979 there were at least a dozen genocides and genocidal massacres that went virtually unnoted.

Two issues arise from the debate reviewed above. First, in their arguments *against* 1959 as genocide (in comparison with 1994), the exiles demonstrated a limited grasp of the content of the UNGC, the convention by which the events of April–July 1994 were recognised as genocide. Second, while the debate concentrates on the events of 1959, there are more compelling arguments that the events of late 1963/early 1964 were genocide (according to the UNGC) and constitute a more relevant precursor to 1994. This raises the question of *why* the Rwandan government chooses to place the emphasis on 1959.

In a number of respects, the exiles are correct in their assertions regarding 1959. First, the violence of 1959 was sparked by an attack by UNAR activists (on 1 November 1959) on Dominique Mbonyumutwa, the Hutu sub-chief of Ndiza who shared the leadership of Parmehutu with Kayibanda (Linden 1977: 271).[1] Second, according to available evidence, the numbers killed in subsequent violence (directed at Tutsi) appear to be no more than 1,000. A UN commission (visiting in 1960) estimated *at least* 200 people had been killed, although it added that 'the number may even be higher since the people preferred to bury their dead silently' (UN 1960: 31; quoted in Lemarchand 1970b: 906).

As regards the targets of the violence, by the end of 1959, 21 Tutsi chiefs (of 43) had been killed, made destitute or gone into exile, while 314 Tutsi sub-chiefs (of 549) had either been killed or fled (Reyntjens 1994: 27). Much of the violence appears to have been 'aimed against those who held administrative posts (such as chiefs and sub-chiefs) and members of the Tutsi aristocracy, rather than directed indiscriminately at all Tutsi' (C. Newbury 1998: 13). Consequently, Barbara Harff and Ted Gurr consider the events of 1959 to be an episode of 'politicide' (1988: 369).[2]

The exiles are also essentially correct in their assertion that Rwanda did not have a 'Hutu government' in 1959. Communal elections were only held in July 1960,[3] with a provisional government being formed on 26 October 1960, with Kayibanda as Prime Minister. The 'coup' in January 1961 (engineered by the Belgians)[4] abolished the monarchy and appointed Dominique Mbonyumutwa as President and Kayibanda as Prime Minister. UN-supervised elections (in September 1961) confirmed the '*de facto* supremacy' of the exclusively Hutu party MDR-Parmehutu, giving it 35 seats out of 44 in the Legislative Assembly (Lemarchand 1970a: 186). A referendum held at the same time, saw 80 per cent of votes in favour of abolishing the monarchy. In October 1961, the new legislative assembly elected Kayibanda as President, with the country becoming independent on 1 July 1962. As the exiles argue, the 'revolution' and the installation of a 'Hutu government' were not simultaneous. In addition, the Belgian authorities were tacitly and actively involved in the 'revolution' of November 1959.[5]

Despite the specific targeting of Tutsi chiefs, the UN also reported non-lethal actions that would now be considered 'ethnic cleansing'. For example, 'the incendiaries set off in bands of ten. Armed with matches and paraffin ... they pillaged the Tutsi houses they passed on their way and set fire to them. ... day after day fires spread from hill to hill. Generally speaking the incendiaries, who were often unarmed, did not attack the inhabitants of the huts and were content with pillaging and setting fire to them' (UN 1960: paras 202–3). There is little evidence, however, of central planning or co-ordination, with many Hutu believing (paradoxically) that the *mwami* was a prisoner of UNAR and had ordered Tutsi huts to be burned (Lemarchand 1970a: 163–4; see Linden 1977: 267–8). There also appears to have been regional differentiation. On the whole, violence 'was primarily focused against property rather than against persons or institutions', but 'where violence did carry some political implications, as in the Gitarama and Ruhengeri districts, it was aimed against individual chiefs, not against the monarchy' (Lemarchand 1970b: 806). Conversely, UNAR attacked opponents, killing the Secretary-General of Aprosoma (Lemarchand 1970a: 166). When UNAR reported that a crowd of Tutsi had been machine-gunned, the accusation was made against the *Belgian* authorities, not against Hutu militants (ibid. 167 n. 35).

There was, however, significant population displacement, with c20,000 Tutsi from the north resettling to Bugesera in the south and more than 10,000 Tutsi fleeing to Uganda, Tanzania, Burundi and the Belgian Congo by the beginning of 1960 (Reyntjens 1994: 27 n. 33). One could argue that the forced displacement of Tutsi corresponds to Article II(b) and (c) of the UNGC: 'Causing serious bodily or mental harm to members of the [ethnical] group; Deliberately inflicting on the group conditions of life calculated to bring about its physical destruction in whole or in part.' Similarly, acts of 'deportation' and 'persecution on political, racial or religious grounds' committed 'against a civilian population' could, at the time, have been considered as 'crimes against humanity' as defined in the 1950 'Principles of International Law Recognised in the Charter of the Nuremberg Tribunal and in the Judgement of the Tribunal' as adopted by the International Law Commission of the UN.

What emerges from statements by exiles (reviewed above) is the limited grasp they had of what constitutes genocide under the UNGC, despite being adamant that 1994 was a case of genocide. On four counts they argued that 1959 was not genocide: not all Tutsi were targeted; the killings were not orchestrated by a 'Hutu government'; the killing of Tutsi was in response to the killing of Hutu leaders; and there were only a small number of victims. *None of these assertions prevents 1959 from being considered genocide under the UNGC*. Given that the convention talks of 'intent to destroy in whole *or in part*, a national, ethnical, racial or religious group' (Art. II, emphasis added) then targeting only the Tutsi élite does not disqualify the events as genocide. Likewise, the convention does not indicate that genocide must be committed by a state, it can equally be committed by private individuals (Art. IV). Similarly, nowhere in the convention are retaliatory killings disqualified from being acts of genocide. Finally, the convention gives no quantitative criteria on the number of victims. It is of concern that although the exiles were adamant that April–July 1994 was genocide, they appeared to possess a limited understanding of the convention by which those events were categorised as such.

Placing the emphasis on the events of 1959 detracts attention from a more pertinent comparison of the 1994 genocide with the events of late 1963/early 1964. By independence (July 1962) an estimated 300,000 Tutsi had been displaced, of which c120,000 were outside Rwanda (Guichaoua 1992: 17). By 1964, a census taken by the UNHCR and IRC (in camps under their control), estimated 336,000 Tutsi refugees were outside the country (of whom 200,000 were in Burundi; 78,000 in Uganda; 36,000 in Tanzania; and 22,000 in the Belgian Congo [ibid.]). As a whole, the figures amounted to 40–70 per cent of the pre-1959 Tutsi population. Consequently, between July 1962 and the UNHCR/IRC report of 1964, the Tutsi refugee population *outside* Rwanda appears to have grown by 216,000. In other words, 64 per cent of Tutsi who found themselves outside Rwanda by 1964 had left between the second half of 1962 and early 1964. What, therefore, had occurred in the intervening period, and can parallels be drawn with the genocide of 1994?

In December 1963, as in October 1990, Tutsi refugees launched an armed incursion (the *'inyenzi'* in 1963, the RPF in 1990). As in 1990, Hutu politicians in 1963 claimed to defend the newly 'liberated *peuple majoritaire*' ('the Hutu') against 'The Tutsis from ... outside the country ... who have not recognised and will never recognise the realities of the Social Revolution of 1959, and are seeking to regain power in Rwanda by any means, including taking up arms' (*communiqué* from Col. Déogratias Nsabimana, 21 September 1992). On this basis, the *'inyenzi'* attack was used as a pretext to launch massive violence against Tutsi inside Rwanda. Although in the 1990s, four years passed between the invasion by the RPF (October 1990) and the 1994 genocide, the massacre of Tutsi began immediately in 1990. From 8 October 1990 onwards, the FAR killed c1,000 Bahima (considered as Tutsi) in Mutara and 348 Tutsi in Kibilira commune (Gisenyi *préfecture*) between 11 and 13 October. In January 1991, c1,000 Bagogwe (considered as Tutsi) were murdered in the *préfectures* of Ruhengeri and Gisenyi (see Chrétien et al. 1995: 175–9). In January and February 1991, further massacre of Tutsi took place in the communes of Mukingo, Kinigi, Gaseke, Giciye, Karago and Mutura. In March 1992, at least 300 Tutsi were killed in Bugesera. Further massacres took place in Kibuye in August 1992 and again in the north-west in December 1992 and January 1993 (see HRW & FIDH 1999: 87ff). Between February and August 1993, a further 300 Tutsi and political opponents were killed in the north-west. Although the 1994 genocide did not immediately follow the RPF attack, anti-Tutsi pogroms (on the basis that all Tutsi were 'accomplices' of the RPF) did begin immediately.

Similarly, the killing of Tutsi in 1963/64 was not solely a response to the attack by the *inyenzi* in December 1963. *Inyenzi* raids had taken place from 1961 onwards and had already resulted in the massacre of Tutsi. After a raid in Byumba in March 1962, 'Between 1,000 and 2,000 Tutsi men, women and children were massacred and buried on the spot, their huts burned and pillaged and their property divided among the Hutu population' (Lemarchand 1970a: 217–19). The widespread massacre of Tutsi in 1963/64 was, like the 1994 genocide, the culmination of intermittent violence directed at Tutsi.

On 21 December 1963, 200–300 armed Tutsi refugees crossed into Rwanda from Burundi. With their numbers swollen to 1,000, they got within twelve miles of Kigali before being stopped by the *Garde Nationale* under Belgian command (see Reyntjens 1985: 461 n. 27). As in 1990 (following the RPF attack), hundreds of influential Tutsi and certain Hutu were arrested (ibid. 463; see Reyntjens 1994: 94–6). As in 1994, killing began with the elimination of political opponents (the leadership of UNAR and RADER).[6] As in 1994, the killing then became indiscriminate. While Kayibanda's government was to admit to 870 dead, it was estimated that in the period 24–28 December 1963, between 5,000 and 8,000 Tutsi were killed in the single *préfecture* of Gikongoro (10–20 per cent of the Tutsi population of that *préfecture* [Reyntjens 1985: 465]). According to figures cited by the World Council of Churches, between 10,000 and 14,000 Tutsi were murdered between December 1963 and January 1964 (see Lemarchand 1970a: 225; Chrétien 1985: 158). These 'cold figures [however] hide the extreme violence of which innocent Tutsi were the victims' (Reyntjens 1985: 468) and 'Never before – not even during the worst periods of the revolution – had the killings reached such frightening proportions. Never before had racial hatred led to such bestial cruelty' (Lemarchand 1970a: 216). Bertrand Russell described these killings as 'the most horrible and systematic massacre we have had occasion to witness since the extermination of the Jews by the Nazis' (*Le Monde* 6 February 1964).

André Guichaoua's observation made in 1992 that a 'veritable "Tutsi-hunt" took place throughout the country' (1992: 9) echoes Degni-Ségui's statement in June 1994 that 'Veritable manhunts [for Tutsi] have been carried out' (UN 1994k para 23). An article in *Le Monde* on 4 February 1964, contained a letter written by an eyewitness (Denis Vuillemin), who wrote 'the repression carried out in the *préfecture* of Gikongoro constitutes a true genocide' (*Le Monde* 1964) while an article in *The World Today* was entitled 'Attempted Genocide in Ruanda [*sic*]' (Reyntjens 1985: 466 n. 48).

Under the *Procureur de la République*, an investigation (launched at the request of the Swiss government) found 89 individuals guilty of inciting/co-ordinating massacres, including two ministers and a number of local officials. Kayibanda refused to accept these findings and ordered a new investigation, which incriminated only a handful of individuals, all of whom received light prison sentences (Lemarchand 1970a: 226).

One can only speculate whether an international tribunal like the ICTR would have found individuals guilty of genocide in 1963 in addition to indisputable crimes against humanity. There is, however, a striking similarity in the way the massacres of 1963 and 1994 unfolded. From March 1992 onwards, various elements close to Habyarimana initiated the organisation of 'self-defence groups' by local officials (see HRW & FIDH 1999: 102–3; 110–11; 139–40). Likewise, in 1963 the organisation of 'self-defence groups' was put in the hands of *bourgmestres* and *préfets* (Lemarchand 1970a: 223). Indeed, the killings in Gikongoro were incited by the *préfet* at the same kind of *ad hoc* 'community meeting' that was common in the 1994 genocide (see Prunier 1995: 137). As in 1994, Théodore Sindikubwabo (interim President during the genocide) travelled to Butare to initiate the massacre of Tutsi, so in 1963 ministers were sent to each *préfecture* to 'clean' the country of a potential fifth column (see Lemarchand 1970a: 223). In 1963 (as in 1994) radio broadcasts asked the population to be 'constantly on the alert' for 'Tutsi terrorists'. In 1963 (as in 1994) references were made in official statements to 'accomplices' of the *inyenzi* and to 'popular, spontaneous anger' as a justification for killing (see Chrétien et al. 1995: 196; 301; Article XIX 1996: 138; UN 1994g para 21).[7] In 1994, the bodies of murdered Tutsi were thrown into rivers. Likewise, in February 1964, Vuillemin stated that bodies were thrown into rivers (*Le Monde* 1964), with *France-Soir* reporting that Tutsi corpses, their legs cut off, were being carried along in the Rusizi river (Chrétien 1985: 158; see Taylor 1999: 128–30).[8] Echoing the failure of the UN in 1994 (see Melvern 2000), a UN mission in 1963 absolved the Kayibanda government by stating that it had not denied there had been 'excesses' (UN 1964).[9] A letter to Kayibanda from the head of the UN mission merely stated that he hoped the government 'would do its utmost to calm and pacify ethnic rivalries' (quoted in Lemarchand 1970a: 227). As an American journalist observed at the time, 'not a finger was raised by the UN, under whose official tutelage the trusteeship region of Rwanda was given its independence' (ibid.).

Given significant similarities between the genocide of 1994 and the massacres of 1963, the latter must be seen as a 'preamble to the planned genocide that was to take place 30 years later' (de Heusch 1995: 5). As Chrétien et al. observe 'the slogans, practices and the international reaction in that period inspired the actors in 1994' (1995: 122). Even if many features of 1963/64 distinguish it from 1994 (for example, that thousands of Tutsi refugees were *allowed* to leave Rwanda), it remains the case that the emphasis on 1959 detracts important comparison between 1963 and 1994. One can envisage a more productive debate concerning the recurring features of genocidal violence in Rwanda, if actors concentrated on comparing (in the context of the UNGC) the events of 1963 with those of 1994.

THE FOCUS ON 1959

There are a number of reasons why the Rwandan government chooses to place the emphasis on 1959 rather than 1963, the most obvious being that 1959 constituted the first episode of generalised inter-ethnic violence and must be accorded pre-eminence. More significantly, the 'social revolution' of 1959 was central to genocidal propaganda from 1990. The interpretation of 1959 was as follows: the 'feudal-monarchical' minority, 'the Tutsi', had oppressed 'the Hutu' and the so-called '*peuple majoritaire*' ('the Hutu') had expressed its 'popular' or 'democratic will' in 1959 by rising against 'the Tutsi'. Even though the monarchy (presented as the symbol of Tutsi 'oppression') was abolished *thirteen months later* in January 1961 and formalised in the referendum of September 1961, genocidal propaganda presented these subsequent events as simply formalising '*le moment fondateur*': the 'social revolution of 1959'. From this interpretation, it followed that the RPF attack of October 1990 was 'an expression' of '<u>the</u> Tutsi' (whether outside or inside Rwanda) desire to reinstate the pre-1959 'oppression' of '<u>the</u> Hutu' by reversing the 'social revolution of 1959'. Consequently, genocidal propaganda argued that the 'liberation' of '<u>the</u> Hutu' in 1959 had to be defended – ultimately with genocide.

Jean-Pierre Chrétien considers the article '*Appel à la conscience des Bahutu*' (December 1990 edition of *Kangura*) to be the 'best expression of *Kangura*'s ideology' and the central role that 1959 played in that ideology. The article attempts to argue that the 'Hutu regime had been founded [on] the "pure democracy" of the "majority people"' against the 'feudal Tutsi minority' (Chrétien 1991: 113):

> At the start of November 1959, the Tutsi provoked inter-ethnic massacres in order to eliminate the Hutu élite who demanded democracy and justice in favour of the Hutu masses who, until then, had been crushed by the feudal power of the Tutsi minority. Since the social revolution of 1959, not a day has passed when Tutsi have given up the idea of re-taking power in Rwanda ... the permanent dream of the Tutsi is to reverse the republican institutions, the legitimacy of which they refuse to recognise, and re-install the power of the Tutsi feudal minority ... Hutu, more than ever, it is now time to rouse yourselves ... and become aware of a new ideology, the ideology of the Hutu, that thrusts its roots into the social revolution of 1959 and jealously defends the gains of that revolution and those of the referendum of 25 September 1961 ... From this moment on, the history of Rwanda, the social revolution of 1959 and the referendum of 1961, must be remembered and taught to all Rwandese, to all generations present and future. Our political life must be based on democratic principles, on the administration of the state by the electoral majority ... The Hutu must stop having pity on the Tutsi! (reproduced in Chrétien 1991: 116–19)

The article ends with the 'Hutu Ten Commandments', of which commandment ten reads: 'The Social Revolution of 1959, the Referendum of 1961, and the Hutu ideology must be taught to all Hutu at all the levels' (see Guichaoua 1995: 605).

The foregrounding of 1959 was not restricted to the pro-genocidal press, but was intrinsic to the very understanding of 'democracy' in Rwanda. The preamble of the 1991 Constitution states: 'Considering the liberation of the Rwandese people accomplished by the social revolution of 1959 and eager to defend the republican form of government resulting from the popular will of January 28 1961 and confirmed by referendum on September 25, 1961' (see Schabas & Imbleau 1997: 231). Again, the Constitution states that '*le moment fondateur*' of 'liberation' is the 'social revolution of 1959'.

At its most fundamental the 1994 genocide was presented as a defence of the 1959 'revolution' against the 'enemy', the 'Tutsi inside or outside the country, extremist and nostalgic for power, who have never and will never recognise the realities of the 1959 social revolution' (*communiqué* from Col. Déogratias Nsabimana, FAR Chief of Staff, 21 September 1992; quoted in HRW & FIDH 1999: 62).

The *historical* events of November 1959 do not constitute the 'social revolution of 1959' as found in genocidal propaganda. The phrase was a metonym. It symbolically represented/condensed the broader 'triumph' of a binary, racial image of Rwandan society: conceived in the 'Bahutu Manifesto' (1957); 'vindicated' in communal elections (July 1960); formalised in the 'coup of Gitarama' (January 1961); 'reiterated' in legislative elections and a referendum (September 1961); institutionalised in the Legislative Assembly's election of Kayibanda as President (October 1961); physically expressed in massive violence against Tutsi (1963/64); endangered by Kayibanda, but revalidated by Habyarimana (1973).

By reducing this series of events to '1959', Kayibanda, Habyarimana and genocidal propaganda were able to elide *decisive* Belgian support in 1960–61[10] and replace it with an image of 'spontaneous empowerment' in 1959. They could efface the fact that UNAR had been a *democratically elected* part of Kayibanda's post-1961 government. They could also ignore the fact that the *inyenzi* were not only unrepresentative of 'the Tutsi', but not even representative of UNAR. By implying that the communal elections of 1960 and referendum of 1961 were merely *post facto* 'rubber-stamping' of the 'popular, spontaneous democratic will' of 1959, the *de facto* destruction of majoritarian democracy by MDR-Parmehutu (between 1962 and 1965) could be conveniently forgotten (especially that MDR-Parmehutu destroyed Aprosoma, its rival for Hutu support). Habyarimana's destruction of MDR-Parmehutu and what it said about the north–south fissure of 'the Hutu' could also be erased. Ultimately,

Kayibanda, Habyarimana and genocidal propaganda placed the emphasis on November 1959, *not because it was the most significant moment*, but because everything that came after was simply inconsistent with the dualistic, racial ideology they wished to convey: '<u>the</u> Hutu' liberating themselves from '<u>the</u> Tutsi'.

It is perhaps to this broader ideological assertion, compressed in the phrase 'social revolution of 1959' – but not restricted to the actual events of November 1959 – that the Rwandan government is referring to when it talks of 'the 1959 genocide'. November 1959 is not the focus by virtue of the historical events, but because of what genocidal propaganda *made* 1959 represent: the triumph of racial ideology. Conversely, exiles appeared to be trying to reduce the meaning of the phrase 'social revolution of 1959' down to the *actual historical events* of November 1959, despite the fact that for 30 years the phrase symbolically signified far more than what actually happened in that month.

The centrality of 1959 to genocidal propaganda, means it is only natural that the current Rwandan government should place the focus on 1959 rather than 1963. At the same time, RPF members of the Rwandan government may wish to avoid drawing attention to the rift within UNAR between 1960 and 1964, between the leadership outside Rwanda (who would settle for nothing less than the restoration of the monarchy) and the leadership inside Rwanda, who had joined the new government (see Lemarchand 1970a: 197ff; Reyntjens 1985: 456–8).[11] Although the exiled UNAR leadership were divided on how the monarchy should be restored, they considered the UNAR leaders inside Rwanda to be 'traitors to the royal cause' because they had signed the *republican* constitution of 1962 (Reyntjens 1985: 462). Because earlier incursions by the *inyenzi* (in March 1962) had led to the massacre of Tutsi, the UNAR leadership *within* Rwanda, and many Tutsi refugees, opposed the December 1963 attack (Lemarchand 1970a: 216; 220). Fearing the consequences, even the exiled *mwami* had forbidden the December 1963 attack (Reyntjens 1985: 469).[12]

Another reason why the RPF may wish to focus on 1959 rather than 1963 is that genocidal propaganda strongly associated the Front with the *inyenzi*. The full name used by Tutsi insurgents in the 1960s was *ingangurarugo ziyemeje kuba ingenzi* ('the brave ones in the service of the king's army'), the name of one of the armies of *mwami* Rwabugiri (1860–95). *Ingenzi* ('brave') appears to have been deliberately transformed into *inyenzi*, the Kinyarwanda for 'cockroach'

(Lemarchand 2001 n. 18). From 1990 onwards, members of the RPF called themselves *inkotanyi* ('the warriors who fight valiantly'). As with *ingenzi*, *inkotanyi* refers to one of *mwami* Rwabugiri's warrior groups, although it is not clear whether the RPF leadership were aware of this historical reference and its monarchist association (Reyntjens 1994: 91 n. 7).

And yet, the character of the RPF was very different from that of the *inyenzi*. While the *inyenzi* had been committed only to the return of Tutsi refugees and the restoration of the monarchy, the RPF's 'eight-point plan' (designed as a minimal political agenda around which broad coalitions could be created [Cyrus-Reed 1996: 485–6]) spoke of 'national unity' and the elimination of corruption, placing the return of refugees as only the fifth objective and omitting any reference to the monarchy (Reyntjens 1994: 91; 146).

Whereas the *inyenzi* were intrinsically monarchist, the same cannot be said for the RPF. As early as 1965, two *republican* groups had been formed by Tutsi refugees: the *Front de libération du Rwanda* (Burundi) and the *Parti Socialiste Rwandais* (Uganda) (Reyntjens 1985: 458–9). In the early 1970s, a group in Uganda, *Imburamajo* ('lost ones'), argued that the right of return to Rwanda should be separated from the restoration of the monarchy. The exiled *mwami* (Kigeli V) convinced Idi Amin that the *Imburamajo* were a threat and they were eliminated (Cyrus-Reed 1996: 482). By the 1980s, the 'monarchist ethos' of the *inyenzi* had clearly faded among Tutsi refugees in Uganda. When in 1980 the *Rwandan Alliance for National Unity* (RANU) was formed in Kampala it called for the abolition of the monarchy (ibid. 484). It was RANU that was to be renamed the Rwandan Patriotic Front in December 1987. Given that many of the RPF cadres had fought in Museveni's 'maoist' NRA, the monarchist position of the *inyenzi* had become a 'ridiculous anachronism' by the late 1980s (Prunier 1993: 126).

Although the RPF's eight-point plan merely side-stepped the anti-monarchical stance of RANU, there remains a clear difference, at the level of discourse at least, between the *inyenzi* and the anti-monarchist position of the RPF, one that has been maintained. In 1999 the exiled *mwami* (Jean-Baptiste Ndahindurwa Kigeli V) publicly denounced the Rwandan government as 'unelected and self-serving masters' and ending with 'Beloved People of Rwanda: Know that your King-*Umwami* will soon be among you' (Kigeli 1999). In addition:

Many of [Kigeli's] Tutsi supporters are genocide survivors who find that the current government fails to satisfy their demands for justice and assistance. These Tutsi deplore the lack of progress in prosecutions for genocide as well as the prosperity of government officials grown rich from corruption while many survivors – particularly widows and orphans – struggle in abject misery. (HRW 2000a)

This rift is demonstrated by the case of Joseph Kabuye Sebarenzi, former Speaker of the Rwandan Parliament (now in exile), a genocide survivor with a large following among *rescapés*:

Although originally a member of the RPF, he was identified more with Tutsi survivors of genocide than with those who had come from outside the country. This identification was strengthened when Sebarenzi moved from the RPF to the Liberal Party, the political group most associated with survivors of the genocide ... In early January [2000], the majority of the members of the National Assembly forced Sebarenzi's resignation. Fellow politicians initially charged him with misconduct specific to his responsibilities within the Assembly, but they later accused him of broader and graver offences, including organising the survivors of genocide against the government, supporting the king, disseminating music cassettes by a singer named Sankara that talked of the return of the king, and encouraging soldiers to leave Rwanda purportedly to join the 'army of the king'. Several weeks after Sebarenzi's forced resignation, General Kagame reportedly said on Radio Rwanda that there was 'credible evidence' of his association with 'royalists' and his distribution of tape cassettes that were contrary to government policy. After his resignation, Sebarenzi feared assassination and fled to Uganda and then to Europe and the United States. Sebarenzi's departure ... underlined both the increasingly important split between the RPF and survivors of genocide and the dissatisfaction of Rwandans of all ethnic groups with the current government. (HRW 2000a; see IRIN 2000i)

Likewise, the assassination of Assiel Kabera, an influential Tutsi *rescapé*, who had worked closely with Sebarenzi:

Political analysts say the murder of presidential adviser Assiel Kabera in Kigali on Sunday [6 March 2000] was 'clearly' a political killing. The BBC Kinyarwanda service said he was shot dead outside his house by three people in uniform. Kabera had apparently told members of his family he feared for his life as Rwandan officials had linked him with the former parliamentary speaker, Joseph Sebarenzi Kabuye, who fled the country, accused of monarchist sentiments. Like Kabuye, Kabera was a genocide survivor and observers note that survivors are becoming increasingly disenchanted with the current authorities in Rwanda. (IRIN 2000ii)[13]

The republican evolution and anti-monarchist character of the RPF sets it apart from the *inyenzi*. This distinction was intentionally obscured by those who committed the genocide: 'the political and ideological history of those who joined the RPF was not of interest, the essential thing was to emphasise that [the RPF] were Tutsi, hence feudalists, and therefore bad' (Chrétien et al. 1995: 127). From 1990 onwards, genocidal propaganda associated the *inkotanyi* with the *inyenzi*. For example, 'they have changed their name, they have changed what they are fighting for; but, in fact, they are the same people' (*Radio Rwanda* 21 April 1994; quoted in Chrétien et al. 1995: 128); 'first they were Tutsi, then they came as *Inyenzi* ... and finally they have come as *Inkotanyi*' (*RTLM* 5 June 1994; quoted in ibid. 130).[14] This misrepresentation of a simple continuity between the *inyenzi* and the RPF is an example of the way in which genocidal movements must 'blend the old with the new so that their lethal ideologies will be effective and make sense to people' (Hinton 2002: 11).

Ultimately, the current emphasis on 1959 is a consequence of the fetishisation of the events of that year by genocidal propaganda as a symbolic expression of the distorted construction of Rwandan society reviewed in Chapter 1. It is regrettable that this emphasis leaves the events of 1963 largely ignored.

3
The Holocaust:
The Comparative Debate

COMPARISON WITH THE HOLOCAUST:
RWANDAN GOVERNMENT

Members of the Rwandan government (and press) appeared acquainted with *aspects* of the UNGC. For example, genocide is described as 'an attempt to make one single group extinct' (Rwandan government spokesperson (RPF), returnee, Kigali, June 1998); that 'the genocide was prepared, organised systematically and methodically executed' (Karasira 1996: 12); and that it was a 'state-sanctioned genocide' (Victor 1998: 1). Although such statements correspond to aspects of the UNGC, none of the members of the Rwandan government interviewed referred to the convention by name. The principal referent was the Holocaust and its associated lexicon. In a (three-page) declaration on 17 July 1994, the RPF described the perpetrators of the genocide as a 'fascist political-military clique'; that the mission and 'special role' of the RPF was 'the struggle against fascism'; that the new political order must be free of those who had demonstrated 'sympathy for fascist or sectarian ideology'; and that the ex-FAR had 'continued to serve fascism' (see Schabas & Imbleau 1997: 304–7). The post-genocide press has continued to describe the Habyarimana regime as 'fascist' (see Visathan 1996; Mikekemo 1996; Munyaneza 1996). Rwandese also describe the 1994 genocide as 'a final solution' (Rwandan government official, Kigali, returnee, June 1998; Gachinya 1996b; UN 1994p) and as a 'holocaust' (UN 1994n; New Times 1996; Mikekemo 1998; Victor 1998).

The 1994 genocide, therefore, is associated with the Holocaust rather than the UNGC. For example:

Two and a half years ago the word 'genocide' was just lying in the history books of the Tsiganes [Roma 'gypsies'], the Armenians and the Jews – and some dictionaries. Then came the end of April 1994 when genocide was already half way in Rwanda and a hot debate erupted in the [UN]. Was it genocide? The [UNSC] finally found no other description of what was happening in Rwanda. The word 'genocide' invaded the world media. (Ruhumuriza 1996: 8)

The word 'genocide' was not 'lying in the history books', but was the subject of an international convention, ratified by 113 states (as of 24 March 1994). Bypassing the UNGC, members (and supporters) of the Rwandan government used analogy with the Holocaust in a number of ways. For example, drawing on a lack of correspondence between contemporary notions of 'ethnicity' and Rwandan social identity (as discussed in Chapter 1) they argued that the 1994 genocide was more proximate to the Holocaust than the Armenian genocide of 1915 (and 1918–23):[1]

A great numbers of deaths, organisation, systematic elimination, this is a genocide. In this way, the Holocaust resembles events in Rwanda, as does the genocide of Armenians. But, the Armenians were killed because they had a different language and culture. In contrast, the Jews had the same language and culture as the Germans, which was also the case in Rwanda. (RPF supporter, non-exile, Europe, July 1999)

Although actors draw attention to differences between the Holocaust and the 1994 genocide, the thrust of their statements is to draw parallels:

There are similarities in its execution. To exterminate a people because of who they are, not because of what they have done. There was no Auschwitz in Rwanda, therefore, it was different. But, people were still killed because of what they were, not what they had done. It is similar [to the Holocaust], because the victims killed in 1994 had never heard about politics. (RPF Representative, non-exile, Europe, February 1999)

Allusions to the Holocaust also figure in the discourse concerning justice. The Rwandan government's announcement in March 1998 that it was to execute 22 people convicted of crimes of genocide[2] generated international calls for clemency. Part of the dismissal of these requests was expressed by reference to the Holocaust:

What about those who were executed at Nuremberg? Did the papers write about people being 'killed' and 'murdered' then? Did the Pope call for clemency? (Rwandan NGO worker, Kigali, May 1998)

After the Second World War, France, England and other European countries judged the people who committed the genocide of Jews. Nobody else could interfere. (Rwandan Roman Catholic Church official, Kigali, May 1998)

Analogies were also made with the Holocaust regarding the ideological foundations of the 1994 genocide:

Habyarimana's reign gave birth to a crop of Hutu intellectuals who were very similar to those that emerged during the reign of Hitler in Germany ... Habyarimana was a primitive fascist who only wanted power at any cost. The Hutu were given to believe that they were a race of supermen, that the world and everything in it was, and will be, for the Bahutu. Hitler used such methods to arouse Germans soon after the First World War. (Gachinya 1996a)

When clear distinctions are drawn with the Holocaust, it is not to suggest a difference *per se*, but to imply that the Rwandan genocide was 'worse' than the Holocaust, both in the speed of killing and the participation of the population. A journalist observed that 'According to some scientists, the methods used here to slaughter Tutsis and opposition Hutus were eight times faster than the gas chambers of the Nazis' (Xinhua 1998). Likewise:

There is a difference in time between Nazi Germany and the long time it took to exterminate six million Jews and over one million killed in such a short time in Rwanda. You can see the level of hatred. (Rwandan NGO worker, returnee, Kigali, May 1998)

The Nazi Holocaust was different to the genocide here in Rwanda because in Germany the state machinery planned and carried out the killing. Here, the state machinery planned the killing, but it was carried out by the population. (Rwandan presidential adviser, (RPF), returnee, Kigali, May 1998)

If you talk with Germans about their war, they will say – it was not us, only the Gestapo who killed. But in Rwanda the population itself killed ... Fifty-six methods of killing were counted before the researchers stopped counting. (Member of the Rwandan Parliament (RPF), returnee, Kigali, October 1998)

A newspaper article described 'Hutu Power' speeches (see Chapter 4) as 'outrageous incendiary statements which would make a Nazi propagandist blush with shame' (Rogers 1996). Other articles imply that the 1994 genocide eclipsed the Holocaust as 'the worst massacres and inhumanity of man to man the world has ever seen' (New Times 1998b) and 'the worst genocide ever because members of communities both caused and were victims of the genocide' (member of the Rwandan Parliament (RPF), returnee, Kigali, October 1998).

COMPARISON WITH THE HOLOCAUST: RWANDAN EXILES

Exiles accepted the fundamental similarity between the Holocaust and the 1994 genocide: 'With the exception of the Nazi genocide, Rwanda is effectively the second case in the twentieth century where a human catastrophe has been identified and classified at the international level as genocide' (Rwandan journalist, exile, Switzerland, June 1999). The exiles also, however, argued for differentiation:

> [The Rwandan government] compares the situation in 1994 with the Holocaust; the situations are not the same. That is to say it is not necessary to compare. It is necessary to take a situation in its own context, where there is an intention to destroy an ethnic group. That is genocide. But, I don't think that it is necessary to compare. It is necessary to consider such things in their own context. (Rwandan NGO worker, exile, Belgium, March 1999)

At a fundamental level the exiles did not deny similarities:

> The Holocaust was the same because they killed innocent people according to their race or because of their convictions, religion etc. and that's terrible. Genocide is unacceptable. We cannot accept what has happened in Rwanda. (Former Rwandan government official, exile, Belgium, March 1999)

> Yes, they resemble one another in some ways, in the sense that, like the Jews, it is the innocent who were killed. It was not the Tutsi who fought against the Hutu, just like the Jews did not fight the Germans. It's the same thing, it was the innocents who were killed, and there was an ideology of extermination. But, for me, the similarities stop there. (Rwandan NGO worker, exile, Belgium, March 1999)

The only comparison is that there are innocent, unresisting victims, whether they were killed fast or slowly. What is important is exterminating a group and the personal suffering each person undergoes. What is common is the innocence of the victims. (Former Rwandan minister, exile, Switzerland, May 1999)

Exiles also argued that the longevity of a formalised ideology also sets the two episodes apart:

When one sees the process of the Holocaust it was a long policy. From Hitler's rise to power it was clear. The exclusion of the Jews was a policy. In contrast, in Rwanda one can say that there was exclusion and ethnic discrimination, but one also saw strong ethnic integration and there was regional discrimination among Hutu. But Hutu and Tutsi always found space for economic and social activities without a problem. That is the great difference. (Rwandan NGO worker, exile, Belgium, March 1999)

While exiles recognised that the civil war (1990–93)[3] and genocide were distinct, unlike the Holocaust the 1994 genocide emanated from an environment in which there had been a genuine conflict between two armed sides (RPF and FAR), an environment that enabled genocidal propaganda to portray the RPF and Tutsi inside Rwanda as one and the same thing. The exiles argued, therefore, that the role of the RPF invasion in creating this environment sets the 1994 genocide apart from the Holocaust:

What happened during the civil war? The Tutsi of the RPF had been in power 30 years before. It was these people who returned armed. This is different to the situation of the Jews in Germany. There is a real difference. I would say therefore, that each genocide is specific. (Rwandan NGO worker, exile, Belgium, March 1999)

The RPF compares the genocide in Rwanda with the genocide committed against the Jews by the Germans, but the Jews did not attack the Germans. (Former Rwandan government official, exile, Belgium, March 1999)

For exiles, in drawing parallels between the 1994 genocide and the Holocaust, the Rwandan government misrepresents the 1994 genocide. As one (ethnic Hutu) exile argued:

[Paul] Kagame is exploiting the Holocaust. Both Tutsi and Jews have suffered, but in a different manner and for different reasons. Rwanda is different. I myself am a *rescapé*. The *interahamwe* killed Hutu, but they are completely forgotten for official reasons. I have no right to say my brothers have been killed. Rwanda is a whole different case to the Holocaust. (Former Rwandan minister, exile, Belgium, February 1999)

According to the exiles, such parallels misrepresent pre-genocide Rwandan society (at least prior to October 1990) and the absence, in their opinion, of a sophisticated ideology as found in Nazi Germany:

In the Jewish case you had the Nazis, you know how their ideology was constructed. We never had such a thing in Rwanda. Some say in Rwanda there was a Nazi system. This is completely wrong. In Rwanda the genocide was caused by the selfishness of a certain élite group wanting to cling to power. There was no theory to that power struggle; one group used fear to cause harm. As such, there was no Hutu hatred for Tutsi or *vice versa*. Yes, there were extremists, but a system constructed on ethnic hatred did not exist. This is a major difference between the two situations. (Former Rwandan minister, exile, Switzerland, May 1999)

The exiles considered there to have been an element of 'politicide' in the events of April–July 1994 (although they do not use this term) and that this sets the Rwandan case apart from the Holocaust:

Genocide has a philosophical basis, a superior race that wants to eliminate an inferior race absolutely, without exception. In 1994 there was a genocide, but a political type in order to maintain political power. Hutu massacred Tutsi because they were seen as political opponents. One cannot, therefore, compare the genocide in Rwanda with the Nazi genocide. (Rwandan journalist, exile, France, July 1999)

In 1994 there were the moderate Hutu and the Tutsi, it was not only a question of ethnicity. It's more correct to say, there were people killed in 1994 and that they were killed by a Hutu group. (Rwandan NGO worker, exile, Belgium, March 1999)

There is a difference in meaning between Rwanda and the Holocaust. In the end we have to call it genocide, although in reality Hutu and Tutsi were killed by the same people. (Former Rwandan minister, exile, Belgium, February 1999)

COMPARISON WITH THE HOLOCAUST: REFLECTION

One critical role of comparison in history is to bring out not only similarities but significant differences. Comparisons that accentuate only similarity are *ipso facto* dubious. (LaCapra 1992: 112)

Interpreting events in the Great Lakes Region through the comparative prism of the Holocaust is not unique to the post-genocide Rwandan government nor the events of 1994. As mentioned, Bertrand Russell described the 1963 massacre of Tutsi as 'the most horrible systematic human massacre we have had occasion to witness since the extermination of the Jews by the Nazis'.[4] Likewise, a broadcast by Vatican Radio on 10 February 1964 called the massacres 'the most terrible and systematic genocide since the genocide of the Jews by Hitler' (quoted in Lemarchand 1970a: 224). The killing of 100,000–200,000 Hutu in Burundi in 1972 by the Tutsi-dominated army is described by Stephen Weissman as 'the first clear genocide since the Holocaust' (1997: 55) and is the subject of an article by Stanley Meisler entitled 'Holocaust in Burundi' (1976; see Lemarchand & Martin 1974; Bowen et al. 1973). The same associations were made in Rwanda as early as December 1991, when an article in *La Griffe* described Hassan Ngeze (editor of *Kangura*) as a dangerous racist, a '"nazi" born half a century too late' (quoted in Chrétien et al. 1995: 48). Likewise, in December 1993 the editorial of *Le Flambeau* reported that 'Rwandan fascists and their chief have decided to apply "the final solution" to their fellow citizens' (quoted in AR 1995: 59). Similarly, the UNCE observed (in December 1994) that it was 'unlikely that the world will ever know the exact number of men, women and children slaughtered in this holocaust' (UN 1994s para 57).

As regards the statement 'Habyarimana was a primitive fascist', films about Hitler and Nazism were reportedly found in Habyarimana's residence in 1994 (HRW & FIDH 1999: 80; Chrétien et al. 1995: 257). According to Christian Scherrer (1999: 24), *Mein Kampf* had been translated into Kinyarwanda by a German missionary at the request of Martin Bucyana (Secretary-General of the racist *Coalition pour la Défense de la République*) and presented to Habyarimana. In a document found in Butare *préfecture*, containing instructions for genocidal propaganda, the author claimed to convey lessons drawn from Joseph Goebbels (HRW & FIDH 1999: 65). Reflecting this, in his introductory remarks at the trial of Jean-Bosco Barayagwiza (a founding member of *RTLM*), Hassan Ngeze (the editor of *Kangura*) and Ferdinand Nahimana (programme controller and broadcaster at *RTLM*) at the ICTR, Deputy Prosecutor Bernard Muna compared the work of these 'hate media' journalists to that of Heinrich Himmler (IRIN 2000xii).

From a detached, analytical perspective one can draw numerous cogent parallels between the Rwandan genocide and the Holocaust (see Levene 1999). And yet, such comparison can border on satisfying what Bauer calls 'some abstract intellectual urge' (1998: 32) detached from how Rwandese themselves refer to the Holocaust and the function such references serve.

Comparing the Rwandan genocide and Holocaust at an analytical level confronts a number of obstacles. First, the Holocaust has been transformed into an 'emblematic horror against which all other horrors are measured' (Novick 2001: 255), one that has 'created an image of victimhood so horrific that all other suffering must be diminished in comparison or inflated to fit its standards' (Bartov 1998: 809). For example, Peter Novick (2001: 231) quotes Al Gore speaking of (in 1989) 'An Ecological *Kristallnacht*' with an 'environmental Holocaust' to follow and refers to anti-Castro activists erecting a monument to the 'Cuban Holocaust' in Miami. While such analogies are simply insensitive, we must recognise that 'Individuals from every point of the political compass can find the lessons they wish in the Holocaust; it has become a moral and ideological Rorschach test' (ibid. 12; see Chalk & Jonassohn 1990: 3). The need for *informed* comparison of the Rwandan genocide and the Holocaust takes place in a distorted environment in which the term 'Holocaust' suffers from 'semantic stretch' (Fein 1994: 95).

Using the Holocaust as the 'apotheosis of genocide' (Fein 1993: 55) encounters two further emotive and intertwined debates. First, was the Holocaust a unique event and second, does the term refer only to the genocide of the Jews? Elie Wiesel has eloquently argued that the Holocaust is a sacred and incomprehensible event, for which no representation is sufficient (1968; see Freeman 1991: 187). If the Holocaust cannot be adequately represented then it is incomparable. At another level, the Holocaust is understood to be the only case in which a state attempted to eliminate a group for purely ideological reasons (Bauer 1978) and whose distinctive bureaucratic and technological methods remain unparalleled (see Rosenberg 1987; Rosenfeld 1999).[5] Whether 'uniqueness' should preclude comparison is not clear, for, as Michael Freeman notes, 'every event is unique; unique events may, however, be similar and comparable ... important events are unique in important respects, but may also be similar in important respects' (1991: 188; see Novick 2001: 9).

As regards whether the term Holocaust refers only to the genocide of the Jews, Bauer argues that two *different* crimes were subsumed under the UNGC: genocide (partial annihilation) and holocaust (total annihilation). While Czechs, Poles, Serbs, other Slavs and Gypsies were victims of a Nazi *genocide*, the murder of Jews was 'the only case where Holocaust would appear fully applicable' because the aim was total annihilation (Bauer 1984: 214).[6] Despite considering 'the Holocaust' to be uniquely Jewish, Bauer does not believe it was a unique event, recognising that to make it unique (hence incomparable) would deny its lessons for the future (1979: 5).

It also appears that the term 'holocaust' has undergone a change of meaning. Novick comments that 'insofar as the word "holocaust" (lowercase) was employed during the [1939–1945] war ... it was almost always applied to the totality of the destruction wrought by the Axis, not to the special fate of the Jews' (2001: 20). While, in Israel, the Hebrew word *Shoah* (whose precise meaning remains ambiguous: see Petrie 2000: 54 n. 71) has been the primary term for the genocide of the Jews (and is now commonly used in the USA) the term 'Holocaust' (understood as *religious* wholesale sacrifice/destruction by fire) has overtaken the secular usage ('holocaust') referring to 'catastrophe' or 'destruction by fire', which until the 1970s was used in reference to nuclear war without alluding to the Nazi genocide (see Petrie 2000). In making 'holocaust', 'Holocaust' it has been imbued with a sacrificial, 'biblical' connotation indicating *total annihilation*, which, for some scholars, restricts its usage to the genocide of the Jews. No comparison can, therefore, be made between the Holocaust and other genocides. The debate still rages, however, of whether 'the Holocaust' refers only to the genocide of the Jews (see Novick 2001: 214ff).

Conversely, making the Holocaust the 'paradigmatic genocide' also has dangers, generating an axiom that only a Western, industrialised state (armed with a sophisticated, pseudo-scientific ideology) can achieve mass murder (Harff & Gurr 1988: 361).[7] As Fein notes, between 1960 and 1979 there were at least a dozen genocides and genocidal massacres, but that these events went 'virtually unnoted in the western press and not remarked on in world forums' (1993: 6). In her opinion, this was (in part) owing to the Holocaust having become the paradigmatic genocide, which 'diminished observation of less planned, less total, and less rationalised cases of extermination' (ibid.). By 'making the Holocaust the emblematic atrocity, have we made resemblance to it the criterion by which we decide what horrors command our attention?' (Novick 2001: 257; see Hirsch 1995: 33–4; Bauer 1998: 32).

Elevating the Holocaust to archetype and assuming genocide follows a mechanically recurring script is 'bound to be misleading' (Fein 1993: 56). We require 'discernment within comparison' (ibid. 54), the recognition that each episode of genocide is distinct as victims, perpetrators, motives, methods and consequences differ (see R. Smith 1998: 4; Hirsch 1995: 34). Such 'discernment within comparison' is critical in designing pre-emptive, generic models of genocide aimed at early-warning and detection, 'as a shield for the future' (Freeman 1991: 194; see Stanton 1998; Hinton 2002: 29–30; Little 1991; Whitaker 1985: 41–5). Genocide should not, however, be reduced to a recurring script, as a *précis* of Roger Smith's typology of genocide demonstrates:

> (1) *retributive genocide*, which is based on the desire for revenge; (2) *institutional genocide*, frequently incidental to military conquest and prevalent in the ancient and medieval worlds; (3) *utilitarian genocide*, motivated by the desire for material gain; (4) *monopolistic genocide*, originating from the desire to monopolise power; (5) *ideological genocide*, motivated by the desire to impose a particular notion of salvation or purification on an entire society and most commonly found in the twentieth-century. (1987: 24–7; see Freeman 1991: 189–90)

Smith's five archetypes are not designed to be mutually exclusive, but represent only the predominant (or verbalised) motive of perpetrators. In any actual case, more than one of these motives will be present (Chalk & Jonassohn 1990: 35). Smith considers the Holocaust to have been primarily 'ideological', although it also involved institutional and utilitarian components. In contrast, the most frequent source of genocide in the twentieth century was the struggle to monopolise power (R. Smith 1987: 26).[8] One could argue that the 1994 genocide in Rwanda had 'retributive',[9] 'monopolistic',[10] 'utilitarian'[11] and (see Chapter 1) 'ideological' components. It is necessary to recognise that the particular coalescence of motives is unique to each genocide. An overemphasis on the ideological component of the Rwandan genocide (in comparison with the Holocaust) may detract attention from its monopolistic features.

Genocide scholars have suggested a further distinction between 'pragmatic' and 'transcendental' genocide (Du Preez 1994: 11; see Freeman 1991: 189). If genocide has a clear economic or political 'pragmatic' purpose it will continue until that purpose is achieved. Pragmatic genocide is devoid of vision.[12] In contrast, 'transcendental' genocide will continue until all members of a target group have been eliminated.[13]

The Nazi genocide was predominantly transcendental.[14] In the Rwandan case there was a clear transcendental element ('racial purity'), but there was also a sense of its pragmatic nature in the desire of Habyarimana and his associates to hold on to power in the context of the Arusha Accords (see Chapter 4).[15] The Rwandan genocide displayed a 'diabolical pragmatism based on fear', and while the Nazis saw extermination of 'lesser races' as a natural expression of Aryan power, 'the Hutu extremists saw elimination of the Tutsi as a practical solution to the political problem of retaining control of the state' (Linden 1997: 48). Over-playing comparison with the Holocaust may obscure this pragmatic component. The archetypes of 'pragmatic' and 'transcendental' are not mutually exclusive (see Du Preez 1994: 67). In order to incite genocide, propaganda must contain both transcendental and pragmatic elements. As with Smith's typology, the relative importance of any element will be unique in each specific case. Each genocide is a unique constellation of components.

A non-exhaustive comparison of the Holocaust and the 1994 genocide does demonstrate the breadth of similarity. Both were preceded by rapid political change; a civil war in the previous ten years and severe economic conditions (see Harff 1987: 43; Fein 1998: 159; Melson 1992). Both Tutsi and Jews were dehumanised/demonised (see Prunier 1995: 143 n. 27). Just as it was widely believed that Jews killed children at Passover and drank their blood (Staub 1989: 102), so Tutsi were portrayed as 'cannibals' (HRW & FIDH 1999: 80; Chrétien et al. 1995: 162; 189; Article XIX 1996: 112). Just as Jews were described as 'vermin', 'rats with human faces' and 'insects', so Tutsi were described as 'hyenas who devour our children' (quoted in Chrétien et al. 1995: 185); as snakes (ibid. 156; 293) and compared to dogs (ibid. 196; 304). Both episodes involved an imagined transnational plot. Like the 'Jewish–Bolshevik conspiracy', genocide propaganda in Rwanda claimed there was a 'Hima–Tutsi' plan to colonise Central Africa with the support of Uganda and Burundi (ibid. 167–75; HRW & FIDH 1999: 111). Just as the forged *Protocole des Sages de Sion* (see N. Cohn 1980)[16] claimed there was a global Jewish conspiracy, so *Kangura* referred to a 'letter' (undoubtedly forged), which it claimed had been found in August 1962 and contained 19 points detailing how 'the Tutsi' should surreptitiously take over the Great Lakes Region (Chrétien et al. 1995: 163ff). There is a resemblance between the concept of *Volksgemeinschaft* (a folk or racial community) and ubiquitous reference to *Rubanda Nyamwinshi*, rule by *le peuple majoritaire*, by the 'ethnic' majority: 'the Hutu'.

Both episodes obfuscated killing with euphemisms. In Nazi Germany *Sonderbehandlung* ('special treatment'), *Evakuierung* ('evacuation') and *Endloësung* ('final solution') were used to obfuscate killing Jews (see H. Friedlander 1980; Hilberg 1985 [1961]: 322–3). In Rwanda, 'bush clearing', 'clearing away tall trees', 'cleaning up', 'our work' (*akazi kacu*), 'community work' (*umuganda*), and 'the tasks that the population is busy doing' (see Chrétien et al. 1995: 192; 298–9; Article XIX 1996: 34) indicated the killing of Tutsi (see also Prunier 1995: 138; 142–3; HRW & FIDH 1999: 89; 460).

In both cases, perpetrators insisted women and children had to be killed to prevent 'future revenge' (Chrétien et al. 1995: 81).[17] There is a parallel between the international silence regarding the massacre of Tutsi in Rwanda in 1963/64, later massacres of Hutu in Burundi and Hitler's question 'Who, after all, speaks today of the annihilation of the Armenians?' (quoted in Bardakjian 1985: 43).[18] In both cases, non-killing demagogues played a critical role, namely Julius Streicher (editor of *Der Stürmer*) and Ferdinand Nahimana (see Chrétien et al. 1995: 51ff). In both cases, perpetrators were obsessed with 'racial hybridity': in Nazi Germany, *Rasenschänder* ('desecrator of the race') and *Mischlinge* ('half breeds'), and in Rwanda *abaguze ubwoko* ('ethnic cheaters') and *ibiymanyi* ('hybrids'). In both cases, a central part was played by élite units associated with the leader: in Nazi Germany the SS (*Schutzstaffel*, 'Protection Squad', Hitler's bodyguard) and Habyarimana's 'Presidential Guard'. Both episodes displayed a paranoiac fear of a 'fifth column': in Nazi Germany, the *Dolchstßlegende* or 'stab in the back' and in Rwanda, *ibyitso* (see Chapter 4). Both episodes displayed a 'dysfunctional madness': paralleling Nazi Germany's commitment of resources to the Holocaust when the war was clearly lost, Taylor points out how the multitude of roadblocks set up by militia and FAR during the genocide defied the 'ordinary logic' by which manpower would have been concentrated on fighting the advancing RPF (1999: 133–4). Just as the mass killings in Nazi Germany began with the murder of political opponents in March and April 1933 (primarily communists and social democrats) so the first victims in 1994 were the non-racially defined political opposition. Just as Hitler used the pretext of a Polish attack to invade Poland – where the 'attackers' were SS dressed in Polish uniforms (Staub 1989: 65) – so the Habyarimana regime staged an 'RPF attack' on Kigali on the night of 4/5 October 1990 as a pretext to arrest Tutsi (see HRW & FIDH 1999: 49). Then there is the most chilling similarity: 70 per cent of European Jewry and 77 per cent of Tutsi were murdered.

There are numerous parallels to be drawn between the Rwandan genocide and the Holocaust, although many of these features (de-humanisation, reverse anthropomorphism, euphemisms) may be generic characteristics of mass killing/genocide and not particular to a Holocaust/Rwanda comparison. What is, perhaps, most revealing is that in drawing analogies between the Rwandan genocide and the Holocaust, Rwandese do not refer to the abundant similarities cited above. This cannot be explained as mere ignorance. Rather, these *detailed* similarities are simply unnecessary for the principal function of drawing analogies with the Holocaust – as a response to *ethnocentrism*.

It has been demonstrated how the international media represented the Rwandan genocide as 'tribalistic savagery', drawing on funda-mentally racist perceptions of Africa (see JEEAR 1996b; Hawk 1992). As early as February 1994, headlines such as 'Tribal Feuds Throw Rwanda in Crisis' (P. Watson 1994) began to appear. During the genocide *Time Magazine* described events as 'Pure tribal enmity' (Michaels 1994a), 'tribal bloodlust' and 'tribal carnage' (Michaels 1994b), and in *The Times* 'tribal slaughter' (Kiley 1994a) and 'tribal pogrom' (Kiley 1994b).[19]

In reviews of Philip Gourevitch's 1998 book (*We wish to inform you that tomorrow we shall be killed with our families*), the phrase 'Heart of Darkness' was used (Soyinka 1998) and appears in the title of Christian Jennings's book (1998) *Across the Red River: Rwanda, Burundi and the Heart of Darkness*. The phrase 'Heart of Darkness' evokes opaqueness, incomprehensibility, the inability to grasp meaning. As Joseph Conrad writes:

The steamer toiled along slowly on the edge of a black and incomprehensible frenzy ... We were cut off from the comprehension of our surroundings; we glided past like phantoms, wondering and secretly appalled, as sane men would be before an enthusiastic outbreak in a madhouse. We could not understand, because we were too far and could not remember, because we were travelling in the night of first ages, of those ages that are gone. (2000 [1899]: 62)

As a journalist wrote in 1998: 'It was the end of April, 1994 ... Rwanda was gripped by a genocidal frenzy' (Swain 1998). When looking for a publisher for this book, an editor from one prestigious university press asked whether there was 'a market for a book which deals with savagery in so rational a way'? The adverb 'savagery' posits the existence of a 'savage'.

Clearly the idea that the genocide was the result of 'primordial bloodlust' – rather than a *modern*, premeditated, well-organised attempt to annihilate Tutsi – was, and remains, prevalent. Such a perception dovetails with Robert Kaplan's warning of 'The Coming Anarchy' (Kaplan 1994a), published two months before the genocide (and faxed to every US embassy [Richards 1996: xv]). While Kaplan begins and ends the article with reference to Sierra Leone, the subtitle reads *How scarcity, crime, overpopulation, tribalism, and disease are rapidly destroying the social fabric of our planet*. Kaplan's argument is Malthusian. Talking of the future, he argues that scarcer resources will engender 'tribal strife', enflame 'ancient tribal hatreds'; he talks of 'tribal ethnicity' and 'tribalistic identity' and he foresees a 're-primitivised man'. On 17 April 1994 (ten days after the genocide began) Kaplan applied his particular vision to Rwanda in an article in the *Washington Post* (Kaplan 1994b). Amidst talking of 'tribal fighting' in Burundi, 'blood feuds overseas' and 'new-age primitivism', he notes that Rwanda is 'one of the most densely populated and over-tilled regions of Africa' and that its 'population will double in 20 years'. He cites the average number of children born to a Rwandan women (eight) and those to a Bosnian women (less than two) as a reason why 'intervention in the Balkans has meaning'. He concludes that 'Rwandas, in varying degrees of intensity, are endemic, built-in ... to the world we inhabit', and that we must put all 'our available financial resources into basic problems such as population control, resource management and women's literacy programs'. In other words, genocides will be prevented if we reverse the Malthusian trend. For Kaplan, overpopulation causes genocide and not the premeditated action by an élite group.[20]

An editorial in *The Economist* in 2000 stated that 'brutality, despotism and corruption exist everywhere – but African societies, *for reasons buried in their culture*, seem especially susceptible to them' (2000: 17; emphasis added). An article in the same edition ('The Heart of the Matter') pondered what made the African situation particularly desperate, for, after all, 'There is tribalism in Bosnia and Ireland.' Such positions (especially Kaplan) bring to mind Chinua Achebe's observation that 'the West seems to suffer deep anxieties about the precariousness of its civilisation and to have a need for a constant reassurance by comparison with Africa' (1988: 17).

The term 'tribal violence' suffers from the same weakness of the supposedly global phenomena of 'ethnic violence', suggesting identical 'recurring scripts' rather than context-specific processes (see Prunier 1995: 141). Likewise, the term 'tribe' suffers from the same definitional ambiguity as 'ethnic group', lacking any consistent meaning (see Lowe 1997). From the perspective of the polythetic characteristics of ethnicity (see Chapter 1) one could argue that 'ethnic group' is merely a euphemism for 'tribe'. If that is the case, then what is the significance, according to context, of using the term 'tribe' *rather* than 'ethnic group'? Although the *positive* concept of a 'multi-ethnic society' is prevalent in Western Europe (*ethnic* groups can live together) no one speaks of 'multi-tribal societies' with the same positive sense (see R. Cohen 1978: 384). It may be argued that Africans *say* they are members of 'a tribe' or '*une tribue*'. To what extent is this an imposed designation? For example, Zulu who learn English are told that the word *isizwe* means 'tribe'; Zulu linguists, however, argue that the word should be translated as 'nation' or 'people' (Lowe 1997).

Why is the use of the term 'tribe' considered derogatory? The term implicitly refers to a concept of social evolution, especially Elman Service's (1962; 1975) 'band → tribe → chiefdom → state' typology (see Tylor 1871; Bock 1979). Thus 'tribes' are well down the 'evolutionary chain', implying that in 1994 Rwanda had not yet reached the level of state formation, that it was merely a 'shell state' (*The Economist* 2000), one of many 'artificial political entities' (Kaplan 1994b), with 'fictitious' sovereignty (Kaplan 1994a) in which the 'paraphernalia of the state' was hollow window-dressing for the real motivating force – *tribalism*.

The use of the term 'tribal(ism)' does three things. First, it obliterates the critical role played in the Rwandan genocide by state-sanctioned actors (see HRW & FIDH 1999: 234) and replaces this role with the image of an ancient, unchanging, all-consuming compulsion that decentres conscious agency from individuals.[21] Second, given that the racialisation of the situation (1990–94) was 'neither a universal nor an instantaneous phenomena' (C. Newbury & D. Newbury 1999: 317), 'tribal(ism)' obscures the concerted, *desperate* efforts of *Kangura*, other pro-genocidal newspapers and *RTLM* (all *modern* technologies) to construct an image of irreconcilable difference. Third, 'tribal(ism)' generates an image of conflict between two monolithic, discrete entities or 'two quasi-nations' (Kagabo & Vidal 1994: 545) rather than *one-sided* mass murder. Media representations that referred to 'tribalism' paralleled genocidal propaganda that evoked the image of a 'final battle' (the *Simusiga*) between '<u>the</u> Hutu' and '<u>the</u> Tutsi' and in so doing obfuscated genocide as 'warfare' (see Chrétien et al. 1995: 192; Article XIX 1996: 102; 112; 118–19; 140). The 'ancient' tribal motif naturalises more recent racial (re)constructions of social distinction in Rwanda. It removes individual accountability from the perpetrators by dispersing responsibility among automatons driven by a semi-mystical, primeval imperative. Ultimately, 'Tribal(ism)' obscures the fact that the genocide was 'a political phenomenon – thought about, spoken about, organised and planned by political actors' who were part of the state and its institutions (Kagabo & Vidal 1994: 545).

A blinker contributing to the perception of the Rwandan genocide as 'tribal savagery' is the method of killing when compared to the Holocaust. A perception of the Holocaust, however, as *only* an 'industrial process' omits the brutal face-to-face torture and killing within and outside extermination camps. On visiting Rwanda (March 1998), President Clinton (1998) observed: 'Scholars of these sorts of events say that the killers, armed mostly with machetes and clubs, nonetheless did their work five times as fast as the mechanised gas chambers used by the Nazis.' By distinguishing between technologies, this statement emphasises that this was an 'African genocide', implicitly setting it apart from the Holocaust. Such statements fail to recognise that the use of machetes and clubs was merely a reflection of 'a certain level of economic functioning rather than cultural barbarity' (Prunier 1995: 140 n. 23). Furthermore, methods of killing are often chosen intentionally:

[T]he use of a low level of technology to destroy hundreds of thousands of victims is done by choice in the twentieth century. Cambodia did have bullets; peasants armed with ritual knives were not the most efficient means of destruction in Indonesia. Rather, the technology chosen was a mirror of the purposes of the perpetrators (to inflict as much suffering as possible) ... and the culture of the particular society (to invoke, for example, the symbolism of an autonomous peasant society, which when it kills uses hoes). (R. Smith 1998: 12)

Two interrelated images of '<u>the</u> Hutu' found in genocidal propaganda, the *Rubanda Nyamwinshi* ('majority people') and *le menu peuple* ('common folk'), implied 'rule' by a peasant majority. Philip Verwimp (2000) demonstrates how Habyarimana glorified the peasantry, stating that manual, agricultural labour was the only work with value (hence the preservation of *Umuganda*[22] and policies to prevent urban migration).[23] The fantasy of '<u>the</u> Tutsi' as 'feudal aristocrats' meant that Tutsi were excluded from this idolised image of a 'peasant republic'. Verwimp demonstrates the correspondence between the organisation of *Umuganda* and the organisation of the genocide (see HRW & FIDH 1999: 249). This is reflected in the tasks of *Umuganda* being used as euphemisms for killing Tutsi: 'bush clearing', 'clearing away tall trees' and cutting 'bad branches'. The genocide, therefore, was presented as an expression of a country in the hands of 'hard-working peasants' . Killing people with machetes, clubs and hoes was not simply a consequence of available objects, but was intended to express symbolically the agency of the 'Hutu peasant republic'. Although a new national 'coat of arms' was introduced in January 2002, the previous emblem showed a hoe, a bow and arrow and a sickle, the 'traditional' tools of the Rwandan peasant. During the genocide, *RTLM* urged people to arm themselves with 'weapons at your disposal ... Take up your traditional "tools"' (quoted in Article XIX 1996: 117).

SUMMARY

Rwandese are pushed and pulled to draw analogies with the Holocaust. Pushed, because of the 'tribalism' projected on to Rwanda by international coverage, and pulled by the privileged place given to the Holocaust in *Western* public consciousness. Although the Holocaust may be a global paradigm, it is also 'the best known genocide *in the Western world'* (Fein 1993: 55; emphasis added), in contrast to other genocidal episodes such as the killing of Armenians (1915–23); Indonesian 'communists' (1966); Biafra (1966); Bangladesh (1971); Cambodia (1975–78); East Timor (1975–2000). This is largely down to ethnocentrically determined empathy. As Novick speculates, 'We can't *know* that one of the reasons Americans have been so moved by the fate of the Jews of Europe is because they were perceived to be "like us". But it seems probable' (2001: 236). Similarly, in the case of Kosovo,

> Western audiences were confronted by refugees to whom they could relate. Here were forced migrants who looked and dressed like them, who fled by car (even facing traffic jams on their trip to safety) and who, through the use of articulate and well-educated translators, could express their suffering in terms that resonated with Western audiences. What made the Kosovans popular refugees was the ability of Westerners to see themselves – and their families, friends, and neighbours – in the Kosovans' suffering. (Gibney 1999)[24]

By drawing analogies with the Holocaust Rwandese legitimately refute the representation of the 1994 genocide as 'a black and incomprehensible frenzy' in the 'Dark Heart of Africa'. No one would contend that the Holocaust – however brutal – was the outcome of primordial tribalism. It was a premeditated act in which irrational 'savagery' gave way to its polar opposite, clinical state bureaucracy. Prior to Clinton's visit a Rwandan journalist hoped that the President would 'acknowledge how the genocide in Rwanda is similar to the genocide in Europe and elsewhere' (Mucyo 1998).

Although such analogies with the Holocaust are legitimate, the price is high. If future genocides are to be prevented or detected and quickly halted, then each episode must be granted equality within a generic framework, a framework found in the UNGC. If the purpose of prosecuting the perpetrators of the 1994 genocide is to end impunity (see Chapter 5) then it is the means by which those responsible are prosecuted (the UNGC) that should take centre stage.

4
Debating Collective Guilt

There is no agreement on how many ethnic Hutu participated in the genocide. Estimates range from 25,000 (Jones 2001: 41), to 80,000–100,000 (Prunier 1995: 342 n. 60) and 75,000–150,000 (Jefremovas 1995: 28). René Lemarchand (2000: 2) suggests around 10 per cent of a Hutu population of c6.5 million participated as organisers, killers or unwilling accomplices, although it is unclear whether he means 10 per cent of all Hutu (c650,000) or 10 per cent of the Hutu 'active population' (c355,000).

COLLECTIVE GUILT: THE RWANDAN GOVERNMENT

Even Lemarchand's higher estimate would leave c5.8 million Hutu who did not participate in the genocide. Despite this, certain members of the current political class in Rwanda appear to globalise guilt according to ethnic identity:

The 1994 genocide involved the whole of the population. (Rwandan human rights worker, Kigali, April 1998)

Even among the Hutu there are people who tell the truth and were against the genocide, but the majority of Hutu were in favour. (Rwandan NGO worker, Kigali, May 1998)

The genocide affected all the people – it was the most complete genocide. Either people themselves or their relatives participated in the genocide, or are survivors of rape and maiming. (Member of the Rwandan Parliament (RPF), returnee, Kigali, October 1998)

One Rwandan summarised this position as: 'there are simply two groups. Hutu are murderers and Tutsi are victims' (Rwandan NGO worker, Kigali, April 1998). Official statements by the Rwandan government appear to preclude such globalisation, insisting that there are only 'Rwandese'.[1] Despite this, certain statements appear to globalise guilt according to ethnic identity implicitly:

On 3 March 1999 ... at the *Université Libre* in Brussels, the Rwandan ambassador to Belgium claimed that there had been two million *génocidaires*, in other words, all adult [Hutu] men ... during the same year, the new minister of Justice declared that, if it became necessary to arrest peasants guilty of crimes of genocide, there will be no one to work on the hills ... On 7 April 1999, at the annual commemoration of the genocide held at Kibeho ... the President of the Republic [a Hutu] announced an 'idea' on which the leaders of the country should reflect: genocide had been committed 'in the name of the Hutu', and even if all of them had not participated, should the Hutu not collectively ask pardon for a crime committed in their name? (Brauman et al. 2000)

A more subliminal issue is the phrase 'Hutu moderate'. Any mention of Hutu killed in April–July 1994 is qualified with the adjective 'moderate'. For example, those who perpetrated the genocide '[planned to] exterminate the Tutsi community in Rwanda and the massacres of the Hutu moderates' (Kamasa 1998); 'Every Tutsi, without exception [would be killed and] any moderate Hutu who might be suspected of disagreeing with the politics of Habyarimana's rabble' (Mukandoli 1998); 'the 1994 massacres that cost the lives of over one million Batutsi and Bahutu moderates' (New Times 1998a).

Although the phrase 'Hutu moderate' is ubiquitous, users do not define to whom it refers other than Hutu killed in April–July 1994 (estimated to number 30,000–50,000 [Lemarchand 2000: 3]) by the FAR, *interahamwe* and Presidential Guard. Those associated with the Rwandan government emphasised that 'Hutu moderates' were not victims of genocide:

They talk of a genocide of Tutsi and of Hutu moderates. This is not right. They killed Tutsi because of what they were and killed Hutu moderates because they considered them traitors. These Hutu were killed because they did something, not because of what they were, as was the case with the Tutsi. They were not victims of genocide. (RPF representative, non-exile, Europe, February 1999)

There were the Tutsi and the Hutu moderates. The first were victims of genocide, the second were systematic massacres. A lot of massacres cannot, therefore, be called genocide. (Rwandan government official, returnee, Kigali, June 1998)

The UNGC does not extend protection to political groups. Consequently, Hutu murdered in 1994 (by those who committed the genocide of Tutsi) cannot be considered victims of genocide. In terms of international law, however, they can be considered victims of 'crimes against humanity' (as defined in the ICTR statute and Rwanda's domestic law) since they were murdered on 'political grounds' as part of 'a widespread or systematic attack against a civilian population'.[2] And yet, assertions regarding the 'victimological status' of the 'Hutu moderates' (see above) make no reference to 'crimes against humanity', underlining the fact that contemporary Rwandan society is understood exclusively through the interpretative lens of genocide. Within this exclusive register, the 'Hutu moderates' are *anomalies*, with ambiguous contemporary relevance and a significance relegated to the past, as one Rwandan observed:

During genocide mourning week, you hear talk of Tutsi who were killed, but you do not hear of Hutu who mourn the Hutu killed. There is a particular terminology, genocide for Tutsi, massacres for Hutu. You don't see Hutu mourning during 'genocide week'. (Rwandan NGO worker, Kigali, May 1998)

COLLECTIVE GUILT: RWANDAN EXILES

The exiles argued that the significance of Hutu killed by those who *simultaneously* orchestrated and committed the genocide of Tutsi has been disregarded. For example, 'Genocide has been executed and Tutsi killed because they were Tutsi. But there is no recognition of the killing of Hutu' (Rwandan academic, exile, France, July 1999); 'On the first day of national mourning in 1994, [the Secretary-General at the Ministry of Justice] said Hutu should not be buried with Tutsi' (former Rwandan minister, exile, Belgium, February 1999).

The exiles believed that responsibility for the genocide had been globalised to all ethnic Hutu. For example, 'All Hutu are globalised as guilty of genocide, but that's not true' (former Rwandan government official, exile, Belgium, March 1999). Exiles considered this globalisation of responsibility to be an implicit function of the phrase 'Hutu moderate'. For example: 'When they speak of "the Tutsi" and "moderate Hutu", I think this is just to divide people' (former Rwandan minister, exile, Belgium February 1999); 'There is an assumption that there are only Tutsi victims and Hutu moderates and the rest of the Hutu are perpetrators. This is very wrong' (former

Rwandan Protestant Church leader, exile, UK, September 1997). The exiles perceived a tension between a collective globalisation of guilt and the judicial principle of individual responsibility. For example:

> There is a globalisation of guilt for Hutu, when not all of them are guilty. The international community has never globalised guilt, but emphasised the principle of personal guilt and that each person should go before the ICTR depending on their individual responsibility. (Rwandan academic, exile, Belgium, February 1999)

The thrust of the exile position was that a binary framework of 'Tutsi are victims, Hutu are perpetrators' cannot capture the reality of the genocide. For example, 'The term genocide is appropriate for the events of 1994 because all Tutsi were targeted. But only some Hutu (some soldiers and militia – but not all Hutu) killed Tutsi' (former Rwandan Protestant Church official, exile, UK, September 1997). The qualities of 'victim' and 'perpetrator' should not, therefore, be assigned according to ethnic identity, as one Hutu exile (targeted during the genocide) observed:

> I consider myself to be a victim, but someone can say he is a victim and I am not. Someone can say that I, as a Hutu, am a killer and he is innocent. I say, therefore, we must look for and establish responsibility at an individual level. (Rwandan NGO worker, exile, Belgium, March 1999)

COLLECTIVE GUILT: REFLECTION

> If readers take from this book the conclusion that 'the Hutu' are devils and 'the Tutsi' are angels, they have not understood anything; hundreds of thousands of the victims of the genocide were Tutsi, but also, a great number were Hutu. The killers were those Hutu who put the fetishisation of their identity before humanity. It is responsibility for this ideological choice that underpins our study, not a crime of birth. (Chrétien et al. 1995: 382)

There is a clear danger that the constructed image of two homogeneous collectivities of 'the Hutu' and 'the Tutsi' central to genocidal propaganda can be easily overlaid by '*génocidaires*' (those who committed the genocide) and '*rescapés*' (survivors of the genocide). In other words, 'To accept the corporatist view of "Hutu"

... is essentially to accept the corporatist constructions of the [genocidal] government' (C. Newbury & D. Newbury 1999: 317).

Social scientists have explored the 'social process of genocide', factoring in motivations not wholly determined by individual, 'rational' choice. Certain versions of this approach argue that one must take into account the 'subconscious', determining influence that 'culture', 'habitus' or 'false consciousness' has on choices individuals make (see Goldhagen 1996 and Hinton 1998 for a critique). Such a deterministic approach borders on suggesting that actors do not *consciously* choose to participate in genocide, and without the presence of agency there is no basis for individual responsibility. If this is the approach one chooses to take, one must dispense with the term 'genocide', because as a contraction of 'the *crime* of genocide' (emanating from Western jurisprudence) the term 'genocide' is inseparable from the concept of individual criminal responsibility. To be able to call a series of events *genocide* one must accept the principle of individual criminal responsibility. As a denunciation and prohibition of mass murder based on collectivisation, the recognition of the *crime* of genocide is required to be resolutely 'anti-collectivisation' and thus based on individual criminal responsibility.

The UNGC affirms the principle of individual criminal responsibility: 'Persons committing genocide or any other acts enumerated in Article III shall be punished whether they are constitutionally responsible rulers, public officials, or private individuals' (Art. IV). The Convention on the Non-Applicability of Statutory Limitations to War Crimes and Crimes Against Humanity (1968) defined 'crimes against humanity' (including genocide) according to the definition contained in the Charter of the International Military Tribunal of Nuremberg (8 August 1945) as a crime 'for which there shall be individual responsibility' (Art. 6; see UN 1994o paras 127–8). In 1950, the International Law Commission codified the 'Principles of International Law Recognised in the Charter of the Nuremberg Tribunal and in the Judgement of the Tribunal', according to which 'Any *person* who commits an act which constitutes a crime under international law is responsible therefor and liable to punishment' (Principle I).

This principle of individual responsibility was emphasised *while the 1994 genocide was underway*. On 30 April 1994, the President of the UNSC stated that regarding breaches of international humanitarian law in Rwanda (including genocide) the Security Council recalled 'that persons who instigate or participate in such acts are individually responsible' (UN 1994e). After visiting Rwanda in May 1994, the UN High Commissioner for Human Rights stated: 'The authors of the atrocities must be made aware that they cannot escape personal responsibility for criminal acts they have carried out, ordered or condoned' (UN 1994g para 32). On 25 May, the resolution of a special session of the UNHCHR 'affirmed' that 'all persons who commit or authorise violations of human rights or international humanitarian law are individually responsible and accountable for those violations' (UN 1994h). On 1 July 1994, the UNSC again recalled that 'all persons who commit or authorise the commission of serious violations of international humanitarian law are individually responsible for those violations and should be brought to justice' (UN 1994l). On establishing the UNCE (26 July 1994) to investigate whether genocide had been committed, the UNSG reiterated that those who violated international humanitarian law were 'individually responsible' (UN 1994m).

The Commission of Experts' interim report (1 October 1994) decisively stated that the Tutsi had been victims of a genocide (UN 1994o paras 44; 124; 148) and argued that those responsible should be tried before an international criminal tribunal (ibid. paras 133–42). The Commission concluded that three 'international legal norms providing for individual responsibility for serious human rights violations' had been breached in the period 6 April–15 July 1994: the Geneva Conventions, crimes against humanity and genocide (ibid. para 85; see 125–8). The principle of individual responsibility was, therefore, intrinsic to the formal *recognition* of the genocide of Tutsi in 1994.

This is reflected in the statute of the ICTR that has the power to prosecute *persons* who have committed the crime of genocide, crimes against humanity and/or violations of Article 3 Common to the Geneva Conventions of 1949 for the Protection of War Victims and the Additional Protocol to the Geneva Convention Relating to the Protection of Victims of non-International Armed Conflicts (Protocol II) of 1977.[3] As regards all three crimes, Article 6(1) of the ICTR statute (entitled 'Individual Criminal Responsibility') states: 'A person who planned, instigated, ordered, committed or otherwise aided and abetted in the planning, preparation or execution of a crime referred to in Articles 2 to 4 of the present Statute, shall be individually responsible for the crime' (UN 1994q). Rwanda's domestic law (30 August 1996) regarding the same three crime-sets refers to both the UNGC and the 1968 'Convention on the Non-Applicability of

Statutory Limitations', thereby accepting the principle of individual criminal responsibility.

The UNSC Resolution (8 November 1994) establishing the ICTR forcefully expressed the need to end impunity in Rwanda and that 'the prosecution of persons responsible for serious violations of international humanitarian law would enable this aim to be achieved and would contribute to the process of national reconciliation' (UN 1994q). It also stated that the 'prosecution of persons' responsible for genocide and other violations of international humanitarian law would 'contribute to ensuring that such violations are halted and effectively redressed'. Although the Rwandan representative at the UNSC voted against the resolution (see Chapter 5) he endorsed the merits of individual criminal responsibility: 'The Tribunal will help national reconciliation and the construction of a new society based on social justice and respect for the fundamental rights of the human person, all of which will be possible only if those responsible for the Rwandese tragedy are brought to justice' (UN 1994p). Individual accountability was accepted in order to 'reject the dangerous culture of collective guilt and retribution, which too often produces further cycles of violence' (Kritz 1996: 591).

In addition, the emphasis on collective responsibility, rather than individuals, is inadequate for survivors of the genocide. As one Rwandan pastor reported, 'people ask "who can we forgive when we don't know exactly who has wronged us?"' Without individual accountability, Bartov's 'elusive enemy' may become the 'elusive perpetrator', who is 'among us yet cannot be unmasked ... the stuff of fear and paranoia and the cause of destructive imaginings and violent eruptions' (Bartov 1998: 779–80).

The principle of individual criminal responsibility is intrinsic to the recognition and prosecution of the crime of genocide. Any statement or insinuation that detracts from or dilutes that principle not only weakens the objective of ending impunity, but brings into question the ontological nature of what we recognise as genocide.

'HUTU MODERATES'

Categories used in the contemporary segmentation of Rwandan society appear inadequate. The phrase 'Hutu moderates' is only used *retrospectively* and does not appear in descriptions of contemporary Rwanda. It is solely an epitaph and may imply that the only 'moderate' (or 'anti-genocide') Hutu are dead. Stripped of contemporary utility, the depiction of this group as an 'extinct category' contributes to a portrayal of contemporary Rwanda according to a crude, binary framework, composed *only* of 'victim–*rescapé*–Tutsi' and 'perpetrator–*génocidaire*–Hutu' (see Prunier 1995: 157 n. 48). This binary segmentation echoes the imagined manichean construction of Rwandan society found in genocidal propaganda.

The phrase 'Hutu moderate' is ubiquitous, its referent apparently self-evident. To whom, however, does it refer? To what extent does the ambiguity of the phrase contribute to a sense that 'moderate' is a transient quality of 'the Hutu' and that what *did* constitute a 'Hutu moderate' need not be defined *because they are no longer relevant*. There is a double jeopardy contained in the phrase. Not only is there a lack of clarity regarding its referent, but 'moderate' suggests its antonym: 'extremist'. According to such a binary framework 'Hutu' can be qualified as either moderate or extremist, and no residual category presents itself.

'MODERATE HUTU', 1990–94

If we are to bring clarity to the meaning of the phrase 'Hutu moderate', we must look to the political evolution of Rwanda during 1989–94 and determine to whom, in this rapidly evolving environment, the phrase refers.

The Rwandan human rights activist Monique Mujawamariya has described what happened in Rwanda 1989–94 as 'a revolution, within which a genocide took place' (quoted in Saint-Jean 1994). In November 1989, a Belgian journalist, Marie-France Cros, spoke of an 'end of the regime atmosphere', with the independent newspaper *Kanguka* (founded in 1989) and the Roman Catholic newspaper *Kinyamateka*, openly criticising the Habyarimana regime (see Bertrand 2000: 37–8; Sibomana 1999: 25–6). In June 1990, Habyarimana attended the Franco-African summit at La Baule, at which François Mitterand made development aid conditional on democratisation. On 5 July, Habyarimana announced the creation of a 'Commission for National Synthesis' designed to 'identify what the concept of democracy means for the majority of the Rwandese population' (quoted in Chrétien et al. 1995: 28). Established on 24 September, the commission was mandated to produce a new 'National Political Charter' upon which political life would be based (see Reyntjens 1994: 104). A week later, on 1 October, the RPF attacked from Uganda. In operations starting on 8 October, the FAR killed c1,000

Bahima (considered as Tutsi) in Mutara and between 11 and 13 October killed 348 Tutsi in Kibilira commune (Gisenyi *préfecture*). Mass arrests then took place of those suspected of sympathy for the RPF, the number rising to 13,000 detainees (90 per cent of whom were Tutsi) (ibid. 94–6).

On 28 December 1990, the 'Commission of National Synthesis' published a draft 'National Political Charter', which proposed a multiparty system, formalised in the Constitution of 10 June 1991. In March 1991, opposition parties (already in existence) were allowed to legally register. These were the *Mouvement Démocratique Républicain* (MDR), the *Parti Social-Démocrate* (PSD), the *Parti Libéral* (PL) and the *Parti Démocratique Chrétien* (PDC). The manifestos of the MDR, PSD and PDC were more or less identical, dedicated simply to the removal of the single ruling party, the MRND, and its president Habyarimana (see Reyntjens 1994: 136). The PL, formed by a multi-ethnic group of businessmen, enjoyed a nationwide, but primarily urban/professional support base, attracting support from those with 'ambiguous' ethnic status (such as *ibiymanyi*) or ethnically mixed couples (Prunier 1995: 125). Unlike the other parties, the PL denounced the exploitation of the 'revolution' of 1959 by the MRND(D) (see below), recognised the legitimacy of the RPF invasion and was explicitly committed to de-ethnicised politics (see Bertrand 2000: 111–12).

It was *within* these four opposition parties that what are now described as 'Hutu moderates' were to be found. At this stage, however, party membership cannot be associated with 'extreme/pro-genocide' or 'moderate/anti-genocide' positions, for as we shall see, a number of these parties (especially the MDR) were to split later along 'moderate' (pro-negotiation/accommodation with the RPF) and 'extremist' (anti-RPF, anti-Tutsi) lines. In this sense, one should conceive of these four parties *initially* constituting the 'Hutu opposition to Habyarimana' *en bloc*, only later dividing (although not along party lines) into 'extremist' and 'moderate' factions, in a large part the result of personal strategies.

In 1991, however, these parties appeared as a *bloc*. On 11 June, the PSD, MDR and PDC issued a joint statement containing demands that became the *leitmotif* of their political action over the following months:[4] principally, that the Habyarimana regime was finished and the war with the RPF was a political *not* an ethnic issue – the result of Habyarimana's bad management of the refugee problem. In July, these parties (by now incorporating the PL) became known as the *Comité de Concertation de Partis Politique Démocratiques* (CDC).

Although the attitude to this group (its purpose and mandate) differed between and within the parties (see Bertrand 2000: 116), it acted as a joint conduit for opposition to Habyarimana, constantly pressing the demands first made in the 11 June statement.

THE 'WAR OF SYMBOLS'

This apparent consensus was, however, built on shaky foundations, principally, how did the parties interpret the so-called 'social revolution' of 1959? As discussed in Chapter 2, Grégoire Kayibanda had established the MSM in June 1957, an all-Hutu party whose programme 'was indistinguishable from that set forth in the [Bahutu] Manifesto' (Lemarchand 1970a: 151). In October 1959, Kayibanda transformed the MSM into Parmehutu. In May 1960, the phrase *Mouvement Démocratique Républicain* was added (to demonstrate the party's anti-monarchical stance), becoming MDR-Parmehutu. In July 1960, MDR-Parmehutu won 70.4 per cent of votes in communal elections. On the basis of this result, on 28 January 1961, the recently elected communal officials formed themselves into a Legislative Assembly; abolished the monarchy and appointed Kayibanda as Prime Minister (the 'coup of Gitarama'). In September 1961, UN-supervised elections gave MDR-Parmehutu 35 seats out of 44 in a Legislative Assembly. A referendum held at the same time (known as *Kamarampaka*), saw 80 per cent of votes in favour of abolishing the 'Tutsi' monarchy. On 26 October 1961, the new legislative assembly elected Kayibanda as President and head of government with Rwanda becoming independent on 1 July 1962.

As President, Kayibanda was to oversee the killings of 1963/64 (see Chapter 2) and further massacre of Tutsi during the 1960s. Furthermore, MDR-Parmehutu was to liquidate all other Hutu parties, declaring Rwanda a one-party state in 1965. Given this history, it is difficult to accept the statement made in March 1991 when the MDR was (re)created: 'MDR-Parmehutu, the party of the common people never betrayed democratic and republican principles: the respect for multipartism, free party membership, free elections at all levels' (quoted in Reyntjens 1994: 28).

Kayibanda's home *préfecture* and power base had been Gitarama (in central Rwanda). By the late 1960s, his single-party government was dominated by people from Gitarama, to the virtual exclusion of those from the north-west of the country. The pogrom of Tutsi of 1973 (which began in Gitarama) was a calculated attempt by

Kayibanda to 'unite' 'the Hutu' against a 'common threat'. The tactic failed, Juvénal Habyarimana taking power in a coup on 5 July 1973. Habyarimana then overtly favoured his own region of Gisenyi between 1973 and 1990. Significantly, when the MDR was (re)created in 1991, its party membership list showed 30 per cent of supporters from Gitarama and 17 per cent from Ruhengeri, the base of Habyarimana's rival faction in the north (Reyntjens 1994: 106). Key figures in the 'new' MDR were drawn from these two areas: Donat Murego from Ruhengeri, Frodauld Karamira and Dismas Nsengiyaremye from Gitarama, while Emmanual Gapyisi and Faustin Twagiramungu were both sons-in-law of Kayibanda, for whose murder they held Habyarimana responsible.

Underpinning the formation of the MDR *contre* the MRND was a 'war of symbols' regarding which party was the *true* inheritor of the MDR-Parmehutu legacy. And yet, was this legacy ethnic (the 'liberation' of 'the Hutu' from the 'oppression' of 'the Tutsi') or political (the triumph of 'democracy')? In an attempt to claim the latter, the MDR dropped 'Parmehutu' from its name when it was (re)created in 1991, attempting to disassociate itself from the anti-Tutsi massacres committed by its previous incarnation (1959–73) and the fact that by the mid-1960s MDR-Parmehutu had become a single, *anti-democratic* party (see Bertrand 2000: 89 n. 15).[5] Despite efforts by the MDR leadership to present itself as a party fighting for democracy for *all* Rwandese, the ambiguous reference to the anti-Tutsi MDR-Parmehutu was dangerous, reinforced by the party's adoption of the MDR-Parmehutu colours and political songs (ibid. 93). Certain actors close to the MDR leadership believed that the association of the 'new' MDR with MDR-Parmehutu was simply too problematic and formed the PSD, with a support base in Butare (in the south of the country) and a membership of whom 15–30 per cent were Tutsi (ibid. 107 n. 54).

A further ambiguity was whether *Républicain*, within *Mouvement Démocratique Républicain*, was merely a constitutional statement or referred to the '*Hutu* Republic'. The formation of the exclusively Hutu, racist *Coalition pour la Défense de la République* (CDR) in March 1992 (its members had to prove 'Hutu ancestry' going back three generations), explicitly resolved this ambiguity, promoting itself as the 'true defenders of the *Hutu* republic' as established in 1959, denouncing the MDR as 'traitors' who had usurped the 'glory' of MDR-Parmehutu and against whom the CDR were 'defending the Hutu' (see Chrétien et al. 1995: 231–4).

Habyarimana always maintained that he was continuing the 'revolution' of 1959 and that his *coup d'état* of 1973 was a 'moral revolution', building upon Kayibanda's 'political revolution' of 1959, whose gains had been betrayed by Kayibanda (see C. Newbury 1992: 195). In order to emphasise this continuity and draw on the ambiguity of the term *Républicain*, the MRND (on 28 April 1991) replaced *Révolutionnaire* with *Républicain* and added *Démocratie*, becoming the *Mouvement Républicain National pour le Développement et la Démocratie* (MRND(D)), thereby making a symbolic claim to the anti-Tutsi legacy of MDR-Parmehutu. Although the addition of *Démocratie* appeared to support the ongoing 'democratic transition', the addition of *Républicain* raised the question of 'democracy for whom?' While elements within the MDR tried (rather unsuccessfully) to shake off association with the anti-Tutsi interpretation of the 1959 'revolution', the MRND(D) was trying to strengthen its claim to continuity with the '*Hutu* revolution' that established the '*Hutu* Republic'.

It was unclear whether the supposed advent of 'democracy' in 1959 (when the 'Tutsi feudal-monarchists' had been driven out) and the idea of 'the Republic' as a '*Hutu* Republic' could be conceptually separated. Central to the interpretation of 'democracy' since independence had been the referendum of 25 September 1961 (*Kamarampaka*) in which 80 per cent of voters supported the abolition of what was considered the 'Tutsi monarchy'. This is demonstrated in the preamble of the Constitution of 1991: 'Considering the liberation of the Rwandese people accomplished by the social revolution of 1959 and eager to defend the republican form of government resulting from the popular will of January 28 1961 and confirmed by referendum on September 25, 1961' (see Schabas & Imbleau 1997: 231). This statement is replete with ambiguity. Does 'liberation' refer to liberation from the monarchy or from 'the Tutsi'? Is 'the republican form of government' simply a constitutional statement, or does it indicate an exclusively '*Hutu* Republic'? As regards the 'referendum' of 1961, for 30 years it had been hailed as an expression of 'Hutu freedom' against 'Tutsi oppression' and not as simple 'democracy'. This ethnic/racial interpretation of 'the Republic' and 'democracy' was made clear by Martin Bucyana (a leader of the CDR) who stated that his party was the result of the 'ethnic war launched against the majority people [the Hutu]' and the failure of the opposition parties to fight against the 'enemies of democracy and the Republic' – the RPF (see Bertrand 2000: 180).

The legacy of MDR-Parmehutu could be interpreted as either the party that achieved democracy *per se* or the party that achieved the 'liberation' of '<u>the</u> Hutu' from '<u>the</u> Tutsi'. While the MDR tried to maintain that the 'revolution' was 'just' in itself and it was merely continuing to fight 'oppression' (by *some* Tutsi in 1959 and by *some* Hutu in 1991 [see Nsengiyaremye 1995: 249–50]), it remained to be seen whether such a delicate nuance could be maintained when the claim of defending 'the masses' against 'oppressive élites' had always been interpreted as defending '<u>the</u> Hutu' against '<u>the</u> Tutsi'. There was a persistent tension within the MDR position (echoing the Bahutu Manifesto) between defining Rwanda's problems as socio-political (vis-à-vis Habyarimana) and ethnic/racial, according to the anti-Tutsi rhetoric of 1959 onwards (Bertrand 2000: 95). The MDR was engaged, therefore, in a precarious balancing-act of trying to cast the 'revolution' in a de-ethnicised light (as the onset of 'democracy' for *all* Rwandese) when 1959 had always been interpreted as the onset of 'democratic' rule by the Hutu, *'le peuple majoritaire'*.

It remained to be seen whether the MDR (or elements within it) could resist seizing the ethnicised mantle of 'defender of the Hutu Republic' seemingly forfeited by Habyarimana. Simultaneously, the government press presented the MDR and MRND(D) as merely a *schism* within the same movement, one that should form a common ethnic front against 'the Tutsi RPF' (see Bertrand 2000: 150; Chrétien et al. 1995: 219; 230; 251). The MDR's position was all the more tenuous when faced with the dilemma of supporting *la patrie* against external 'aggression' (the RPF invasion) while simultaneously opposing the head of state (and military chief) who chose to define the RPF 'invaders' in ethnic/racial terms.

Ultimately, individuals within the MDR could no longer resist the 'ethnic temptation', and chose to resolve the party's ambiguous stance, unequivocally emphasising that the war with the RPF was an 'ethnic war' requiring a 'common Hutu front' to defend the *'Hutu Republic'* against 'Tutsi invaders'. Given that the MDR, MRND(D) and CDR appealed to the same legacy of MDR-Parmehutu (in different ways) it was easier, at a later date, for elements within the MDR to adopt an ethnicised stance.

APRIL 1992

On 29 March 1991, a cease-fire was agreed between the Rwandan government and the RPF at N'Sele, Zaïre. After the FAR broke this agreement by shelling RPA positions, a second cease-fire was agreed at Gbadolite, Zaïre on 16 September 1991 (Jones 2001: 55–6).

On 13 October 1991, Habyarimana *appeared* to respond to the demands of the opposition parties (CDC) and relinquished some of his *formal* authority by appointing Sylvestre Nsanzimana to the new post of Prime Minister, whose cabinet was (finally) named at the end of December. Nsanzimana's so-called 'multiparty' cabinet contained only one opposition minister (from the PDC), the other parties refusing to participate unless the Prime Minister was drawn from an opposition party. On 8 January 1992, the CDC organised demonstrations in Kigali at which party leaders demanded a *real* multiparty government while the PDC threatened to leave the government unless a *true* multiparty cabinet was installed.

At this point, Habyarimana tried to deflect attention from his increasing political isolation. In late February/early March, Hassan Ngeze (editor of *Kangura*) visited the Bugesera region several times and distributed leaflets warning of infiltration by *'inyenzi'*. On 1 March, following a local PL meeting in Bugesera, a pamphlet accusing the party leadership of being 'rebels' (RPF) was distributed (from a vehicle belonging to the local authorities), ending with the phrase 'they must not escape us' (Reyntjens 1995b: 268). Meanwhile, Presidential Guards in civilian clothes and *interahamwe* had been transported into the area in government vehicles. On 3 March, *Radio Rwanda* broadcast five times the contents of a fictitious 'letter' (dated 3 February 1992 and probably written by Ferdinand Nahimana) said to come from the *Commission interafricaine de la non-violence*, claiming that the PL was the local headquarters of the RPF and was involved in a plan to assassinate Hutu leaders from the MDR, MRND and PSD (see Guichaoua 1995: 611–13).[6] Following these broadcasts, from the night of 4/5 until 9 March, at least 300 Tutsi in Bugesera were systematically massacred (see ibid. 613–14). As soon as the massacres began, an Italian woman living in the area (Antonella Locatelli) phoned the Belgian Embassy, the BBC and *Radio France Internationale* (Sibomana 1999: 48). She was assassinated the following day.

The Bugesera massacre (and the fake letter in particular) were designed to enable Habyarimana to call for a 'common Hutu front' (principally the MDR and MRND) against the 'RPF/*inyenzi* threat'. To achieve this, Habyarimana had to break the cohesion of the CDC and isolate the multi-ethnic PL. Then, he had to forcibly resolve the MDR's ambiguous relationship with MDR-Parmehutu (see above). To this end, the February 1992 edition of *Kangura* portrayed a vision of

Kayibanda visiting Rwanda, being shocked that 'Parmehutu' has been removed from 'MDR' and calling on his son-in-law, Twagiramungu, not to betray the Hutu. After the massacres, however, the MDR denounced the Nairobi *'communiqué'* as a fake, criticised *Radio Rwanda* for broadcasting it and demanded the removal of Ferdinand Nahimana (director of ORINFOR and *Radio Rwanda*) as well as the dismissal of the Ministers of the Interior and Information and the *sous-préfet* and *bourgmestre* of the commune where the massacres took place (Bertrand 2000: 148–9). Once it was clear that the MDR (especially Twagiramungu) would not capitulate, the CDR was formed (on 1 April 1992) as the 'true' reincarnation of MDR-Parmehutu.

His attempt to break the CDC and create a 'common Hutu front' having failed and under pressure from the US and Belgian ambassadors in Kigali, Habyarimana was forced (on 13 March 1992) to reach a 'Protocol of Understanding' with the MDR, PL, PSD and PDC, agreeing that a coalition cabinet (nine from the MRND(D), eleven from the four opposition parties) would be formed, with the Prime Minister being drawn from the largest opposition party: the MDR (see Reyntjens 1994: 108ff).[7]

Dismas Nsengiyaremye (the MDR's candidate) was appointed Prime Minister on 2 April 1992, announcing his cabinet and programme on 16 April.[8] The new cabinet took a number of immediate actions: replacing the ethnic/regional 'policy of equilibrium' (by which access to government schools was controlled in favour of the northern *préfectures*) with entrance exams (see Bertrand 2000: 25);[9] dismantling the secret service (*Service Central de Renseignements*); replacing the worst *préfets*; and removing Ferdinand Nahimana (whose broadcasts had incited the massacre of Tutsi in Bugesera in March 1992) from the directorship of the government information service (ORINFOR), which controlled the only radio station, *Radio Rwanda*. Habyarimana was also forced to relinquish his position as chief of the armed forces.

Between September 1992 and July 1993, Nsengiyaremye wrote a number of letters to Habyarimana (parts of which were reproduced in the press) detailing the way in which affiliates of the MRND(D) (including the *interahamwe*) were destabilising the country (see Prunier 1995: 187) and criticising Habyarimana for his 'double language' regarding negotiations with the RPF (see Bertrand 2000: 196ff).

Nsengiyaremye was to be denounced by the pro-genocidal press as a 'traitor' (Chrétien et al. 1995: 257). Of the eleven members of his cabinet drawn from the opposition parties (all of whom, but one were Hutu) Félicien Gatabazi (Secretary-General of the PSD) was assassinated on 21 February 1994, probably by the Presidential Guard, and three other ministers killed in the first few days of the genocide[10] (as was the single Tutsi minister, Landoald Ndasingwa (PL)).

Nsengiyaremye's government made negotiation with the RPF a priority. In addition to an official meeting at Kampala on 24 May 1992 between the Foreign Minister (Boniface Ngulinzira (MDR)) and RPF vice-chairman Patrick Mazimpaka (to set a date for starting negotiations), representatives of the MDR, PSD and PL held talks with the RPF in Brussels on 29 May–3 June (see Bertrand 2000: 190–2), at which point the three parties combined under the name *Forces Démocratiques du Changement* (FDC). With the refusal of the MRND(D) to attend the Brussels meeting; the RPF's decision to renounce the armed struggle; and the common denunciation of Habyarimana by the RPF, MDR, PSD and PL as 'the major obstacle to peace', the meeting appeared to unite the internal and external opposition against Habyarimana. The PSD representative at the meeting, Théoneste Gafaranga, stated that he no longer considered the RPF as 'enemies', but as 'brothers' (Bertrand 2000: 201).

On 6 June 1992, the RPF and the official Rwandan government delegation reached agreement in Paris on the technicalities of a peace process, and talks began soon after in Arusha, the first agreement being signed on 12 July.[11] As well as including a cease-fire (to begin 31 July), the agreement called for the rule of law; respect of human rights; democratic pluralism and a system of power-sharing in the form of a 'Broad-Based Transitional Government' (BBTG). On 18 August, an agreement was signed, which detailed elements of 'the rule of law' and declared as inalienable the right of Tutsi refugees to return to Rwanda.[12] On 30 October, an agreement was signed on the formation of the BBTG, incorporating the RPF in to the existing coalition government.[13] New articles were added to this agreement on 9 January 1993, giving details of the distribution of cabinet posts and seats in the Transitional Assembly among the political parties and the RPF.[14] The agreements of October 1992 and January 1993 stripped Habyarimana of all meaningful power, reducing him to a ceremonial head of state (even the content of presidential addresses would be decided by the cabinet) (Reyntjens 1994: 249–50). The October 1992 agreement also strengthened the independence and authority of the judiciary (especially a recreated Supreme Court), which could hold Habyarimana and others accountable for massacres since 1990.[15]

These agreements appeared to demonstrate a delineation between those committed to non-violence and inclusive democracy and those committed to an ethnicised/racialised, anti-RPF/anti-Tutsi stance. Article 14 of the October 1992 agreement read: 'The political parties in the Coalition Government established on 16 April 1992, [MRND(D) MDR, PSD, PL, PDC] as well as the [RPF] shall set up the [BBTG and] shall decide by consensus, on the other political formations which may participate in that Government.' In other words, these parties would have to agree to admit the CDR. Such a move was unlikely, given that Article 61 of the January 1993 agreement read: 'political parties that do not participate in the [BBTG]' but would want to sit in the Transitional Assembly, would have to 'avoid engaging in sectarian practices and in any form of violence'. Article 80 of the same agreement read: 'the political forces called upon to participate in the Transitional institutions shall ... Abstain from all sorts of violence and inciting violence, by written or verbal communication ... and undertake to fight [and reject] any political ideology or any act aimed at fostering discrimination based on ethnic, regional, sexual or religious differences.' Clearly, the MRND(D), its *interahamwe* militia and its association with the CDR did not fulfil this undertaking. Equally, at a local level, the MDR did not avoid 'any form of violence' (see Wagner 1998).[16] But in terms of the official policy of the opposition leaders, the *bloc* of opposition parties named in the agreements corresponded, at this stage, to 'Hutu moderates', understood (with hindsight) as 'anti-genocide'.

THE RISE OF 'HUTU POWER'

In January 1993, the leadership of the opposition parties *appeared* to be a single *bloc*. How, therefore, did it fragment into two factions: one committed to the Arusha agreements and the other becoming anti-RPF/anti-Tutsi 'Hutu Power'?

Nsengiyaremye did not become Prime Minister in April 1992 by virtue of being the 'leader' of the MDR. At the time, there were six MDR 'presidents', each in various degrees of competition with one another. Only in August 1992, did Twagiramungu become the party's official president. By proposing Nsengiyaremye (in April 1992), the other 'presidents' may have sought to avoid the potential failures of the first multiparty government (Bertrand 2000: 173). By the end of his mandate, however, Nsengiyaremye had proved himself a contender to Habyarimana, thereby raising the stakes higher for rivals within his own party. The seeds were sown by which 'Hutu Power' would emerge *within* the MDR by virtue of personal opportunism.

Frodauld Karamira and Jean-Marie Vianney Nkezabera (both members of the National Committee of the MDR) had denounced the meeting between the CDC (which included their MDR colleagues) and the RPF in Brussels in June 1992 (Bertrand 2000: 202). Given that the MDR had yet to hold a national congress to elect a *de jure* leadership, they could argue that positions taken by the *de facto* leadership (in Brussels) were not those of the party *in general*.

On 21 January 1993, in an attempt to topple Nsengiyaremye's government and restart the war, the MRND(D) rejected the January Arusha agreement, arguing that Ngulinzira (MDR Foreign Minister) did not have the mandate to negotiate power-sharing with the RPF. MRND(D) activists and *interahamwe* then committed massacres in the north-west until 26 January (with at least 300, predominantly Tutsi, killed and 20,000 displaced). The RPF broke the cease-fire (on 8 February), advancing to within 30 km of Kigali, killing 100–250 civilians in the process (see HRW 1993: 24–5).[17] On 20 February, the RPF unilaterally declared a new cease-fire and returned to their pre-offensive positions. To some within the opposition parties, the offensive indicated that the RPF's negotiations at Arusha were merely a manoeuvre to take power (HRW & FIDH 1999: 109). Those who did not believe this found it increasingly difficult to maintain opposition to Habyarimana lest they be seen as condoning RPF aggression.

In response, the opposition parties (MDR, PSD, PL, PDC) sent a delegation to meet the RPF in Bujumbura (25 February–2 March), resulting in a joint *communiqué* calling for: a new cease-fire; withdrawal of French troops; the return of IDPs to their homes; and legal action against those responsible for recent massacres. Simultaneously, Habyarimana organised a 'national conference' attended by representatives of the MRND(D), CDR *and* the MDR, PSD, PL and PDC. In direct opposition to the Bujumbura *communiqué*, this meeting condemned the 'RPF-*inkotanyi*' for 'trying to take power by force of arms'; thanked the FAR for their 'bravery'; welcomed the French military presence; and called for the government to mobilise the population in civil defence (Prunier 1995: 179).

Divisions within the main opposition parties were clear, given that members had attended two different meetings that released diametrically opposed *communiqués*. Three of the four opposition delegates who had attended Habyarimana's conference were personal challengers of their party presidents.[18] Given that the basis of the BBTG was in place, actors were now jockeying *within* parties for who was to represent the party in the new cabinet and national assembly. The danger of personal politicking appeared to be averted when the presidents of the four opposition parties[19] issued a joint *communiqué* stating that those who had attended the 'national conference' had 'neither the mandate nor the power to start such negotiations' (quoted in Prunier 1995: 181).

With a meeting between Nsengiyaremye and the RPF at Dar es Salaam (6–8 March 1993) the Arusha process resumed. But within the MDR, personal ambition and animosity was not so easily resolved (especially the personal animosity of Karamira for Twagiramungu). Twagiramungu had been elected MDR president in August 1992 and was thus *de jure* leader, with Nsengiyaremye as first vice-president, Karamira as second vice-president, Murego as secretary-general, while Gapyisi was head of the party's 'Political and Ideological' Commission (Bertrand 2000: 209).

Gapyisi remained the main rival to Twagiramungu and Nsengiyaremye. In March–April 1993, Gapyisi began to recruit support from *all* the opposition parties to create an anti-Habyarimana *and* anti-RPF (anti-Arusha) group, the *Forum Paix et Démocratie* (FPD). Although the movement opposed Habyarimana, it also resolved the ambiguity of the MDR's official, non-ethnic/racial position, by stating clearly that 'democracy' corresponded to the 'ethnic majority' ('the Hutu') in whose hands power must remain. Habyarimana, seen as incapable of defending 'the Hutu', should be side-stepped. The FPD was the 'common front of Hutu' that Habyarimana was incapable, or unwilling, to create. On 18 May 1993, Gapyisi was assassinated, probably by those associated with the MRND(D), who saw in him a rival who, 'unsullied' by Habyarimana's 'sell-out' at Arusha, was well placed to claim the 'defender of the Hutu' mantle (see Prunier 1995: 185).

Elements within the MDR maintained the position taken by Gapyisi before his death. Considering negotiations with the RPF to be treason, they denounced Twagiramungu and Nsengiyaremye as traitors, the former for having initiated negotiations with the RPF (in Brussels May/June 1992), the latter for having made these negotiations government policy (in Paris). In July 1993, Murego (second vice-president of the MDR) denounced both his 'colleagues' as 'traitors and enemies of our country' (quoted in Bertrand 2000: 225).

Nsengiyaremye's mandate (of April 1992) ended on 16 Apryil 1993, but was extended for three months to complete the Arusha negotiations. Although Nsengiyaremye wanted to remain in the post, on 16 June, Habyarimana, the presidents of the PSD, PL, PDC *and* Twagiramungu (as president of the MDR) issued a joint *communiqué* refusing to extend his mandate any further (despite the fact that he was the MDR's official candidate). Furthermore, Twagiramungu, in consultation with Habyarimana, unilaterally proposed Agathe Uwilingiyimana as Prime Minister (which she became on 18 July 1993). Twagiramungu appears to have blocked the reappointment of Nsengiyaremye in order that he himself could become prime minister once the BBTG was installed (Bertrand 2000: 222). In so doing, Twagiramungu, for personal strategic reasons, assisted Habyarimana in splitting the MDR. With the agreement to form the BBTG (and the possibilities of power that entailed) personal strategies had come to the fore.

At this point, there were three groupings within the MDR. First, those who believed that the party should be Hutu, anti-RPF/anti-Tutsi, 'true' to its MDR-Parmehutu roots. Second, those loyal to Twagiramungu (including the MDR ministers) who continued to assert that the 'democratic' legacy of the 1959 'revolution' could remain a de-ethnicised principle. Finally, those who, although repelled by the emerging ethnic ideology, considered Twagiramungu to be a dangerous opportunist (Bertrand 2000: 235). Paradoxically, although Twagiramungu and Nsengiyaremye had, until then, been in ideological agreement (pro-Arusha)[20] their personal schism provided a void into which the anti-Arusha/anti-RPF/anti-Tutsi MDR faction could step. This faction, always hostile to negotiations with the RPF, now constructed a clear division between the pro- and anti-Arusha wings within the party. In July 1993, having received death threats, Nsengiyaremye withdrew from being the MDR's official candidate for the premiership of the BBTG and left Rwanda. With his exit, internal rivalry within the MDR became more pronounced regarding who would replace Uwilingiyimana as the 'official' MDR candidate for prime minister of the BBTG, given that Twagiramungu was acting unilaterally, Nsengiyaremye was out of the country and Gapyisi was dead. The way was now clear for the ethnicised anti-RPF/anti-Arusha/anti-Tutsi wing to take control, led by Karamira, who denounced the Arusha Accords as a 'surrender to the RPF' (ibid. 237).

The explicitly ethnic discourse of the CDR was now echoed within the MDR, as Karamira and Murego denounced Twagiramungu for having betrayed MDR-Parmehutu and thus 'the Hutu' (Bertrand 2000: 237). Although Karamira had wanted Nsengiyaremye to be the MDR's candidate for the premiership of the BBTG (as a way of excluding Twagiramungu from future presidential elections) when Twagiramungu excluded Nsengiyaremye by appointing Uwilingiyimana, Karamira proposed Jean Kambanda as prime minister of the BBTG. On 20 July 1993, the Political Commission of the MDR named Kambanda as the party's candidate. On the same day, in a letter to Habyarimana and the RPF, Twagiramungu (still officially president of the MDR) unilaterally proposed himself as the MDR candidate for the premiership of the BBTG, a proposition accepted by Habyarimana. Although this action could be interpreted as opportunism, it would also prevent an anti-Arusha (anti-RPF/anti-Tutsi) MDR candidate acceding to the premiership. At an (illegal) Extraordinary Congress of the MDR (26 July 1993), called and chaired by Karamira, the membership voted to expel Twagiramungu from the party (with a narrow margin 217 for, 201 against); made Nsengiyaremye party president and declared Kambanda the party's 'official' candidate for the premiership. Nsengiyaremye, uncomfortable with the legality of the extraordinary congress, refused to take up the position, preferring to wait for a legal congress, which could make him the MDR candidate in a future presidential election. Consequently, Karamira declared himself president of 'MDR-Power'.

The congress also expelled Uwilingiyimana (the Prime Minister) and the MDR ministers in her cabinet, all of whom remained loyal to Twagiramungu. With Twagiramungu destined to become Prime Minister by virtue of being the *official* president of the MDR (the party to which the post was assigned by the Arusha Accords) and his agreement with Habyarimana and the RPF, Karamira could not allow the BBTG to be installed and what had become 'MDR-Power' refused to suggest candidates for its allotted posts in the BBTG, thereby undermining the viability of the new government and the whole Arusha settlement.

On 4 August 1993, Habyarimana signed the peace agreement at Arusha, which set out the arrangements for the BBTG that would come into power by the end of the year with Twagiramungu named as Prime Minister. And yet, with the MDR 'proper' (led by Karamira) espousing an anti-RPF/anti-Arusha stance and refusing to name the four MDR candidates for ministerial posts in the BBTG, Habyarimana could feel assured that the new government would never come into existence or at least not as envisaged in the Arusha Accords. Despite this, the signing of the peace agreement was greeted with relief among the general population, especially the hundreds of thousands of IDPs.

On 21 October 1993 the first elected President of Burundi, Melchior Ndadaye (a Hutu), was assassinated by Tutsi army officers.[21] At least 50,000 people were killed in ensuing violence (60 per cent Tutsi, 40 per cent Hutu), 150,000 Tutsi internally displaced and 350,000 Hutu fled to Rwanda (see HRW et al. 1994).[22] A UN commission of inquiry concluded that 'acts of genocide had been perpetrated against the minority Tutsi' from 21 October by militants and leaders of FRODEBU (UN 1996e para 483; 496) and that an international tribunal should be given competence over these crimes. Echoing the multi-ethnic BBTG envisaged in the Arusha Accords, Ndadaye had appointed Sylvie Kinigi, a Tutsi from the opposition party (UPRONA) as Prime Minister (and a third of the cabinet were Tutsi). There was clear symbolism in that Ndadaye's attempt to transcend ethnic division had led to so little (symbolically emphasised by the fact that both the Rwandan and Burundian prime ministers were women). The position of pro-Arusha politicians in Rwanda was seriously undermined, with anti-Arusha factions within the Rwandan opposition parties arguing that the RPF may (like their 'Tutsi brothers' in Burundi) not respect the principle of multi-ethnic government as envisaged by the peace settlement (see Prunier 1995: 200; Chrétien et al. 1995: 133).

On 23 October 1993, at an MDR rally (attended by members of the MRND(D), CDR and PL) Karamira declared that the RPF were among those who had plotted to kill Ndadaye and it would do the same in Rwanda (HRW & FIDH 1999: 138). Rejecting the Arusha Accords, Karamira denounced Twagiramungu and Uwilingiyimana as *inyenzi*, as 'puppets of the Tutsi', stating that 'the enemy is among us', that 'we have plans "to work"' (kill Tutsi) and calling on Hutu to unite and mobilise against the Tutsi 'invaders' (Bertrand 2000: 247). In conclusion, he shouted 'Hutu Power! MRND Power! CDR Power! MDR Power! *Interahamwe* Power! JDR Power![23] All Hutu are one Power!' (quoted in HRW & FIDH 1999: 138).

The anti-Arusha/anti-RPF/anti-Tutsi wing of the MDR now coalesced with the CDR and MRND(D). The ethnic/racialised understandings of 'the Republic' and 'democracy' were now ascendant, with 'Hutu Power' presenting itself as the 'true custodians' of the legacy of the 1959 'revolution', interpreted as the victory of the 'Hutu majority', '*le peuple majoritaire*'. The contemporary situation was now presented unequivocally as a conflict between 'the Hutu' and 'the Tutsi'. A large part of the MDR were now associated with the CDR and MRND(D), who in turn were associated with elements among the military, media and administration who were engaged in widespread violence and establishing the machinery of genocide.[24] Meanwhile, Twagiramungu and Uwilingiyimana tried to maintain the MDR's original position of fighting for 'freedom and democracy' for *all* Rwandese (based on the Arusha Accords).

Similar personal rivalries and politicking were seen within the PL regarding who would be the party's candidate for President of the Transitional National Assembly (a post assigned to the PL by the Arusha Accords). Given that Mugenzi (President) and Ndasingwa (First Vice-President) were Hutu and Tutsi, respectively, the division between supporters of the candidates was quickly ethnicised (Bertrand 2000: 250). Mugenzi, a notorious opportunist, crippled by debts, had secretly agreed to support Habyarimana and became the anti-Arusha/'Hutu Power' leader within the PL (see Prunier 1995: 130). In contrast, the PSD leadership resisted ethnicising/racialising the situation.

By the end of 1993, party allegiance was fading in the face of 'Hutu Power' and its ethnicised/racialised representation of the situation. In the political environment of 1993, following the RPF offensive and the killing of Ndadye, it was the ethnic/racial interpretation of MDR-Parmehutu's 'legacy' that proved most effective in attracting support. The 'Power' groups now moved closer to the CDR and the hard-line wing of the MRND(D). It was to be the 'Power' representatives of these parties who would form the 'Interim Government', which was to oversee the genocide, with Jean Kambanda ('MDR-Power') as Prime Minister.[25]

THE GROUPING OF THE *IBYITSO*, *INYENZI* AND 'THE OPPOSITION'

The evolution of the opposition parties demonstrates that the use of the epitaph 'Hutu moderate' disguises great complexity. In tandem with shifting allegiances there was also a meta-discourse that denounced *any* opposition to Habyarimana. Opposition politicians were presented as RPF 'collaborators' *en bloc*, with only those who explicitly associated themselves with 'Hutu Power' able to shake off this association.

Given its extensive Tutsi membership, the PL was denounced as a 'Tutsi' party, a 'snake with a thousand heads' fighting to undo the gains of the 'revolution' and a 'natural branch of the RPF' (see Chrétien et al. 1995: 225; 234; 253; 255; Article XIX 1996: 36). The *communiqué* from a fictitious organisation based in Nairobi mentioned above (3 February 1992) and broadcast five times on *Radio Rwanda* to incite the Bugesera massacre of March 1992, warned that:

> Foreign terrorist agents (Arabic and African) have just been recruited here [in Nairobi]. They are to be infiltrated into Rwanda under different disguises (businessmen, tourists) and on arrival will immediately contact the local HQ of the RPF, the leadership of the *Parti Libéral*, led by Mr Justin Mugenzi. Different personalities will be murdered: politicians, businessmen, servicemen, all members of Hutu parties ... a Hutu leader of one of these political parties will be murdered ... [The RPF] is in direct and permanent contact with its branch in Kigali under the control of the [PL]. (see Guichaoua 1995: 612)

Although Mugenzi, a Hutu, was president of the PL, the party's other main leader, Ndasingwa (first vice-president) was Tutsi. Ndasingwa, therefore, would seem a more obvious candidate to be denounced as *ibyitso* (an RPF collaborator). And yet, Mugenzi as a Hutu was, at this stage, more dangerous as he could undermine the ethnicised/racialised discourse of 'the Hutu vs the Tutsi'. In 1992, it was more important for anti-Tutsi elements to mention and discredit Mugenzi explicity. The irony is that Mugenzi, denounced in March 1992 as *ibyitso*, was to later lead the 'Hutu Power' wing of the PL.

Genocidal propaganda claimed that all Tutsi in Rwanda were 'accomplices' (*ibyitso*) of the RPF and were planning to exterminate the Hutu (see HRW & FIDH 1999: 78).[26] In December 1990, *Kangura* stated that the 'extremist Tutsi' who had attacked Rwanda in October (the RPF) counted on the 'complicity of the Tutsi of the interior' (Chrétien 1991: 116). In July 1991, *Kangura* claimed that 85 per cent of the Tutsi population were linked to the RPF (Chrétien et al. 1995: 149). This denunciation of *ibyitso* was 'the fundamental obsession of *Kangura*' (ibid. 248) and expressed in the fictitious 'Simbananiye Plan'.[27]

Although *ibyitso* was used primarily to refer to 'Tutsi of the interior', the term was expanded to incorporate the opposition parties. In December 1991, two *communiqués* from *La Direction des opérations militaires des forces armées rwandaises* (a fictitious body [see Reyntjens 1995b: 267–8]) condemned those who 'knowingly or unknowingly, aided the enemy under the cover of political party activities' and called on the security services to 'neutralise all collaborators identified with the enemy' (quoted in HRW & FIDH 1999: 61). In February 1992, *Kangura* admonished the MDR for working with the PL, stating that the MDR and the PSD were working with *inyenzi* (Chrétien et al. 1995: 227). When in August 1992, Gatabazi (PSD Secretary-General) denounced massacres in Kibuye, he was denounced by the CDR as *ibyitso* (Prunier 1995: 162). Although the memorandum issued by Col. Déogratias Nsabimana (FAR Chief of Staff) on 21 September 1992 stated that 'The principal enemy is the Tutsi both inside and outside the country', it also stated that the 'enemy' was recruited from among those 'Hutu dissatisfied with the regime in power' (HRW & FIDH 1999: 63).

In his speech on 22 November 1992 (see Chapter 1) Léon Mugesera stated that the MDR 'as well as those who share its opinions are *ibyitso* of the *Inyenzi*', and continued:

> We must protect ourselves against the traitors and those who want to do us harm ... Having arrived at Brussels, the MDR, PL and the PSD agreed to hand over the *préfecture* of Byumba [to the RPF][28] they discussed how they could demoralise our soldiers ... The punishment for such persons is clear: 'Any person who is guilty of acts aiming at sapping the morale of the armed forces will be condemned to death' ... Why should we not kill such a person? Nsengiyaremye must be brought before the courts and ... condemned to death ... In all truth I tell you that the representatives of these parties, who collaborate with the *Inyenzi*, only want to exterminate us: they have no other objective ... the representatives of these parties who collaborate with the *Inyenzi*, namely the MDR, the PL, the PSD, the PDC and the other small groups ... all these parties, as well as their representatives should go and live in Kayenzi with Nsengiyaremye;[29] so we shall know where to find those with whom we are at war ... As for what they are going to say at Arusha it is the same as what those *ibyitso* of the *Inyenzi* who live here went to say in Brussels. [At Arusha] it is *Inyenzi* who negotiate with *Inyenzi*. (my translation from a French translation by Thomas Kamanzi)

Following the June 1992 meeting between MDR, PSD and PL and the RPF, the *Interahamwe* newspaper (MRND(D)) called for the arrest of the 'traitors' who had attended (see Chrétien et al. 1995: 255). Mugesera implies that the members of the Rwandan government's negotiating team at Arusha drawn from the opposition parties, Boniface Ngulinzira (the MDR Foreign Minister) and Landoald Ndasingwa (PL), are *inyenzi* (see Jones 2001: 72).

Elsewhere in the speech, Mugesera states that Tutsi are *ibyitso* and that this 'scum should be exterminated'. But, in the extract above, he explicitly brackets the opposition parties with the *inyenzi*/RPF and their 'accomplices' (*ibyitso*). Similarly, in a letter to Habyarimana on 20 January 1993, *Amasasu* (*Alliance des militaires agacés par les séculaires actes sournois des unaristes*)[30] declared that it would 'detect and destroy' the politicians and others who supported the RPF 'from within' and would deliver 'an exemplary lesson to these traitors from inside' (HRW 1993: 8). The following day, *Kangura* stated that the CDR was the true inheritor of the MDR-Parmehutu legacy and that 'The other parties ... have chosen to collaborate with the RPF' (quoted in Chrétien et al. 1995: 134).

Those who remained committed to a de-ethnicised, pro-Arusha stance (and resisted 'Hutu Power') were, within the genocidal mentality, bracketed with Tutsi as *ibyitso*. When the commitment of Hutu politicians to the Arusha process demonstrated the absurdity of a simple, ethnic/racial dichotomy of 'the Hutu vs the Tutsi', those who were to perpetrate the genocide shifted these anomalous individuals into the *ibyitso* category in order to maintain the simple binary segmentation they required. This demonstrates, again, that when 'matters out-of-category disturb the entire structure [they] must be either corrected or effaced' (Geertz 1983: 180). Members of the non-'Hutu Power' factions of the opposition parties were 'corrected' by turning them 'into objective *ibyitso*, no better than the Tutsi' (Prunier 1995: 231).

The bracketing of opposition Hutu and all Tutsi as a single, homogeneous target of genocide is obscured by the contemporary qualification of these 'Hutu' with the adjective 'moderate'. The forced amalgamation by the perpetrators of the genocide of opposition Hutu with the Tutsi into an undifferentiated, single target of genocide – required by the perpetrator's binary construction of Rwandan society – has now been separated into Tutsi and 'Hutu moderate'.

THE KILLING OF THE 'HUTU MODERATES'

The enormous gains of the CDC and Nsengiyaremye's government (especially the Arusha Accords) were acquired by the opposition parties *en bloc*, from which pro-genocide elements would later emerge. The ubiquitous, undefined phrase 'Hutu moderate' disguises this evolution. It appears that the contemporary term 'Hutu moderate' signifies those within opposition parties who were killed for having chosen to resist the anti-Arusha/anti-RPF/anti-Tutsi position (for ideological or opportunistic reasons). Half an hour after Habyarimana's plane was shot down, *RTLM*

> did not immediately designate the Tutsi as a target, but rather the Hutu opponents of the regime, who less than an hour later were attacked by the Presidential Guard ... the radio then made a quick change of strategy, calling for the extermination of the *Inyenzi* of the RPF, their accomplices ('*Ibyitso*', Tutsi of the interior), the 'traitors' (Hutu democrats) and all those who gave them shelter and assistance. (Chrétien et al. 1995: 78)

The 'Hutu moderates' killed included the following (see Guichaoua 1995: 777ff):

Agathe Uwilingiyimana, Prime Minister, MDR, killed 7 April 1994 by the Presidential Guard.

Boniface Ngulinzira, former Foreign Minister (named as the Minister of Information in the new BBTG), MDR, killed 14 April 1994 by the Presidential Guard.

Faustin Rucogoza, Minister of Information, MDR, killed 7 April 1994 by the Presidential Guard.

Félicien Ngango, Vice-President of the PSD (nominated to be the President of the new National Assembly), killed 7 April 1994 by the Presidential Guard.

Frédéric Nzamurambaho, Minister of Agriculture, President of the PSD, killed 7 April 1994 by the Presidential Guard.

Joseph Kavaruganda, President of the Constitutional Court, associated with the MDR, killed 7 April 1994 by the Presidential Guard.

Théoneste Gafaranga, Second Vice-President of the PSD, killed 16 April 1994 by the *interahamwe*.

The Tutsi vice-president of the PL and Minister of Work and Social Affairs, Landoald Ndasingwa, was also killed (with his family) by the Presidential Guard on 7 April 1994. The Foreign Minister, Anastase Gasana (MDR, Hutu) was targeted, but was still in Tanzania, although his *chef du cabinet*, Déogratias Havugimana (MDR, Hutu), was killed by the Presidential Guard on 7 April. Virtually the whole leadership of the PSD was killed (see Guichaoua 1995: 778), although Marc Rugenera (Hutu) managed to escape (see AR 1995: 179–81) as did Jean Népomuscène Nayinzira (PDC, Hutu) nominated as a minister in the BBTG (ibid. 194–5). Twagiramungu only survived because the killers had the wrong address, although most of his family were killed (Guichaoua 1995: 777). When *RTLM* announced the creation of the interim government on 8 April, the announcer laughingly stated that the former members of the cabinet 'could not be found' (Article XIX 1996: 110).

One assumes it is to these *visible* politicians that the contemporary term 'Hutu moderate' refers. It may equally refer to Hutu journalists killed for their anti-genocidal statements. Forty-nine journalists were murdered in 1994, more than half of the journalistic community (see Sibomana 1999: 46). Although many of them were Tutsi (for example, Charles Karinganire of *Le Flambeau*; Marcellin Kayiranga of *Kanguka*; Aloys Nyimbuzi of *L'Observateur* and Gratien Karambizi of *Imbaga*), Hutu journalists, such as Vincent Rwabukwisi of *Kanguka*, Emmanuel-Damien Rukondo of *Rubyiruko-Rubanda* and Tharcisse Rubwiriza of ORINFOR were killed because they had criticised the genocidal movement. Gaspard Karamera, editor of *Imbaga*, only just survived (AR 1995: 204–6) as did Sixbert Musangamfura, editor of *Isibo* (ibid. 206–9).

The term 'Hutu moderate' may equally refer to human rights activists murdered in 1994. By 1994, six human rights organisations were co-operating under CLADHO (*Collectif des Ligues et Associations de Défense des Droits de l'Homme*) (see Reyntjens 1994: 162). Human rights activists were among the first to be killed in the genocide. Again, many were Tutsi, such as Fidèle Kanyabugoyi of *Kanyarwanda*, Charles Shamukiga, of AVP (*Association pour les Voluntaires de la Paix*) and the Jesuit priest Chrysologue Mahame (see AR 1995: 213–19). Many, however, were Hutu, including Ignace Ruhatana of *Kanyarwanda*, Félicien Ngango, first vice-president of the PSD and ARDHO (*Association Rwandaise pour la Défense des Droits de l'Homme*). Alphonse-Marie Nkubito,[31] the Attorney-General and President of ARDHO, was targeted, but managed to escape. François-Xavier

Nsanzuwera, Deputy Attorney-General and deputy-secretary of ARDHO, was on the list of those to be killed, but also managed to escape (see AR 1995: 720–4).

It is unclear whether the term 'Hutu moderate' extends to the countless *non-visible* Hutu who saved Tutsi once the genocide began. Not only did many Hutu risk death by protecting Tutsi, but there are 'many, many cases of Hutus who died to protect Tutsi' (AR 1995: 590; see AR 2002; Jefremovas 1995; Rutayisire 1995). As used, the term 'Hutu moderate' appears to indicate Hutu who actively resisted at a *visible*, political level the violence perpetrated (and planned) by the 'CDR constellation' (Prunier 1995: 182). These Hutu were killed because they explicitly refused to condone acts committed 'in their name', their murder a '"destruction of alternatives" ... the elimination of people who represented those alternatives' (Bringa 2002: 213). If 'Hutu moderate' signifies only *visible* actors at political level, why is there no collective term for the 'ordinary' Hutu who resisted the genocide?

CONTEMPORARY FUNCTION OF THE TERM 'HUTU MODERATE'

From the complexity of Rwandan politics (1990–94) one can provisionally isolate those to whom the ubiquitous, contemporary phrase 'Hutu moderate' applies. And yet, the passive term 'Hutu moderate' fails to communicate the pro-active resistance these actors demonstrated.

These Hutu, both those killed and those who survived, demonstrate that the genocide perpetrator's binary construction of Rwanda ('the Hutu vs the Tutsi') was not 'natural', but had to be imposed. While one must recognise that opportunism and personal politicking were prevalent among the political class in 1990–94 (see Guichaoua 1995: 7), the acknowledgement of Hutu who resisted 'Hutu Power' remains a powerful rejection of the vision of Rwandan society proclaimed by the perpetrators of the genocide. And yet, is the phrase 'Hutu moderate' the best means? As one Tutsi *rescapé* stated:

> Anybody who was against Habyarimana and his regime was tagged as an enemy of the Hutu. This also explains the killing of those who came to be known as 'Hutu moderates', but the right term would be 'Hutu opposing Habyarimana and his power'. This correction needs to be made as the use of the term 'moderate' for only Hutu who were killed does not do justice to many Hutu, the

majority in fact, who were not involved in the killings. (Personal communication, Kigali, March 1998)

'Hutu moderates' are anomalous to prevalent, binary understandings of post-genocide Rwanda (there are only victims *or* perpetrators). Because the phrase is a qualification of a group that *still exists*, but the phrase is only used (persistently) to refer to an event *in the past*, then that qualification becomes a purely retrospective quality. This group, one that demonstrates the absurdity of the genocide perpetrator's manichean construction of Rwandan society, may be mentioned, but it is anterior and prefatory to the 'manageable, schematised form' (Hinton 2002: 12) by which contemporary Rwanda is understood. The phrase 'Hutu moderate' may then imply a deceased 'righteous minority', 'exceptions to the rule' that serve to damn the remaining 'unrighteous majority' (Novick 2001: 180).

There is an additional danger inherent in the term 'Hutu moderate'. Used only retrospectively it implies that Hutu are, by default, 'extremist' – for 'moderate' inevitably suggests its antonym. While 'Hutu moderate' is used exclusively as a retrospective term, the phrase 'Hutu extremist' is widely used in describing the contemporary situation with a 'subliminal impact':

> After deconstructing the term ['Hutu extremist'] we find a word denoting an ethnic group and a word for an ideological bigot or fanatic. Re-coupled, we have a choice of meanings: (1) a bigot or fanatic belonging to the Bahutu ethnic group, or (2) a member of the bigoted and fanatical Bahutu tribe. Doubtless meaning (1) is what most 'informed' observers would claim that they intend to convey. Nevertheless, by choosing this form of words they must take some share of the responsibility for the occasions when meaning (2) is actually understood [which] leaves an impression of a consensus that political formations in Rwanda are defined almost entirely by ethnic association ... In other words, Hutu cultural identity has now been conflated with genocidal political ideology. (Stockton 1996: 4)

With the term 'Hutu moderate' consigned to *the past*, the use of the term 'Hutu extremist' *in the present* may strengthen a global conflation of '<u>the</u> Hutu' and '<u>the</u> Tutsi' with *génocidaire* and *rescapé*. Commenting on Karamira's 'Power Speech' (see above), in which he associated the RPF with the leaders of the Burundian *coup* (thereby globalising guilt to all Tutsi), Jordane Bertrand observes that 'the assimilation of the whole of an ethnic group with certain members of it is at the root and is the perversity of the argument' (2000: 247). The inanimate character of the term 'Hutu moderate' and animate character of the term 'Hutu extremist' may generate understandings of Rwandan society segmented along simple, binary lines – the same simple, binary lines deployed by the perpetrators of the genocide.

Ultimately, genocide and individual criminal responsibility are indivisible. The globalisation of guilt according to ethnic identity not only resonates with the construction of Rwandan society on which the genocide perpetrators depended, but undermines the contribution that the recognition of genocide (indivisible from individual criminal responsibility) should make to 'the process of national reconciliation and to the restoration and maintenance of peace' (UN 1994q).

5
Unresolved Allegations and the Culture of Impunity

The judicial recognition of 1994 as genocide (especially in the Akayesu judgment) entirely reconfigures how 'ethnic' violence in the Great Lakes Region *should* be interpreted, placing individual accountability centre stage. As a denunciation and prohibition of mass murder based on constructed collectivities, the recognition of the *crime* of genocide is required to be resolutely 'anti-collectivisation' and thus based on individual criminal responsibility. Individual responsibility is needed to refute unequivocally the massive distortions of empirical reality found in genocidal propaganda (see Chapter 1) and end the 'dangerous culture of collective guilt and retribution, which too often produces further cycles of violence' (Kritz 1996: 591).

Individual responsibility is the final *coup de grâce* to a mode of thought that has poisoned Rwandan society from colonialism to the genocide of April–July 1994. And yet, the caricature of manichean, collective categories still permeates representations of Rwanda. It cannot be overstated that giving contemporary credence to this simplistic image grants a posthumous victory to those who planned, propagated and perpetrated the 1994 genocide, based on the image of a 'final battle' (the *Simusiga*) between two, essentialised 'quasi-nations' (Kagabo & Vidal 1994: 545).

The pressing need for individual responsibility to efface wholly assertions of collective guilt is demonstrated by three issues considered in this chapter. All three have been pursued within the context of international human rights law, based exclusively on individual responsibility. For anyone who has accepted that the events of April–July 1994 were genocide (a concept indivisible from the principle of individual responsibility) pursuing these three issues is unproblematic. Their pursuance is only troublesome to those who remain tempted to mutate individual agency into collective agency, a temptation central to the genocidal propaganda of 1990–94.

For some actors it is expedient to simply ignore these three issues and respond with silence. And yet, these issues feature prominently in how Rwandan exiles and international observers interpret post-genocide Rwanda. In addition, two of the issues are the subject of active judicial investigations, while a third (given the seriousness of the allegations) will probably become so in the future. The three issues are: alleged massacres committed by the RPA in Rwanda 1990–94; responsibility for the attack on the plane carrying President Habyarimana in April 1994; and the involvement of the RPA in the alleged massacre of Rwandan refugees in Zaïre (now the Democratic Republic of Congo) in 1996–97.

ALLEGED MASSACRES COMMITTED BY THE RPA IN RWANDA OCTOBER 1990–APRIL 1994

On this subject, only the exiles expressed an opinion:

> Before they took power, the RPF committed massacres in the north; in Byumba and Ruhengeri. (Former Rwandan government official, exile, Belgium, March 1999)

> Why was there no condemnation of the Byumba massacres of 1990? (Former Rwandan minister, exile, Belgium, February 1999)

> The RPF killed the Hutu population of Byumba in the zone they controlled. (Rwandan academic, exile, Switzerland, June 1999)

There is a paucity of information regarding allegations of massacres committed by the RPA in the period October 1990–April 1994. Some authors argue that this is because the movement of journalists and human rights workers was closely controlled by RPF 'guides' in the area it controlled (see AI 1994: 2; Dorsey 2000: 343). When the *International Commission of Inquiry into Human Rights Abuse in Rwanda* visited the RPF-controlled zone for a few hours in January 1993, commission members were able to interview who they wished, but only in the company of an RPF official (HRW et al. 1993: 31). Those interviewed did not complain of human rights abuses by the RPF. Testimony collected by the commission *outside* the RPF zone did contain reports of alleged killings by the RPF, but were few in number. AI, however, stated that it had received 'numerous reports of human rights abuses committed by the RPA' since October 1990, including 'hundreds of deliberate and arbitrary killings ... "disappearances" of captured combatants and unarmed civilians suspected of supporting the [Habyarimana] government' (AI 1994: 2).

There is little available evidence that the RPA committed systematic massacres between October 1990 and April 1994, although isolated human rights abuses (including arbitrary killings) appear to have been committed. It is not clear on what basis the exiles make their accusations.

In a letter to the President of the UNSC on 28 September 1994, the post-genocide Rwandan government requested that an international tribunal with jurisdiction over Rwanda be established 'as soon as possible' (UN 1994n). The government argued that the tribunal's jurisdiction should cover the period 1 October 1990–17 July 1994 so that it could 'investigate the crimes committed against Tutsis and moderate Hutus since the beginning of the war in 1990 up until the final victory of the [RPF]' (ICG 1999: 22). The government objected, therefore, to the proposal that the tribunal's jurisdiction would cover the period *after* 17 July 1994 (the date on which the RPF established a Government of National Unity) and that it would not cover October 1990–December 1993 (see UN 1994p). Ultimately, the ICTR's jurisdiction covers the period 1 January–31 December 1994. This strict, temporal delineation is in contrast to the ICTY, whose mandate covers crimes committed anytime '*since* 1991'. It appears that the UNSC chose this period to enable the tribunal to investigate violations of international humanitarian law committed by the RPA *after* July 1994. The statute of the ICTR was based, in a large part, upon the findings of the UNCE's interim report (1 October 1994), which stated there were 'substantial grounds' to conclude that the RPA had committed serious breaches of international humanitarian law and crimes against humanity between April and early September 1994 (UN 1994o paras 79–83).

The ICTR's jurisdiction does not cover the period 1990–94 (as requested by the Rwandan government) but does include the period *after* 17 July 1994 up to 31 December 1994 (as rejected by the Rwandan government). This was one of the reasons why Rwanda was the only member of the UNSC to vote against Resolution 955 (8 November 1994), which established the tribunal.[1] The ICTR cannot, therefore, investigate the massacre of 2,000-plus Tutsi in 1990–93, nor the killing of Hutu opponents of Habyarimana during the same period. Likewise it cannot confirm or refute the allegation of human rights abuses by the RPA during the same period. In contrast to the ICTR, Rwanda's domestic genocide law (30 August 1996) covers acts of genocide, crimes against humanity and violations of the Geneva Conventions committed 'since 1 October 1990' (Art. I).[2] It would be unlikely, however, for Rwanda's domestic courts, at this stage, to investigate allegations against the RPA.

ALLEGED MASSACRES COMMITTED BY
THE RPA IN RWANDA APRIL–DECEMBER 1994

It is puzzling that the exiles interviewed concentrated on arguing that the RPA committed large-scale massacres prior to April 1994 given that human rights organisations have published substantial allegations that the RPA committed such massacres *after* the start of the genocide (6 April 1994).

As AI made clear in its report of 20 October 1994, 'Given the horrendous scale of massacres committed by forces loyal to the former government [the genocide of Tutsi], there could never be any comparison between those massacres and other human rights abuses committed by the RPA' (1994: 1).

In a report in August 1994 AI stated 'hundreds – possibly thousands – of unarmed civilians and captured armed opponents of the RPF have been summarily executed or otherwise deliberately and arbitrarily killed' since 6 April 1994 (ibid. 3). Following a mission in September 1994, HRW reported detailed specific massacres and 'disappearances' by the RPA since June and concluded that 'substantial numbers – at least hundreds – of persons' had been killed after being taken away by soldiers (1994: 9). The report specifically documented the alleged massacre of hundreds of civilians by RPA soldiers in Mukingi commune during 19–21 June 1994 (ibid. 6). Paul Kagame told HRW that Major Sam Bigabiro 'may have been in command at Mukingi' when the massacre had taken place and that Bigabiro was under arrest for killing civilians (ibid. 7).

The interim report of the UNCE (1 October 1994) authoritatively declared that Tutsi had been victims of a genocide (UN 1994o paras 44; 124; 133; 148). The commission also stated that there were 'substantial grounds' to

> conclude that mass assassinations, summary executions, breaches of international humanitarian law and crimes against humanity were also perpetrated by Tutsi elements against Hutu individuals and that allegations concerning these acts should be investigated further [although] the Commission has not uncovered any evidence to indicate that Tutsi elements perpetrated acts

committed with intent to destroy the Hutu ethnic group as such within the meaning of the [UNGC]. (ibid. para 82)

The commission's ethnicisation of these allegations (use of the term 'Tutsi elements' rather than RPF or RPA) is distorting and regrettable, but it is clear that the commission possessed evidence. The commission had also received reports of 'violations of the right to life' by the RPA 'from August to early September 1994' and was actively investigating these allegations (UN 1994o para 83). Subsequently, in its final report (9 December 1994), the commission stated that it had received from UNHCR

information concerning massacres alleged to have been perpetrated by members of the [RPA] on a systematic basis against a number of Hutus. In all alleged cases, the victims included not only men, but also women and children. Most of the massacres do not seem to have been provoked by individuals suspected of participation in the massacres of Tutsis carried out in April 1994. (UN 1994s para 44)

In this final report, the commission reiterated that it had been unable to uncover any evidence that the killings by 'Tutsi elements' were intended 'to destroy the Hutu ethnic group as such within the meaning of the [UNGC]' (UN 1994s para 98) or that the 'killings of Hutus perpetrated by a certain number of RPF soldiers were systematic, sponsored, or even approved of by Government officials or army commanders' (ibid. para 185). The commission recommended, however, that 'an investigation of violations of international humanitarian law and of human rights law attributed to the [RPF] be continued by the Prosecutor for the [ICTR]' and that it would hand over 'all relevant files' to the UNSG (ibid. para 100).

After the Government of National Unity was established (17 July 1994), UNHCR sent a three-person mission, led by Robert Gersony, to explore ways in which the 2 million refugees in neighbouring countries could be repatriated. Given that the objective of Gersony's team was to facilitate repatriation (a goal of the new government) the mission was allowed to travel freely without the presence of official 'guides'. Between 1 August and 5 September, Gersony's team visited 91 sites and gathered information about ten others, conducting 200+ interviews and 100 group-discussions at these sites and in nine refugee camps. By 23 September 1994, an internal

UNHCR memo (as seen by HRW) stated that the RPF had committed 'systematic murders and persecution of the Hutu population in certain parts of the country' (quoted in HRW & FIDH 1999: 727).

It is to the UNHCR memo that the UNCE appears to refer in its interim report (1 October 1994), stating that it had received from UNHCR 'extensive evidence of systematic killings and persecution ... of Hutu individuals by the [RPA]' (UN 1994o para 30; see AI 1994: 4). On 10 October 1994, the commission was to meet with UNHCR officials *including* Gersony (UN 1994s para 20).

The September UNHCR memo estimated that the RPA had killed 'thousands of persons a month' (quoted in HRW & FIDH 1999: 728). Gersony himself reportedly estimated that in the period April–August 1994 the RPA had killed 25,000–45,000 people (ibid.).

Gersony sent a report to the UN High Commissioner for Refugees who in turn informed the UNSG. The UNSG then instructed Kofi Annan (at that time head of Peacekeeping Operations) to visit Rwanda. On arrival in Kigali (18 September), Gersony briefed Annan, Shaharyar Khan (UNSG's Special Representative to Rwanda) and UNAMIR commanders. Gersony stated that, between June and August, he had spoken to witnesses who had escaped alleged RPA massacres, that he had visited the sites where killings had allegedly taken place and counter-checked evidence (Khan 2000: 51). He was convinced that the 'RPA had engaged in the calculated, systematic, pre-planned killings of around 30,000 Hutus' mostly in the southern belt of Rwanda bordering Burundi and Tanzania (ibid.). It should be noted that, although the UNCE gave credence to the UNHCR memo, they found no evidence that killings had been systematic or ordered by the RPA high command (UN 1994s para 98).

Annan, Gersony, Khan and a UNHCR representative then met with the Rwandan Prime Minister (Faustin Twagiramungu), the Minister of Foreign Affairs (Jean-Marie Vianney Ndagijimana) and the Minister of the Interior (Seth Sendeshonga) to whom Gersony presented his findings (Khan 2000: 52). The three Rwandan ministers admitted there had been individual reprisal killings, but rejected Gersony's assertions regarding the scale and systematic nature of the alleged massacres (HRW & FIDH 1999: 729). Both the UN Military Observers and UN Rwandan Emergency Office reported that there had been revenge killings, but also rejected the idea of 'systematic, preordained massacres' (Khan 2000: 53). Khan implies, however, that there were hardly any UNAMIR troops or NGOs operating in the area in which Gersony claimed the majority of massacres had taken place (ibid.).

Once Gersony's allegations were known, UNAMIR despatched 100 peacekeepers to the south-eastern region (HRW & FIDH 1999: 730).

Khan convinced Sendeshonga and Twagiramungu to establish a joint UN/government investigation team. The next day the investigation team left 'late in the day' (HRW & FIDH 1999: 730) and travelled to Kibungo (two hours by road). There they visited one mass grave identified by Gersony which, the team concluded, dated back to April or May (Khan 2000: 54). This was the sum of the team's activities. According to HRW and FIDH, 'One witness connected with the group dismisses the investigation as a sham from the beginning, saying that no one wanted the truth known' (1999: 730).

According to HRW and FIDH (1999: 730–1) Gersony was instructed not to write a report. When, in April 1996, a representative of the UNHCHR Special Rapporteur (René Degni-Ségui) requested a copy of the 'Gersony Report', he received a letter from the UNHCR office in Rwanda stating that 'the Gersony Report <u>does not exist</u> [n'existe pas]' (ibid. 726; underlined in original).

Brief visits to the field by UN and US officials and the one-day investigation did not confirm Gersony's findings, 'neither were they extensive enough to invalidate them' (HRW & FIDH 1999: 731). Whether Gersony's estimates are exaggerated remains unresolved. HRW and FIDH believe that 'partial and tentative' estimates put the 'minimum death toll' at between 25,000 and 30,000 killed by the RPA in 1994, although the two organisations admit that it is impossible to say how many of those killed were active participants in the genocide or were engaged in any military action against the RPA when killed (ibid. 734). Irrespective of exact numbers, HRW and FIDH conclude that:

> These killings were widespread, systematic, and involved large numbers of victims and participants. They were too many and too much alike to have been unconnected crimes committed by individual soldiers or low-ranking officers. Given the disciplined nature of the RPF forces and the extent of communication up and down the hierarchy, commanders of this army must have known of and at least tolerated these practices. (1999: 734–5)

Unlike accusations of RPA abuses before 1994, alleged massacres in 1994 come under the temporal jurisdiction of the ICTR and would fall under serious violations of the Geneva Conventions or (depending on their scale and whether systematic) crimes against humanity. The UNCE recommended (in December 1994) that the ICTR Prosecutor further investigate these allegations (UN 1994s para 100). In September 1998, Judge Laity Kama (President of the ICTR) stated that 'All parties, including the RPF, who have committed crimes against humanity must be prosecuted. It is a simple question of equality. The credibility of international justice demands it' (quoted in Hazan 1998).

In an interview on 13 December 2000, Carla del Ponte (at that time Chief Prosecutor at the ICTR) stated that she had opened (in 1999) an investigation into alleged war crimes committed by the RPF during 1994 and had informed the Rwandan government at the time. On 9 December 2000, del Ponte had held a private meeting with President Kagame at which he had agreed to co-operate fully with the investigation into three specific cases of alleged massacres (IRIN 2000xiii). Del Ponte hoped that the investigation would be completed 'during the next year' (ibid.). Asked whether the independence of her investigation was damaged by discussing these issues with the commander of the RPA at the time of the alleged massacres (Kagame), del Ponte stated that the Rwandan government had its own relevant dossiers on the alleged massacres and that: 'I need access to witnesses ... Being realistic, without their co-operation I can get nowhere' (ibid.; see Edwards 2000a).

In April 2001, Kagame reportedly agreed to hand over to the tribunal any army officers suspected of committing crimes in 1994 (IRIN 2001ii). In April 2002, however, del Ponte's spokesperson announced that the she was 'not satisfied' with the level of co-operation received from the Rwandan authorities and was dissatisfied with access to archives, documents and witnesses in Rwanda, although she hoped to issue an indictment by the end of the year (IRIN 2002ii).

In a letter to the UNSC on 23 July 2002, del Ponte complained that the Rwandan government was impeding the progress of the ICTR's prosecutions, by making it difficult for witnesses to travel from Rwanda to Arusha, witnesses 'whose testimonies are crucial to the prosecution of ongoing [genocide] cases' (UN Wire 2002). Del Ponte stated that tensions between the tribunal and the Rwandan government had escalated since December 2001 when the ICTR 'indicted an unnamed member of the [RPF]' (quoted in ibid.; see Lynch 2002). Whether this was misreporting and referred only to del Ponte's *intention* to indict, or alternatively that 'sealed' indictments (which remain secret until the indicted individual has been apprehended) had already been issued, is unclear. At the end of October 2002, del Ponte presented a report to the UNSC detailing what she considered as obstruction by the Rwandan government, while the ICTR President (Navanethem Pillay) registered a formal complaint.

In mid-October 2002, the Rwandan government suddenly increased its co-operation with the tribunal, leading to reports that del Ponte had suspended investigation into the RPA cases (HRW 2002b; Nicholas 2003). Del Ponte explained, however, that she had stopped the investigation because 'It was the moment for me to ask [the investigators] to assess what they had uncovered, to see what has come out of the investigations and what can be used' and that the full investigation had resumed in November 2002 (Grellier 2002; see Fondation Hirondelle 2002ii). When asked (on 4 December 2002) whether she would be able to issue indictments against RPA soldiers before the end of the year, del Ponte replied: 'For the moment, we do not have enough evidence. I have drafts of indictments, but will issue them when I am ready. I will not say when, but it is still a pressing subject' (quoted in Grellier 2002).

The Rwandan government argues that RPA soldiers accused of human rights violations in 1994 should be tried by military courts in Rwanda and not at the ICTR. In April 2002, Paul Kagame stated: 'Carla del Ponte and others should take into consideration the attitude of the RPA which has severely punished those responsible for these crimes ... a number of our soldiers have been judged guilty, condemned and executed' (quoted in ICG 2002a: 14–15).

The RPA has indeed tried soldiers accused of committing human rights abuses. In January 1998, four RPA soldiers were sentenced to death for killing their commanding officer in 1997 (IRIN 1998i). In the same month, two RPA soldiers were executed for killing civilians and in September 1998 three RPA soldiers were sentenced to death for killing two civilians in August of that year (IRIN 1998iv). None of these cases involved crimes committed in 1994, crimes that would give rise to prosecution before the ICTR.

As regards the ICTR's jurisdiction, it is alleged crimes committed by RPA soldiers *during* 1994 that are of relevance. The RPA high command has never denied that some individual soldiers killed civilians in 1994. In September 1994, 64 RPA soldiers were under arrest, some charged with killing civilians (HRW 1994: 7). Likewise, in his November 1994 report, René Degni-Ségui stated that he had received a fax from the Rwandan Minister of Justice stating that 100 RPA soldiers had been arrested for human rights abuses committed in 1994 (UN 1994r para 44c). Also in 1994, Kagame told the UNCE that 70 RPA soldiers had been arrested (including three majors), which 'the Government intended to try and punish for private acts of revenge against Hutus, acts the Government insisted were not only unauthorised, but subject to heavy military discipline and punishment' (UN 1994s para 99).

Military courts, however, appear to have tried only a handful of soldiers accused of crimes in 1994. In January 1998, Major Sam Bigabiro, the only senior officer to be tried, confessed to and was convicted by a military court of having directed the killing of 30–40 civilians in June 1994 (HRW 1994: 7; HRW & FIDH 1999: 709; 733). Although Paul Kagame had indicated that Bigabiro was in command at Mukingi where hundreds of civilians had been killed on 19–21 June 1994 (see HRW 1994: 7), Bigabiro was tried for a massacre at Runda on 2 July 1994. Bigabiro was sentenced to life imprisonment, while a subordinate was given a 45-month sentence (HRW & FIDH 1999: 733). According to HRW (2002a), Bigabiro appealed and was released. By November 1994, 21 other RPA soldiers had been charged with killing civilians (HRW & FIDH 1999: 733). Six were tried in June 1998 and all found guilty, but received relatively light sentences (three to five years). These trials appear (according to available evidence) to be the sum of prosecutions. HRW (2002a) state that 'Most Rwandans know nothing of these RPA trials or discount their importance because of the small number and light penalties involved.' Furthermore, del Ponte has stated that the massacres being investigated by her investigators are not the same episodes as those for whom RPA soldiers have already been tried (Maupas 2000).

Reference to the allegations of human rights abuses by the RPA in 1994 referred to above is interpreted, by some parties, as a denial of the genocide or of proposing 'double genocide' (see ICG 2002b: 17). As regards the first accusation, it is the same bodies who have *definitively* demonstrated that the Tutsi were victims of genocide in 1994 (UNCE, HRW, FIDH, AI, ICTR judgments) that have also stated the RPA has a case to answer. As regards 'double genocide', none of the bodies cited above have accused the RPA of committing genocide. As Alison des Forges (2003) of HRW has observed: 'There is no equivalence between RPF crimes and the 1994 genocide, but there is an equivalence in the rights of victims. If we cannot agree on that, we cannot talk about a rule of law and justice.'

An example of the way in which allegations against the RPA are interpreted as genocide denial can be found in a statement by Martin

Ngoga (Rwanda's Special Envoy to the ICTR) following del Ponte's announcement in December 2002 that RPA officers would be indicted. Ngoga stated that 'the prosecutor is deeply immersed in the ethnic arithmetics and negationist theories of "equal guilt"' and that the ICTR should try genocide suspects before it should indict 'individuals that committed crimes of revenge as they tried to stop the genocide' (quoted in Fondation Hirondelle 2002i). On her part, del Ponte has made it clear that her priority is to prosecute those responsible for the 1994 genocide of Tutsi and that investigations into the RPA are 'purely technical', based on evidence and are not a 'political matter' (Fondation Hirondelle 2002ii).

Given that while del Ponte was Chief Prosecutor at the ICTR, seven defendants were successfully found guilty (out of a total of twelve at the time of writing) of genocide, complicity in genocide or crimes against humanity against Tutsi in 1994; that 23 new indictments were issued against persons accused of these crimes; and 53 accused were being prosecuted by del Ponte and her team, one wonders in what sense she could be described as a 'negationist/denier' of the 1994 genocide. Likewise, if asserting that RPA soldiers committed human rights abuses in 1994 equates with negationism, then where should one place Paul Kagame's statement to the UNCE (quoted above) that he was committed to trying RPA soldiers in military courts for such crimes?

The risk that such allegations can be used to deny the genocide of Tutsi in 1994 is, of course, real (see AI 1994: 2). And yet, leaving such allegations free to circulate, but *unresolved* by a formal, transparent judicial investigation, provides those who would deny the 1994 genocide of Tutsi with a greater room for manoeuvre. Leaving these allegations unresolved allows those who would deny the genocide of Tutsi the freedom to inflate the size and nature of RPA abuses in order to argue for parity between the genocide and alleged crimes committed by the RPA.

As AI states, there can 'never be any comparison' between the genocide and human rights abuses committed by the RPA, but 'this fact should not be allowed to prevent the truth about alleged RPA abuses from being uncovered' (1994: 1). As we shall see below, both the ICTR and the Rwandan government have expressed a commitment to ending the 'culture of impunity'. And yet, 'Allowing the [RPA's] crimes of 1994 to go unpunished would send a dangerous message of impunity' (ICG 2001: 10).

THE SHOOTING DOWN OF PRESIDENT HABYARIMANA'S PLANE

In the opinion of the exiles interviewed, little attention has been paid to who shot down President Habyarimana's plane on 6 April 1994.

> Why do they not investigate the attack on the President's plane? They try to give little importance to that act. However, for me that is the determining act of the genocide. Without that act, I cannot believe that the genocide would have been able to proceed. (Rwandan NGO worker, exile, Belgium, March 1999)

> First of all search for who killed Habyarimana. They are primarily responsible for what has happened in Rwanda. If President Habyarimana had not been killed, there would not have been the genocidal massacres. (Former Rwandan government official, exile, Belgium, March 1999)

On 6 April 1994, Habyarimana was returning to Kigali from a summit in Dar es Salaam where he apparently consented to establish the BBTG (HRW & FIDH 1999: 181). His aircraft was shot down around 8:23 p.m., having been hit by surface-to-air missiles launched from a location near Kigali airport. On board the plane were President Habyarimana, President Ntaryamira of Burundi, Bernard Ciza and Curiaque Simbizi (both Burundian ministers), Major-General Déogratias Nsabimana (FAR Chief of Staff), Major Thadée Bagaragaza, Colonel Elie Sagatwa, Juvenal Renzaho (a senior adviser to Habyarimana), Dr Emmanuel Akingeneye (Habyarimana's physician) and three French crew.[3] There were no survivors.

It appeared that elements opposed to the Arusha Accords (the 'CDR constellation') had shot the plane down to prevent the BBTG being installed (see HRW & FIDH 1999: 183). Above all, if the Arusha agreement had been implemented, the RPF would have taken control of the Ministry of the Interior and command of the *gendarmerie*. This would have severely restricted the planned campaign of massive violence against Tutsi and the elimination of the political opposition.

That the plane was shot down by the 'CDR constellation' was borne out by the fact that within 45 minutes of the plane being shot down and *before* the news was reported on national radio, *interahamwe* militia had established roadblocks throughout Kigali (UN 1994o para 52). Eyewitnesses assert that Presidential Guard units had erected roadblocks in the district inhabited by government ministers *before or a few minutes after* the plane was shot down (HRW & FIDH 1999: 183).

The identity of who shot the plane down remains unresolved. The weight of available evidence, however, suggests that those who planned and perpetrated the genocide of Tutsi also shot the plane down (see Prunier 1995: 213–29; Guichaoua 1995: 675ff; HRW & FIDH 1999: 181–5; Reyntjens 1995a).

The interviews on which this book draws were completed in July 1999. At the time, speculation remained rife as no official (or at least public) investigation had been undertaken. What follows is an overview of more recent 'revelations', which, in the absence of an official investigation, continue to fuel speculation.

The lack of any subsequent UN investigation is surprising, given the importance the organisation initially attached to the incident. The day after the attack, the President of the UNSC called on the UNSG 'to collect all available information [on the crash] with all means at his disposal and report to the Council as soon as possible' (UN 1994a). This request was reiterated by the UNSC on 21 April (UN 1994c) and 17 May (UN 1994f) and by UNHCHR on 25 May (UN 1994h). On 28 June, Degni-Ségui urged that the attack must be examined to determine any links between those 'who ordered it and those responsible for the massacres' (UN 1994k para 64). UN bodies have continued to argue the importance of establishing who shot the plane down (see UN 1996c).

On 1 March 2000, the *National Post* (Canada) published an article that claimed that UN documents contained evidence that the RPA had shot down the plane (Edwards 2000b). According to a leaked UN memo (dated 1 August 1997), three RPA soldiers had told investigators working for the ICTR Prosecutor, that they had been part of a ten-person strike team and that the attack was 'carried out with the assistance of a foreign government' under the overall command of Paul Kagame. The three informants had, it was reported, provided detailed descriptions of the operation and that two of them were willing to work with the ICTR if given protection. According to the *National Post*, the investigators gave the information a high credibility rating ('probably true, but untested').[4] According to the documents seen by the *National Post*, the investigation had been in existence for a year (since mid-1996), but when (in 1997) the information was presented to Louise Arbour (then ICTR Chief Prosecutor) in the form of a memo, she terminated the investigation on the basis that the attack did not fall within the Tribunal's mandate.

The Rwandan government (on 6 March 2000) described the *National Post* article as 'a classical revisionist piece of work designed to justify the 1994 genocide'; part of a campaign by those threatened by the 'efforts of Ms Carla del Ponte, in tracking down the perpetrators of the genocide'; and that the UNSG's spokesperson (Fred Eckhard) had denied the memo's existence (Bideri 2000). Joseph Mutaboba (Rwandan Ambassador to the UN) denounced the article as 'disinformation', the work of 'revisionists' supporting and harbouring genocide criminals (IRIN 2000iii).

On 29 March 2000, Eckhard announced that the UN had 'found' a 'three-page internal memorandum', but emphasised that there was 'no report as such' (IRIN 2000iv). There was, however, a 'memo' written by Michael Hourigan, the former leader of an ICTR investigative team who, while subsequently engaged on 'a short-term contract' at UN headquarters, had 'committed to paper his thoughts, as well as information conveyed to him' in the form of an 'internal memo', which had 'got buried in a file' (ibid.). Bernard Muna (Deputy Prosecutor at the ICTR) likened Hourigan's report to jotting down personal opinions and stated that 'The attack has nothing to do with the genocide and our mandate is based on the genocide' (Cruvellier 2000a). This is in contrast to Ken Fleming (prosecuting at the ICTR) who, in March 2001, described the attack as 'a starter's flag for one of the most barbaric events in the history of mankind' (IRIN 2001i).

The UNSG ordered the three-page memo sent to the ICTR (IRIN 2000v). Given that the document related to issues that may be raised before a Trial Chamber, the President of the Tribunal directed that the document, and accompanying correspondence, be placed under seal in the President's chambers 'so that if the matter is raised before the Tribunal, the appropriate Trial Chamber could decide if the document is relevant to the defence of any of the cases on which the attorneys are working and, if so, determine under what circumstances and conditions the document can be released' (ibid.).

There is confusion, however, over *which* documents were delivered to the ICTR. It has been claimed that, in addition to the three-page memo, there is also a four-page (undated) 'internal memorandum', which, according to the *National Post*, contains the 'details of the attack' (including the names of those involved) and it is this document that was originally delivered to Arbour in 1997. According to Thierry Cruvellier (2000a), this document *has not been* delivered to the ICTR. As a consequence, 'the document handed over to the Tribunal most likely does not contain the information that is needed in order to verify the allegations and to thoroughly assess the credibility of this investigative lead' (ibid.).

Although Eckhard stated that Hourigan was a minor official in the UN, Hourigan had in fact been a divisional inspector in New South Wales and, as a lawyer, a Crown Prosecutor in Adelaide, South Australia. In an Australian Broadcast Corporation programme in March 1999 (ABC 1999) Hourigan emphasised that the genocide was co-ordinated by state officials and criticised the failure of the UN in Rwanda. In addition to the infamous 'genocide fax' sent by General Roméo Dallaire, UNAMIR's commander, on 11 January 1994 (see HRW & FIDH 1999: 150ff), the UN ignored warnings of catastrophe from a delegation of Rwandese who visited UN headquarters in New York in mid-to-late 1993. Hourigan concluded that 'given the unique position and the intelligence information that [UN headquarters] received ... they should've been in a far better position to deal with the catastrophe once it broke out'. Hourigan, with the Belgian senator Alain Destexhe, later put pressure on the UN to establish an independent investigation into the organisation's failure to prevent the genocide (Cruvellier 2000a; see Carlsson et al. 1999).

In the 1999 interview, Hourigan also stated that in the course of investigating genocide suspects, 'we received accurate information about who was responsible for that plane crash, and that the information was very detailed and involved a good number of people' (ABC 1999). According to Hourigan, when the information was handed to the ICTR 'the senior members of the war crimes tribunal were very excited by it. But within a week there was great concern about it and my inquiry was stopped' (ibid.).

According to James Lyons (former Commander of Investigations for the ICTR), Hourigan was made Team Leader of a 'National Investigation Team' (Lyons 2001). The principal tasks of the team were to investigate Col. Théoneste Bagasora (considered the mastermind of the genocide); those responsible for the killing of political opponents in the first 72 hours of the genocide; and those responsible for shooting down Habyarimana's plane.[5]

In December 1999, del Ponte argued that although the attack 'set everything in motion' it did not fall under 'the articles that give us jurisdiction' (quoted in Cruvellier 2000a). Lyons, however, believes the attack comes within the ICTR's mandate on the basis of the UNSC's request to the UNSG (quoted above) and the fact that Article 4(d) of the ICTR's statute covers 'acts of terrorism' as a violation of Article 3 Common to the Geneva Conventions and Additional

Protocol II (see UN 1994q). According to Lyons, when Hourigan first briefed Arbour she did not indicate that the attack was outside the tribunal's mandate. Lyons states that he was present at the US embassy in Kigali in late February 1997 when Hourigan called Arbour at The Hague to brief her on the progress of the investigation, and that she had appeared pleased with its progress and asked Hourigan to travel to The Hague to discuss the matter. According to Lyons, it was at that meeting that Arbour instructed Hourigan to close the investigation because it was outside the tribunal's mandate.

Since March 1998, the French anti-terrorist Judge Jean-Louis Bruguière has conducted an investigation on behalf of the families of the French crew killed in the attack. On 23 May 2000, Bruguière requested a copy of the UN 'report'. On 5 June, Judge Pillay (President of the ICTR) replied: 'we would be going beyond our mandate if we provided you with the document' (quoted in Afrik'Netpress 2000; see IRIN 2000xi). Earlier in May, however, Bruguière was given permission to interview Hassan Ngeze (former editor of *Kangura*) and six other defendants regarding the attack in the presence of representatives of the chief prosecutor (see IRIN 2000vi; 2000vii). In June 2000, del Ponte reiterated that the attack was outside her jurisdiction, but that 'if facts emerge [from Bruguière's inquiry], then I will take over that inquiry' (quoted in Maupas 2000). In October 2000, a French magazine reported that Bruguière had gathered enough evidence to call for an international arrest warrant against Kagame (Péan et al. 2000). Del Ponte rejected this report (Willum 2000), as did the Rwandan government (IRIN 2000xii). In any case, since the 'Yérodia' ruling in February 2002, national jurisdictions are no longer able to indict ministers or heads of state currently in office.[6] If Bruguière did have evidence against Kagame, only the ICTR would be able to issue an indictment.

At a press conference on 13 December 2000, del Ponte stated:

The investigation [into the attack] has not been opened [by the ICTR] because there is an issue of jurisdiction. Judge Bruguière has begun an enquiry and has requested our cooperation. I am working with Bruguière ... I am following him closely. His results will allow me to decide whether or not we open an investigation. I think that by the beginning of next year we'll be able to make an informed decision and we will make public the reasons why the enquiry is or is not launched. (quoted in ICG 2001: 9)

In response, the Rwandan government issued a statement that the 'The [RPA] and President Paul Kagame, had no hand in the downing of the plane' (IRIN 2000xiv). The statement continued: 'In the interests of truth and to finally put the matter to rest, the government of Rwanda supports a full investigation conducted by the ICTR involving all political and military groups that were present in Rwanda in 1994 ... the Rwandan government will co-operate, as it has done in the past' (ibid.).

In April 2001, Bruguière conducted a further six interviews at Arusha. At the time, del Ponte indicated that she was moving 'towards opening an investigation' into the attack on the plane (Cruvellier 2001). In August 2002, the ICG reported that Bruguière's inquiry was near completion (ICG 2002a: 15). In an interview in December 2002, del Ponte said that she had met Bruguière in September and as he had not yet completed his inquiry, they had agreed to meet in January 2003 (Grellier 2002). Del Ponte stated:

> I will need to find out the details of the enquiry in order to decide whether I have jurisdiction to accept it or not. I asked him not to reveal the results of the enquiry until we had discussed it. If I have jurisdiction, I will certainly take up the case. (ibid.)[7]

It is essential to place the attack on Habyarimana's plane in context. The statements by the exiles above, that the genocide would not have occurred unless the plane had been shot down, do not stand up to scrutiny. Preparations for the genocide had been a long time in the making, including the formation, arming and training of militias, the establishment of *Kangura* and *RTLM* and the preparation of target lists (see UN 1994s paras 58; 62). The massacre of Tutsi since 1990 demonstrates that, in a sense, the genocide was already under way (see AI 1992).

As discussed in Chapter 2, in October 1990 the FAR had killed c1,000 Bahima (considered as Tutsi) and 348 Tutsi in Kibilira commune (Gisenyi *préfecture*). In January 1991, c1,000 Bagogwe (considered as Tutsi) were murdered in the *préfectures* of Ruhengeri and Gisenyi. In January and February 1991, further massacres of Tutsi took place in the communes of Mukingo, Kinigi, Gaseke, Giciye, Karago and Mutura. At least 300 Tutsi were killed in Bugesera in March 1992. Bugesera was unlike any previous massacre, foreshadowing the genocide: it was preceded by an incitement on *Radio Rwanda* (repeated five times); it was co-ordinated by local officials; roadblocks were established to stop the targeted population escaping (see Guichaoua 1995: 613–14); and it involved Presidential Guard units and *interahamwe* militia transported into the region in government vehicles (Reyntjens 1995b: 268). Further massacre of Tutsi took place in Kibuye in August 1992 and again in the north-west in December 1992 and January 1993 (see HRW & FIDH 1999: 87ff). Between February and August 1993 a further 300 Tutsi and political opponents were killed in the *préfectures* of Gisenyi, Ruhengeri, Kibuye and Byumba (UN 1993 para 27; HRW 1993). As HRW and FIDH observe:

> Responsibility for killing Habyarimana is a serious issue, but it is a different issue from responsibility for the genocide. We know little about who assassinated Habyarimana. We know more about who used the assassination as the pretext to begin a slaughter that had been planned for months. (1999: 185)

As one prosecution lawyer at the ICTR observed: 'The attack neither absolves, nor lessens the crime [of genocide] committed. The accident is not an excuse, nor is it absolutory. It is another crime' (quoted in Cruvellier 2000a).

Not only does the bulk of available evidence indicate that the plane was shot down by the perpetrators of the genocide, but it is difficult to provide a convincing explanation of why the RPF would wish to carry out such an attack (see Prunier 1995: 220). It is for these reasons that the Hourigan memo has taken on such importance. By leaving its contents public but unresolved, the memo feeds the arguments of those who wish to deny the genocide (by denying it was an intentional, premeditated act) or attribute responsibility. The way in which the vacuum left by the lack of an official investigation can be exploited has been demonstrated at the ICTR. In a letter to the UNSG on 19 March 2000, defence lawyers at the ICTR (acting for 27 defendants) requested a copy of the Hourigan memo:

> This report is essential for the defence of the accused and undermines one premise of the Prosecution that the 'genocide' was meticulously planned. Can a meticulous plan to exterminate be a conspiracy when it was incomplete, when the enemy triggered the apparent 'extermination' as part of its own coherent military strategy to undermine the Arusha Accords? (Quoted in Cruvellier 2000a; see IRIN 2000viii)

Likewise, in May 2000, Jean Degli, defending Gratien Kabiligi, called on the prosecutor to open an investigation into the attack, arguing: 'We cannot accuse people of planning the genocide and refuse to investigate that which constitutes the point of departure of the genocide' (quoted in Cruvellier 2000b; see IRIN 2000viii; 2000x).

The lack of a transparent, judicial investigation into the attack serves the cause of those who seek to deny *the indisputable reality* of a premeditated genocide against Tutsi in 1994. Although the revelation of Hourigan's memo appears to indicate RPA culpability, such responsibility must be proven (or disproven) according to the same rigorous judicial mechanism as employed in the prosecution of those accused of crimes of genocide. Even if it were established that the RPA shot the plane down, such a fact would be immaterial in the face of the overwhelming evidence that state officials planned (from at least 1993), incited and co-ordinated the genocide of Tutsi. The priority of demonstrating this at the ICTR continues to be unnecessarily hampered by the hearsay and rumour that exists in the void left by the lack of a formal investigation.

ALLEGED MASSACRES IN ZAÏRE/DEMOCRATIC REPUBLIC OF CONGO, OCTOBER 1996–MAY 1997

Exiles asked why the alleged massacre of Rwandan refugees in Zaïre (now the Democratic Republic of Congo [DRC]) in 1996–97 had not received the same international and judicial attention as the Rwandan genocide of 1994:

Why when Tutsis are killed that is recognised as genocide, but if 200,000 Hutu refugees are killed in Zaïre that is not genocide? (Rwandan NGO worker, exile, Belgium, March 1999)

[Paul] Kagame planned the killings in 1996. He said this in the *Washington Post* [see below]. Therefore, it was a genocide. A planned attack on Rwandans and the refugee camps in which 200,000 were killed. (Rwandan academic, exile, France, July 1999)

There have been massacres of refugees in Congo [Zaïre] and the international community? They have said nothing, they have done nothing. (Rwandan NGO worker, exile, Belgium, February 1999)

The international community did not condemn the massacre of 200,000 refugees in Zaïre. Why does the so-called international community keep silence? You kill – silence. You attack – silence. (Former Rwandan government minister, exile, Belgium, February 1999)

These alleged massacres must be understood in the context of persistent violence in eastern Zaïre since 1993. Along the western border of Rwanda, the Kivu region of the DRC (Zaïre until 1997) was home to a substantial population of Kinyarwanda-speakers whose antecedents arrived in four migratory movements from what is now Rwanda. As early as the seventeenth century Kinyarwanda-speakers migrated to what is now North Kivu (Fairhead 1989: 5). In the latter half of the nineteenth century (although possibly much earlier) Tutsi pastoralists migrated to the Itombwe area of South Kivu (see Pottier 2002: 16ff). Famine in Rwanda in 1928/29 and 1943 forced more Rwandese to migrate to Kivu, while 'assisted migrations' in the 1930s–1950s brought an additional 85,000 to North Kivu (Pottier 2002: 11). A further 150,000 Tutsi fled to Kivu following the violence of 1959–64.

The right to Zaïrian citizenship of *some* of these Kinyarwanda-speakers remained in doubt. As the 1964 Constitution granted Congolese nationality (from 30 June 1960) to anyone 'one of whose forefathers was a member of a tribe or of a part of a tribe established on Congolese territory before October 18, 1908' (Art. VI; see Peaslee 1965: 104), descendants of Kinyarwanda-speakers who had migrated in the nineteenth century (or earlier) were undoubtedly Zaïrian. The western boundaries of Congo/Zaïre, however, were not demarcated until the Brussels Convention of 11 August 1910 (between Germany and Belgium) (see Smis 2000: 195). Parts of North Kivu were, until then, under the nominal control of the Rwandan *mwami* (Linden 1977: 87; D. Newbury 1997). Despite this ambiguity, the 1964 Constitution appeared to grant collective Congolese nationality to all Kinyarwanda-speakers in Kivu, with the exception of Rwandan immigrants (1930s–1950s) and refugees of 1959–64.

The 1964 criteria were confirmed in a 1965 decree and left unchanged in the 1967 Constitution. In 1971, a decree conferred collective Zaïrian citizenship upon all persons who had originated from the former Belgium colony of Ruanda-Urundi and who had been resident in Congo on 30 June 1960, thereby extending citizenship to Rwandese migrants of the 1930s–1950s and refugees of 1959. Article I of the Nationality Act of 1972 reiterated the 1964 Constitution. Article XV, however, changed the 1971 criteria, adding a caveat that only migrants from Ruanda-Urundi who had been resident in Kivu from *before* 1 January 1950 until 30 June 1960 held Zaïrian nationality (requisite ten-year residency). Although the law excluded Rwandan refugees who had arrived in 1959, it confirmed that those who had migrated to Kivu prior to 1 January 1950 were Zaïrian, while those whose antecedents had migrated to Congo from the seventeenth century onwards continued to possess Zaïrian citizenship according to the 1964 Constitution.

The 1981 Nationality Law, however, repealed Article XV of the 1972 law and declared as Zaïrian (as of 30 June 1960) any person whose ascendants had been members of 'a tribe' established in Zaïre as defined by its frontiers of '1 August 1885, modified by subsequent conventions'. In addition, in 1982, Decree 061 cancelled the certificates of nationality issued under the 1972 law. Descendants of Rwandan migrants of 1885–1950 were thereby stripped of their citizenship, an illegal act under international law (UN 1997a paras 129–33). Under the new law, each individual would have to submit a formal application for naturalisation. Although many Kinyarwanda-speakers would qualify, proving ancestry back to 1885 (on an individual basis) would be difficult.

The 1981/82 law and decree were not actively enforced, with the National Sovereign Conference (which had passed the law) ruling that a transitional government should respect citizenship rights already acquired (UN 1996d para 26), while identity cards of Rwandan immigrants (1930s–1950s) were not revoked (HRW & FIDH 1997: 8). Kinyarwanda-speakers were, however, prevented from standing as candidates or voting in the 1982 and 1987 parliamentary elections and were excluded from the National Sovereign Conference in 1991.

Whatever the detail of the law, by 1991, the 1981 law had become an expression of a generalised discourse deployed by politicians in Kivu who, foreseeing the imminent advent of representative democracy, used an ethnic discourse both to solidify their own support base and attempt to exclude the numerically significant Kinyarwanda-speakers from the electoral process. This discourse made no distinction between Kinyarwanda-speakers whose ascendants had arrived *before* the creation of 'the Congo' and those who had arrived in the first half of the twentieth century. Neither did this discourse distinguish between Hutu and Tutsi. All Kinyarwanda-speakers were considered as 'foreigners'.

NORTH KIVU 1993–96

Kinyarwanda-speakers (Banyarwanda) constituted around 50 per cent (40 per cent Hutu, 10 per cent Tutsi) of North Kivu's population of 3 million, the remainder belonging to self-styled 'autochthonous' groups: Hunde, Ntembo, Nande and Nyanga (HRW 1996: 4). With the onset of a 'transition to democracy' in the early 1990s, it became clear to the leadership of 'autochthonous' groups that if Banyarwanda were allowed to vote in forthcoming elections their numerical superiority (at least in some areas) would mean a loss of power.

In March 1993, the Governor of North Kivu stated that Zaïrian security forces should assist Nyanga and Hunde to 'exterminate' Banyarwanda (HRW 1996: 7). Several days later, 'autochthonous' militia (Mai Mai and *Bangirima*)[8] began ethnically cleansing Banyarwanda (Hutu and Tutsi) from Masisi, Walikale, Rutshuru and Lubero, often assisted by *gendarmes* and local government officials (see AI 1993; UN 1996a para 23). After several months, Zaïrian Hutu (the main targets of the attacks) formed militia. Ethnic cleansing by 'autochthonous' and Zaïrian Hutu militia began, whereby previously multi-ethnic areas become mono-ethnic, the majority group driving out the minority in any given area. Depending on the area, Zaïrian Tutsi were left unmolested or were attacked by the 'autochthonous' militia and/or Zaïrian Hutu militia (HRW 1996: 7). By September 1996, 350,000 people had been internally displaced and 7,000–40,000 killed, the majority Zaïrian Hutu (ibid.; see UN 1996d para 95).

Following the 1994 genocide in Rwanda, c1.2 million refugees fled to Kivu.[9] Estimates suggest 6 per cent were *initially* armed (20,000–25,000 ex-FAR and 30,000–40,000 *interahamwe* [Emizet 2000: 165]). This proportion probably grew, with as many as 80 per cent of young people in Mugunga camp (Goma) belonging to militia by December 1994 (UN 1994t para 96). These elements actively rearmed (see HRW 1995; AI 1995b; UN 1996b) with arms deals amounting to US$17 million (IRIN 1996xxxiv; 1996xxxvii; 1997ii). The politico-military leadership, responsible for the 1994 genocide, controlled the camps and intimidated refugees who wished to return to Rwanda, killing as many as 4,000 (JEEAR 1996a).

Many refugees were prepared to return to Rwanda, and by January 1995, c200,000 refugees had repatriated themselves (Pottier 1999: 163ff). Others had genuine concerns for their security on return (see AI 1994; 1995; 1996a; 1996b). By September 1996, the majority of refugees in Goma appear to have lost faith in the politico-military leadership in the camps and were prepared to return home (Pottier 1999: 165).

Human rights organisations, humanitarian agencies and the Rwandan government repeatedly demanded that armed elements be separated from *bona fide* refugees. In November 1994, the UNDPKO proposed sending 5,000–7,000 troops to undertake this task. The plan was scrapped when no UN states were prepared to contribute troops (see Jones 2001: 141ff). By mid-1995, ex-FAR/*interahamwe* were launching incursions into Rwanda, ostensibly to kill 'genocide witnesses', but indiscriminately targeting all ethnic Tutsi (see AI 1995a; 1996a; AR 1996). By July 1996, senior members of the Rwandan government were talking of 'taking the war to Goma' (Jones 2001: 147).

The Rwandan genocide and the arrival of the refugees divided Banyarwanda in North Kivu. Zaïrian Hutu militia formed joint *interahamwe* militia with Rwandan refugees and began to attack both Zaïrian Tutsi and 'autochthonous' groups with weaponry provided by the Zaïrian government (HRW 1996: 10).

The 'new *interahamwe*' and 'autochthonous' militia not only fought one another, but both attacked Zaïrian Tutsi and Tutsi refugees who had left Rwanda in the 1960s/70s. Although attacks had tapered off by July 1995, the threat by Zäire's President Mobutu to repatriate refugees forcibly prompted refugee leaders to talk of making Masisi a 'Hutu-land' – an alternative to returning to Rwanda. Violence re-erupted and by December 1995 the 'new *interahamwe*' had killed 4,000 Hunde and Nyanga in Masisi, displacing 250,000 autochthones in the process (Pottier 2002: 41). In November 1995, the FAZ chief of staff reiterated that 'autochthones' had the right to expel all 'foreigners'. Again, 'autochthonous' militia attacked *all* Banyarwanda, while the 'new *interahamwe*' attacked Hunde and Zaïrian Tutsi. Thousands of Zaïrian Tutsi were killed and by December 1995, c12,000 Tutsi refugees of the 1960s/70s had fled back to Rwanda (HRW 1996: 12). In early 1996, *interahamwe* and 'autochthonous' militia killed hundreds more Zaïrian Tutsi, and by July 15,000 more had fled to Rwanda (ibid.). By this time there were 250,000–400,000 IDPs in North Kivu (UN 1996d para 106). The main instigators of the violence had been the 'new *interahamwe*' often aided by the FAZ (ibid. paras 38; 75ff).

SOUTH KIVU, 1995–96

By 1996, the Tutsi population on the Itombwe high plateaux had become known as 'Banyamulenge' (see D. Newbury 1991; 1997).

Given the lack of census data, Banyamulenge numbers were put at anything between 15,000 and 400,000 (UN 1997a n. 6; 1996a para 33). Although it is agreed that Tutsi were established at Itombwe by the mid-nineteenth century, it has been suggested that the ethnonym 'Banyamulenge' was adopted in the early 1970s by descendants of long-term Tutsi residents in order to distinguish themselves from Tutsi who had fled Rwanda in the 1950s/60s/70s and in response to anti-Tutsi sentiment following the 1972 massacres in Burundi (Vlassenroot 2000: 274 n. 21; see HRW & FIDH 1997: 8). Conversely, in the mid-1970s, later Tutsi refugees may have adopted the name to strengthen claims to Zaïrian citizenship (Pottier 1999: 154). Whatever the case, by mid-1995, politicians in South Kivu had mobilised against *all* Tutsi, referred to indiscriminately as 'Banyamulenge' (see Vlassenroot 2000: 272).

A resolution of the Zaïrian *Haut Conseil de la République – Parlement de Transition* (28 April 1995) called for the 'repatriation, uncondi-tional and without delay, of all Rwandan and Burundian refugees and immigrants' from South Kivu (see UN 1996a para 27). The resolution referred to Banyamulenge as recent immigrants 'who had acquired Zaïrian nationality fraudulently' (IRIN 1996i; see AI 1996d: 20). A report of 19 October 1995 (signed by a government official in Uvira) spoke of an 'ethnic group *unknown* in Zaïre called the Banyamulenge [whose leaders] will all be expelled from the country' (UN 1996a para 35; emphasis added). The ethnonym 'Banyamulenge' had now become an 'omnibus term' for *all* those considered 'Tutsi' in South Kivu (Pottier 2002: 43). In late 1995/early 1996, Tutsi/Banyamulenge were evicted from their land, and the UN warned that 'local tribes [*sic*] were arming in readiness for a struggle against the Banyamulenge, forcing the latter to do the same' (UN 1996a para 37).

In early September 1996, militia from the Bembe ethnic group (often with FAZ support) attacked 'Banyamulenge' communities, killing and raping (HRW & FIDH 1997: 10). Following a demonstra-tion in Uvira on 9 September (which called for 'foreigners' to leave) Banyamulenge were attacked and a number killed (IRIN 1996i), prompting c1,000 Tutsi/Banyamulenge to flee to Rwanda and Burundi (see AI 1996c).

On 13 September 1996, the Zaïrian government accused Rwanda and Burundi of training and arming Banyamulenge (IRIN 1996i). On 8 October, the deputy governor of South Kivu told 'all Banya-mulenge to leave Zaïre within a week', and that those remaining 'would be considered as rebels and treated as such' (quoted in AI 1996d: 14). Although the deputy governor was suspended, his statement was interpreted by ethnic militia and government security forces as a pretext to attack Tutsi. Clashes between the FAZ and armed Banyamulenge were reported in the Uvira district and, by 11 October, the FAZ Chief of Staff declared: 'Zaïre is at war in South Kivu' (IRIN 1996ii).

THE 'WAR OF LIBERATION', OCTOBER 1996–MAY 1997

Reports on 13 October 1996 stated that c19,000 Rwandan refugees had fled from a camp near Uvira following armed attacks by what were described as 'Zaïrian Tutsi' (IRIN 1996iii). On 21 October, c220,000 refugees abandoned twelve camps around Uvira, following fighting between the FAZ and Banyamulenge (IRIN 1996iv). By 26 October, an estimated 80,000 refugees were moving north towards Bukavu with c500,000 refugees/IDPs on the move in South Kivu (IRIN 1996vi).

In North Kivu, Kibumba camp (25 km north of Goma) was attacked on 25/26 October 1996 (IRIN 1996v), prompting its population of c194,000 to flee towards Mugunga camp (Goma) (IRIN 1996vii). On 28 October, Katale camp (55 km north of Goma) came under mortar fire, although the c202,000 refugees remained in place (IRIN 1996v; xxvi). By 29 October, however, the entire population of Kahindo camp (pop. c115,000, 60 km north of Goma) was fleeing south towards Mugunga (IRIN 1996viii).

On 23 October 1996, a Banyamulenge spokesperson, claiming to represent the Democratic Alliance of the People, said they were fighting with 'other opposition groups'[10] to overthrow President Mobutu and intended to take Bukavu and link up with forces fighting in North Kivu (IRIN 1996v). On 25 October, the group was referred to as *Alliance des forces démocratiques pour la libération du Congo-Zaire* (AFDL) (IRIN 1996vi), and by 2 November, Laurent-Désiré Kabila had emerged as its spokesperson (IRIN 1996ix).

On 29 October 1996, the AFDL attacked camps around Bukavu, prompting Rwandan refugees to flee northwards (UN 1997c para 42). By 1 November the population of Katale camp (c210,000) were reported to be moving towards Mugunga (IRIN 1996ix). By the following day, refugee numbers in Goma were estimated at 717,000, and it was reported that the RPA had entered Goma in support of the AFDL (IRIN 1996x). On 4 November, UNHCR reported it had lost contact with c520,000 Rwandan and Burundian refugees in South Kivu (IRIN 1996xi).

At the same time, having prevented journalists and aid personnel from entering Mugunga camp (c400,000 refugees), AFDL troops were preparing to attack the camp, defended by ex-FAR/*interahamwe* and FAZ (IRIN 1996xvii; xviii). On 8 November, heavy artillery was heard in the direction of Mugunga while c175,000 refugees from Kahindo and Katale were reportedly fleeing westwards (IRIN 1996xix; xx). On 9 November, some Mugunga residents fled westwards, only to be stopped by Mai-Mai and instructed to return to Rwanda or be imprisoned/killed (Pottier 1999: 151). Heavy fighting was reported around Mugunga until 11 November (IRIN 1996xxi), and by 12 November the 'front line' had apparently moved westwards with the AFDL in control of immediate access to Mugunga (IRIN 1996xxiii). Although foreign journalists confirmed on 13 November that there were still refugees in Mugunga camp the AFDL denied access to both journalists and aid workers (IRIN 1996xxv).

On 11 November 1996, the UNHCR did not know the whereabouts of c75,000 refugees from the Uvira camps (IRIN 1996xxii). The following day, aid agencies complained that satellite imagery (requested by UNHCR five days earlier) had not been made public (IRIN 1996xxiii), despite the fact that a senior US official later admitted that from the start of the crisis US satellite and aerial reconnaissance had provided daily assessments of the number and location of refugees (HRW & FIDH 1997: 35; IRIN 1997v).

On 13 November, reports indicated that refugees from Katale camp (pop. c202,000) were encamped around Masisi (75 km north-west of Goma) and that hundreds were dying each day from dehydration, diarrhoea and lack of food (IRIN 1996xxvi). The following day, it was reported that ex-FAR/*interahamwe* were ordering refugees to gather at Mugunga camp to act as a 'human shield' (IRIN 1996xxviii). The same report stated that Mugunga camp was 'well hemmed in' by rebel forces and that an 'élite force ... seemingly consisting of Rwandan soldiers' was positioned to the west of the camp. By the end of 14 November the AFDL/RPA had taken Mugunga and by noon the next day, the camp was 'empty' and tens of thousands of refugees were fleeing through Goma and arriving at the Rwandan border (IRIN 1996xxix). Although Mugunga had held up to 400,000 refugees, it was unclear whether all the refugees were returning to Rwanda; how many were retreating westwards with the ex-FAR/*interahamwe*; or how many had been killed (ibid.). By 3 p.m. on 15 November, c70,000 refugees were waiting to cross into Rwanda (IRIN 1996xxxi). Meanwhile, unconfirmed reports stated that c80,000 refugees were near Walikale (80 km west of Goma), while c490,000 refugees from Bukavu and Uvira remained unaccounted for (IRIN 1996xxx). Further reports emerged that ex-FAR/*interahamwe* had forced refugees at Mugunga to retreat with them, killing those who refused (ibid.; Pottier 1999: 150).

By 10:30 a.m. on 16 November 1996, 100,000 refugees had crossed into Rwanda and a further 300,000 were reportedly on the way from Mugunga and further west (IRIN 1996xxxii). *At this point, refugees were no longer being screened/registered at the border.* By 19 November, UNHCR estimated 575,000 refugees had arrived in Rwanda (IRIN 1996xxxv; xxxviii), but reports on 17 November stated that c500,000 refugees remained in South Kivu with unconfirmed reports of c300,000 refugees in the Masisi area (IRIN 1996xxxiii; xxxiv).

While UN Special Envoy, Raymond Chrétien (on 17 November 1996) estimated up to half a million refugees remained in Zaïre (CNN 1996), Paul Kagame stated (on 20 November) that the 'majority' of refugees had returned (IRIN 1996xxxix). On the same day, UNHCR gave the following estimates of concentrations of people based on 'Western' satellite photos and aerial reconnaissance: c50,000 20 km west of Masisi; c100,000 north of Sake; c200,000 70 km north of Bukavu; c250,000 70 km south of Bukavu; and c100,000 people at Fizi (100 km south of Uvira) (Drogin 1996; see IRIN 1996xxxvi; xxxix). Although cautioning that the figures were not precise, the agency argued that it had an overall picture of the whereabouts of c700,000 refugees remaining in Zaïre (Bond 1996; IRIN 1996xl).

The Rwandan government, however, continued to question the accuracy of these figures on the grounds that the UNHCR had not completed a census of the refugee camps. As regards Uvira and Bukavu, UNHCR (1996) argued that refugee figures were based on two 'elaborate registration exercises' in 1995 and 1996. In Goma, the UNHCR admitted that attempts to conduct a census, in February 1995 and September 1996, had been obstructed by the politico-military leadership in the camps and had been abandoned. UNHCR figures, therefore, were based on food distribution cards issued to each refugee *family* in January 1995. The agency admitted that camp leaders had inflated family size in order to acquire more food aid (often sold to purchase weapons). And yet, in October 1996, a joint food assessment mission, comprising UNHCR and WFP officials (accompanied by US and EU observers) 'was able to verify Goma's population figures', thereby verifying the overall figure of c1.2 million (ibid.)

For the Rwandan government, the refugee population had never risen beyond 800,000 of whom 600,000 had returned to Rwanda by 20 November 1996. According to the Rwandan Ambassador to Belgium (on 19 November) those who remained in Zaïre were 'criminals' (quoted in Pottier 1999: 148). On 21 November, a Rwandan minister stated that his government's assessment of refugees remaining in Zaïre (that the 'vast majority' had returned) was based on the (rather strange) logic that neither UNHCR nor the Rwandan government had carried out a physical count of refugees crossing the border and that the camps in *North* Kivu were empty (IRIN 1996xli).

The insinuation that refugees remaining in Zaïre were 'criminals' was also found in a US Committee for Refugees statement on 26 November, which stated that c300,000 refugees remained in Zaïre (USCR 1996). The USCR noted that 'Some observers estimate that 100,000 to 200,000 of these Rwandans might be directly or indirectly implicated in the 1994 genocide, calling into question their refugee status' (ibid.). While according to the 1951 UN Convention relating to the Status of Refugees this is true,[11] the right to receive humanitarian assistance and have one's human rights protected (including the right to a fair trial) is not dependent on a civilian or disarmed combatant possessing refugee status.

On the same day that the Rwandan government declared that the vast majority of refugees had returned (21 November 1996), the US Ambassador to Rwanda stated that those remaining in Zaïre 'appear to be in the tens to twenties of thousands rather than in vast numbers' (IRIN 1996xli). And yet, on 4 December the ambassador's colleague, Phyllis Oakley (Assistant Secretary of State, Bureau of Population, Refugees, and Migration) stated that aerial surveillance 'has indicated that there are concentrations of people in Eastern Zaïre adding up to over 200,000'. Overall, Oakley estimated 200,000–400,000 refugees remained in Zaïre (US Congress 1996). On 6 December, UNHCR (1996) stated that although c562,000 refugees had returned to Rwanda, aerial reconnaissance indicated c250,000 people 75 km–100 km west of Lake Kivu, with a 'substantial numbers of refugees' unaccounted for.

It appears that throughout the crisis the US government possessed aerial and satellite data regarding the number and location of refugees/IDPs. Nicholas Stockton (Emergencies Director, Oxfam) refers to a meeting on 20 November 1996 at which Oxfam staff were shown US aerial reconnaissance photos that:

> [C]onfirmed, in considerable detail, the existence of over 500,000 people distributed in three major and numerous minor agglomerations. (Whether these were refugees or displaced Zaïrois could not be confirmed.) This information, also made available to the [UN], was the non-attributed source of the UNHCR press release of 20 November [see above] ... Yet, incredibly, in a press conference in Kigali on 23 November, the US military claimed they had located only one significant cluster of people which 'by the nature of their movement and other clues can be assumed to be the ex-FAR and militias.' (Stockton 1996: 2)

For Stockton, as many as 400,000 refugees and unknown numbers of Zaïrian IDPs had 'in effect, been air-brushed from history' (ibid.).

The apparent attempt to downplay the number of refugees remaining in Zaïre must be understood in the context of the planned multinational intervention force (MNF). Calls by MSF for such a force (to create safe havens and disarm armed elements) on 4 November 1996 were immediately rejected by the Rwandan government (IRIN 1996xii; xiv). On 5 November, however, an OAU-sponsored summit called for a UN-sanctioned MNF (IRIN 1996xv; xvi). On 9 November, a UNSC resolution established a MNF 'for humanitarian purposes in eastern Zaïre' and called on member states to draw up plans for the proposed force. A central concern was whether the force would separate ex-FAR/*interahamwe* from *bona fide* refugees, given that both the US and Canada pledged involvement on the condition that they *did not have to disarm these groups* (IRIN 1996xxvii). On 12 November, the Canadian government offered to lead the MNF (IRIN 1996xxiv) and by 14 November nine African states and eight North American/European states had committed troops to a force 10,000–15,000 strong (IRIN 1996xxvii). Although the UNSC authorised the deployment of the force on 15 November (IRIN 1996xxxii), the following day the Rwandan Ambassador to the UN announced that such a force was 'no longer relevant' (quoted in ibid.; see IRIN 1996xlii). On 20 November, the Canadian Prime Minister agreed there was no longer a need for military intervention, and by 15 December his government announced the force was to be disbanded (IRIN 1996xxxviii; xliii).

The crisis was not, however, over. By 9 January 1997, UNHCR had located c330,000 refugees in Lubutu (170 km south-east of Kisangani) (IRIN 1997i), while on 27 January, Refugees International reported 200,000 refugees divided between Lubutu and Shabunda 'clinging tenuously to life' (IRIN 1997iii; iv). The AFDL attacked the Shabunda camps in mid-January 1997 (MSF 1997: 7) and on 6 February it was reported that c40,000 refugees had fled west (IRIN 1997vi). On 21 February, UNHCR estimated c193,000 refugees were encamped at Tingi-Tingi, Kalima and Punia (south-east of Kisangani), while c189,590 Rwandan and c39,675 Burundian refugees remained unaccounted for (IRIN 1997x). The following day, the AFDL attacked Amisi camp (south-east of Tingi-Tingi) and c40,000 refugees fled towards Ubundu (130 km south of Kisangani). Tingi-Tingi camp (c150,000) was abandoned on 28 February and refugees fled towards Kisangani (IRIN 1997ix; xiii).

By mid-March 1997, c140,000 refugees were moving towards Ubundu. By mid-April 69,000–86,000 refugees were encamped in a number of concentrations south of Kisangani (at Kasese, Biaro and Obilo), in appalling conditions, although the AFDL limited access by humanitarian agencies (MSF 1997: 4–5). Between 21 and 23 April, the AFDL attacked the Kasese camps, assisted by local people (ibid.). On 23 April, UNHCR officials and journalists were allowed to enter Kasese camp and found it empty – 'all the refugees [45,000–55,000], including the sick and 9,000 children had disappeared' (ibid.; see Pomfret 1997a; AI 1997c: 17). Gunfire nearby meant it was not possible 'to take a closer look at the suspected mass graves' (MSF 1997: 5). Visiting Biaro camp on 28 April, MSF found no trace of 6,250 refugees who in the agency's opinion would have been 'too weak or ill to flee', the agency concluding that 'some 85,000 refugees had disappeared from the camps at Kasese and Biaro' (ibid. 6). Although by early May, 30,000 refugees had reappeared at Biaro (many of them bearing bullet and machete wounds [AI 1997c: 17]), it was unclear what proportion of the missing refugees were hiding in the forest; had been killed; or had died of disease and malnutrition. As of 16 May 1997, MSF estimated that at least 190,000 refugees remained unaccounted for (ibid. 1). By 2 July, 234,000 additional Rwandan refugees had been repatriated and UNHCR had located a further 52,600 in Zaïre or neighbouring countries, leaving an estimated 213,000 refugees unaccounted for (HRW & FIDH 1997: 10).

ACCUSATIONS OF MASSACRES

On 21 November 1996, CNN reported that the AFDL had massacred Rwandan refugees fleeing westwards from Goma (Bond 1996). On 26 November, it was reported that 500 unarmed Rwandese refugees and Zaïrian IDP's had been massacred at Chimanga camp (60 km south of Bukavu) on 18 November (AI 1996e). Equally, reports of gross violations of human rights committed by the FAZ continued to emerge (see AI 1997a).

In a statement on 3 December 1996, the US State Department (1996i) said it was 'deeply concerned about allegations of human rights abuses' committed by the AFDL, and called on the alliance to allow 'objective observers from the international community free and unfettered access' to investigate 'these very serious allegations'. On 4 December a 'very clear message from the United States' was delivered to the AFDL, requesting that it 'halt any operations that would take the life or victimise the innocent civilians who are trying to make their way back to Rwanda' (US State Dept 1996ii). On the same day, a State Department official said that these allegations had been raised with the governments of Uganda and Rwanda and that instructions had been issued 'to urge restraint on their part' (US Congress 1996). This was despite the fact that as late as February 1997, the US embassy in Kigali denied there were Rwandan troops in Zaïre (HRW & FIDH 1997: 36).

In January 1997, the UN Special Rapporteur for Human Rights in Zaïre (Roberto Garretón) detailed violations of Article 3 Common to the Geneva Conventions of 1949, committed by the FAZ (UN 1997a paras 191–6), especially against Zaïrian Tutsi and by the ex-FAR/*interahamwe* (ibid. paras 203–6). His report also noted 'many reports of atrocities committed by the AFDL' (ibid. para 197).

In an interview on 22 February 1997, the Belgian Minister for Co-operation (Reginald Moreels) stated: 'I have eyewitness accounts that a new genocide [*volkerenmoord*] is under way in Eastern Zaïre' and that mass graves had been found (Van der Kelen 1997). On 26 February, *Le Monde* revealed that a 14-page report, written by a 'western eyewitness' to events in Kivu, had been sent to the UNSC, Amnesty and the Belgian government (*Le Monde* 1997; see IRIN 1997xi). The report's anonymous author alleged that thousands of Rwandan refugees had been systematically killed by the AFDL; that she/he had personally visited mass graves at Mugunga, Kibumba, and Katale and had been given the location of other graves 'containing thousands of bodies' (see Loos 1997). On 20 December 1996, she/he had asked a senior UNHCR official at Goma why the agency had not denounced the massacres and was told 'we know very well that the refugees have been killed in the forest in their tens of thousands; what can we do? We're not an army' (quoted in *Le Monde* 1997). On 28 February 1997, the field co-ordinator for UNHCR (based in Goma) stated that, although some refugees had been killed, 'there was nothing to prove organised massacres' (IRIN 1997xii).

UNITED NATIONS INVESTIGATIONS

On 6 March 1997, the UN High Commissioner for Human Rights (José Ayala-Lasso) said he was 'deeply concerned' about unconfirmed reports he had received of massacres of Rwandan Hutu refugees in Zaïre and had instructed Garretón to conduct a preliminary investigation (IRIN 1997xiv). Between 25 and 29 March, Garretón visited (and confirmed the existence of) four mass graves in North Kivu (UN 1997b). In his report (2 April 1997) Garretón gave the location of 40 possible sites of massacres by the AFDL, accusing the alliance of intentionally blocking humanitarian assistance to refugees (ibid. paras 35–6). Garretón also reported massacres committed by the ex-FAR/*interahamwe* and FAZ (ibid. paras 43–4) and recommended that the UNHCHR launch a full investigation into 'gross violations of life committed in Eastern Zaïre against refugees and the local population' (ibid. para 55).

On 24 March 1997, AI stated there was 'mounting evidence' that the AFDL had carried out 'a deliberate campaign of arbitrary killings of refugees ... and of Zaïrian Hutu' (1997b: 4), and that mass graves located in or near refugee camps contained victims whose hands were tied behind their back and who had been shot in the head. The report also detailed human rights violations by the FAZ, including systematic looting, killing of unarmed civilians and widespread rape (ibid. 5–7; see AI 1997c: 22–3). Rape committed on a widespread, systematic basis is a crime against humanity (see UN 1994q; 1994s paras 142–5).

On 15 April 1997, the UNHCHR asked Garretón to head a joint mission to investigate allegations of 'grave and massive violations of human rights, especially the right to life, particularly article 3 common to the Geneva Conventions' in eastern Zaïre since September 1996 (UN 1997c para 9a). The members of the joint mission chose to 'concentrate on verifying whether the acts committed had been systematic and planned and whether some of them constituted acts of genocide under the terms of the [UNGC]' (ibid. para 10).

Although the UNHCHR received assurances from the AFDL that it would co-operate with the mission (UN 1997c para 3), the alliance later objected to the participation of Garretón, arguing that his April 1997 report had not been 'impartial' (ibid. para 6). Refused entry to Kivu, the mission collected evidence in Kigali and issued a report on 2 July 1997. The report stated that following attacks on refugee camps in Kivu (October–November 1996), at Shabunda (mid-January 1997) and Tingi-Tingi/Amisi (February 1997) witnesses reported that refugees 'almost all of whom were Hutu' had been massacred and that c140,000 refugees remained unaccounted for (ibid. para 42).

The report repeated accusations that the AFDL had blocked the provision of humanitarian assistance to refugees, with 'extremely serious consequences', and had announced the arrival of humanitarian agencies to lure refugees out of the forest in order to kill them (UN 1997c paras 45; 53; see MSF 1997: 3). The report stated that such action 'prompts the suspicion that it is a more subtle but no less effective tactic aimed at eliminating the Rwandan refugees', and it was 'not just a question of sporadic violence, but rather of a skilfully applied stratagem' (ibid. para 54).

The joint mission gave the location of 134 sites of alleged massacres of Rwandan refugees or Zaïrian Hutu, 'most of them carried out by AFDL and the Banyamulenge rebels' (UN 1997c para 59). According to evidence available to the joint mission, the targets of AFDL attacks were:

> Very often ... neither *Interahamwe* combatants nor soldiers of the former FAR: they were women, children, the wounded, the sick, the dying and the elderly, and the attacks seem to have had no precise military objective. Often the massacres were carried out after militia members and former FAR soldiers had begun to retreat. (Ibid. para 46)

For the joint mission, it was 'unacceptable to claim that more than 1 million people, including large numbers of children, should be collectively designated as persons guilty of genocide and liable to execution without trial' (ibid. para 41) and that 'testimony accusing AFDL of human rights violations often refers to [RPA] complicity' (ibid. para 73).

The report also stated that on 13 May 1997, at Mbandaka in western Zaïre (where fighting had not taken place) Rwandan refugees, 'most of them women, children and unarmed men were murdered' (UN 1997c para 47). The refugees were unarmed because the local military governor (a Mobutu appointee) had disarmed both refugees and FAZ deserters, a fact confirmed by the new governor appointed by Kabila (Pomfret 1997a; see AI 1997c: 12). The case of Mbandaka was to be pursued by a subsequent investigation (see below). The report also contained allegations of extensive human rights violations committed by the FAZ (ibid. paras 62–5) and the ex-FAR/*interahamwe* (ibid. paras 66–7), the latter having killed refugees who had tried, or simply announced an intention, to return to Rwanda.

It should be noted that on 18 May 1997, the AFDL had captured Kinshasa, Laurent Kabila declaring himself President, renaming the country the Democratic Republic of Congo (DRC).

Given that *officially* the conflict was 'internal', the joint mission believed it was covered by Article 3, common to the four Geneva Conventions of 1949. Article 3 reads:

> In the case of armed conflict not of an international character occurring in the territory of one of the High Contracting Parties, each Party to the conflict shall be bound to apply as the minimum, the following provisions: (1) Persons taking no active part in the hostilities [unarmed civilians], including members of the armed forces who have laid down their arms and those placed *hors de combat* by sickness, wounds, detention, or any other cause, shall in all cases be treated humanely, without any adverse distinction founded on race, colour, religion or faith, sex, birth or wealth, or any other similar criteria. (Quoted in UN 1997c para 84 n. 25)

Thus, 'violence to life and person, in particular murder of all kinds, mutilation, cruel treatment and torture [shall] remain prohibited at any time and in any place whatsoever with respect to the above-mentioned persons' (ibid.). Given that Zaïre had ratified all four Geneva Conventions on 14 February 1961 ('occurring in the territory of one of the High Contracting Parties'), then *all* parties to the conflict were required to respect the provisions of Article 3. Rwanda had ratified the Geneva Conventions in 1964. Even if neither Zaïre nor Rwanda had been party to the Geneva Conventions, it is acknowledged that Article 3 has become part of international customary law binding non-parties (see UN 1994o para 87 n. 5). If the conflict was regarded as inter-national, Article II of the Geneva Conventions would apply.[12]

The joint mission asked whether reported incidents constituted crimes against humanity. The mission concluded that the 'concept of crimes against humanity could also be applied to the situation which reigned and continues to reign in the [DRC]' (UN 1997c para 88), taking the definition from the 1996 'Draft Code of Crimes Against the Security and Peace of Mankind', of which the relevant parts of Article 18 read:

> A crime against humanity means any of the following acts, when committed in a systematic manner or on a large scale and instigated or directed by a Government or by any organisation or group: (a) murder; (b) extermination; (c) torture ... (e) persecution on political, racial, religious or ethnic grounds ... (g) arbitrary deportation or forcible transfer of population; (h) arbitrary imprisonment; (i) forced disappearance of persons; (j) rape, enforced prostitution and other forms of sexual abuse; (k) other inhumane acts which severely damage physical or mental integrity, health or human dignity, such as mutilation and severe bodily harm. (Quoted in UN 1997c para 87)

The mission stated that in terms of the number of allegations of violations of international humanitarian law (Article 3 of the Geneva Conventions) received, the majority had been committed by the 'AFDL, the Banyamulenge and their allies' (68.02 per cent) (UN 1997c para 95); and as regards other parties: FAZ (16.75 per cent); ex-FAR/*interahamwe* (9.64 per cent); RPA (2.03 per cent); the armed forces of Burundi (2.03 per cent); and mercenaries fighting for the Kinshasa government (1.52 per cent). The mission suggested that those responsible could be brought to trial before an international tribunal as 'in the case of the former Yugoslavia and Rwanda' (ibid.).

The report stated that available evidence suggested violations had been systematic in nature and that advance planning '[could not] be ruled out' (UN 1997c para 77). Given that the victims were 'mostly Hutu from Burundi, Rwanda and Zaïre [the] mission's preliminary opinion is that some of these alleged massacres could constitute acts of genocide' (ibid. para 80). Although the mission felt unable to issue 'a precise, definitive opinion', it called for 'in-depth, impartial and objective investigations that the question of genocide warrants' (ibid. para 96).

An MSF report (6 May 1997) stated that the AFDL had used the promise of humanitarian aid to lure refugees out of the forest so they could be killed and that this was 'a deliberate strategy by the AFDL, aimed at the elimination of all remaining Rwandan refugees, including women and children' (MSF 1997: 10; see HRW & FIDH 1997: 16; USCR 1997: 5; PHR 1997; AI 1997c: 33).

As the UNHCHR mission had been refused entry to DRC, the UNSG established his own investigation team at the beginning of July 1997 to 'investigate grave violations of human rights and of international humanitarian law which have been committed in [DRC] since the 1 March 1993' (UN 1998a para 10). The team's interpretation of their mandate was to establish whether Article 2 of the UNGC was applicable and whether war crimes or crimes against humanity had been committed (ibid. para 11a). Although the team recognised that at least one neighbouring country (Rwanda) had 'participated actively in the conflict' (ibid. para 16), they remained undecided whether the conflict should be considered internal or inter-national. They concluded, however, that Article 3 Common to the Geneva Conventions was applicable to all armed conflict (ibid. para 16).

The mission arrived at Kinshasa in mid-August 1997. In mid-September, the DRC government restricted investigations to the east of the country (UN 1998a para 33). This would prevent further investigation at Mbandaka, 1,220 km west of the DRC–Rwanda border, significant because:

Killings in the east, near Rwanda, could perhaps be written off as random acts of overzealous or vengeful [RPA] soldiers. But for Hutu refugees to be tracked down and killed at the opposite end of this huge country, when Kabila's victory in the war was already assured, would strongly suggest deliberate extermination. (French 1998; quoted in Emizet 2000: 171)

Refused authorisation to visit Mbandaka, the team withdrew on 1 October 1997, returning to DRC on 11 November (UN 1998a para 35). Although the team believed that the number killed at Mbandaka was small in comparison with the 'total number of persons killed during and after the attacks on the [refugee camps]' (ibid. para 41), it decided to begin the investigation at Mbandaka because:

> Information concerning the circumstances in which these massacres had taken place was categorical, including ... the identity of the forces responsible and that the victims were unarmed. We had precise information of the location of mass graves and, in contrast to the eastern provinces, there was no indication of fighting in the region. (Ibid.)

After a three-week wait, the team was allowed to travel to Mbandaka on 8 December 1997, only to receive information that in late-November/early December, DRC authorities had excavated mass graves (UN 1998a para 42). Despite obstruction the team confirmed the existence of one mass grave at nearby Wendji (from which bodies had been removed after several months). Following further obstruction, the mission moved to Goma to collect testimonies, most of which concerned human rights violations committed by Rwandan refugees (ibid. paras 58; 64). The UNSG withdrew the team on 17 April 1997, following the detention and expulsion of a member of the team (ibid. paras 61–3).

The mission interviewed Rwandan refugees in neighbouring countries and received substantial documentation from journalists, diplomats, aid agencies and human rights organisations (UN 1998a para 72). The mission chose to base its conclusions on evidence it had itself collected and on corroborated testimony from other sources (see ibid. 'Report Summary'). Information deemed 'original' would remain confidential until it was 'possible to undertake a full investigation' (ibid. para 72). Consequently, the information contained in the appendix to the team's report of 28 June 1998[13] ('Summary of Allegations') contains only information *already* published.

Although the team was unable to quantify the number of victims, it was clear that a 'large number of actors' had committed massacres and other atrocities since March 1993, including the FAZ, 'the rebels', 'tribal militias', the RPA and 'Zaïrian mobs' (UN 1998a para 19). The team conceded it was impossible to confirm or refute most allegations, but was certain that grave violations of human rights had taken place and that, in the majority of cases, it was possible to make 'general conclusions' regarding the identity of perpetrators and in certain cases specific military units or individuals (ibid. para 76).

The report stated that from mid-October to mid-November 1996 the AFDL and 'elements of the [RPA]' had attacked the refugee camps in Kivu' (UN 1998a 'Report Summary'). Although the team had not obtained 'sufficient information', they believed the attacks had resulted in numerous civilian casualties. They had evidence that 'in certain cases' during 'systematic attacks' on refugee camps, unarmed refugees (especially women and children) had been executed; 'hundreds' following the attack on Mugunga camp (ibid. para 80). AFDL soldiers had played a 'predominant role' in these attacks while 'the Rwandese Government [has] publicly admitted that Rwanda had participated in these operations' (ibid.). Furthermore, 'a large number' of refugees had been 'hunted down and killed' by the AFDL and Mai Mai while fleeing westwards, although 'the extent of Rwandan participation in the massacre of camp residents who were in flight is not sufficiently documented' (ibid. para 81). The report also stated that FAZ soldiers had killed unarmed civilians as had the ex-FAR/*interahamwe* (ibid. paras 84–5).

According to the report, following attacks on camps at Amisi, Tingi-Tingi, Kasese and Obilo, 'tens of thousands of Rwandan Hutu had disappeared' and that AFDL soldiers had killed unarmed (fleeing) civilians (UN 1998a para 86). Again, 'the extent of Rwandan participation in these attacks is not known' (ibid.). As regards attacks on camps in Kivu and south of Kisangani: 'These massacres constitute a violation of international humanitarian law, and given their systematic character, strongly imply that they constitute crimes against humanity' (ibid. 'Report Summary').

According to the report, 'hundreds' of unarmed 'Rwandan Hutu had been massacred at Mbandaka and in the neighbouring village of Wendji' in May 1997 by AFDL soldiers, 'apparently under the command of the Rwandan army' and that corpses had been removed from a mass grave at the site (UN 1998a paras 87; 89; see AI 1997c: 11–13). The mission had received 'numerous credible indications' that 'strongly suggested' such 'cleaning' operations had taken place elsewhere (UN 1998a para 89). Eyewitnesses reported AFDL combatants using a truck to remove bodies from the Goma camps and that heavy machinery and trucks had been used south of Kisangani in April 1997 to remove/bury bodies (HRW & FIDH 1997: 16; 26; AI 1997c: 17; Pomfret 1997a; IRIN 1997xv).

The report concluded that acts of pillage and killing committed by the FAZ (October 1996 onwards) constituted 'grave violations of the right to life and property' as protected by human rights treaties ratified by Zaïre, while the killing of civilians violated international humanitarian law (UN 1998a para 90) Likewise, the massacre of civilians by ethnic militia in North Kivu in 1993 and by *interahamwe* and Mai Mai militias from October 1996 onwards constituted 'grave violations of international humanitarian law' (ibid. paras 91; 94).

In the team's opinion, evidence strongly indicated that:

> [A]t least the massacres committed by the AFDL and its allies during the period October 1996 to May 1997 and the refusal of humanitarian aid to displaced Rwandan Hutu have been systematic practices, including murder and extermination, which constitute crimes against humanity as defined by the statutes of the [ICTR and ICTY]. (UN 1998a para 95)

Although the team recognised that an objective of attacking the Kivu camps had been to force refugees to return to Rwanda and that this had been voluntary to 'a certain extent' (UN 1998a para 96), it was 'also clear that at certain times and in certain places, attacks against populations who had left the camps and who had fled westwards ... did not have the objective of forcing them to return to Rwanda but to simply eliminate them' (ibid.). Certain evidence, therefore, tended 'to demonstrate an objective of physically eliminating Rwandan Hutu who had decided to remain in Zaïre' and that this could be interpreted in two possible ways:

> a decision to eliminate these groups rather than repatriate them, for whatever reason; or a decision to eliminate them because the destruction of the camps had physically separated 'good' Hutu from 'bad', in the sense that ... those who fled rather than return [to Rwanda] were those who had participated in the genocide or who had supported it. *In either case,* the systematic massacre of Hutu who stayed in Zaïre was a heinous crime against humanity, but the motive behind these decisions is important in order to determine whether these murders constitute genocide ... a decision to eliminate, in part, the Hutu ethnic group. The motive behind the massacre of Zaïrian Hutu in North-Kivu is also important. (UN 1998a para 96; emphasis added)

In contrast to attacks on camps in Kivu, attacks against camps in the interior of Zaïre (Amisi, Tingi-Tingi, Shabunda, Kasese, Biaro, Obilo and Mbandaka) demonstrated

> that the intention was to eliminate Rwandan Hutu who had remained in Zaïre. A possible interpretation of this phase of the

operations led by the AFDL with the support of Rwanda is that it had been decided to eliminate this part of the Hutu ethnic group as such. If this is confirmed, it would be an act of genocide. (UN 1998a 'Report Summary')

The report recommended that a new investigative team be created, to investigate further crimes committed by all parties and in particular establish the extent of 'direct participation' by the RPA in AFDL operations from October 1996 onwards (UN 1998a 'Recommendations' para 7c) and the intention behind the massacre of Zaïrian and Rwandan Hutu from October 1996 onwards (ibid. para 7e).

In letters to the UNSG, the DRC government dismissed the report as 'a collection of unfounded allegations' (UN 1998b para 11), while the Rwandan government categorically denied that the RPA had committed any human rights violations in Zaïre and that such an 'incomplete, biased and totally misleading report does not serve the human rights cause, and would compromise the possibility of getting the truth of what happened' (UN 1998c).

Throughout the 1996/97 conflict, the movement of international journalists (and aid agencies) was tightly controlled by the AFDL/RPA (see Gowing 1998). Paul Kagame is reported to have said: 'we used communication and information warfare better than anyone' (quoted in IRIN 1998iii). By the beginning of October 1998 (by which time Rwanda and Laurent Kabila had parted company) the Rwandan foreign minister was urging that steps be taken against Kabila whose regime 'incites the populace to genocide' (IRIN 1998v). At the end of October 1998, the Rwandan embassy in Washington was warning of a 'second genocide' (committed by Kabila) and that the world's silence over the conflict in DRC 'reflects the double-standard that is by now all too familiar in Africa ... While photojournalists find their way to the battlefront to photograph Kosovo Albanians, the visual account of what is happening right now in the eastern DRC remains unseen' (IRIN 1998vi).

The UNSC took no decisions after receiving the July 1998 report, although the Council's president requested that the Rwandan and DRC governments immediately investigate the allegations and inform the Council of any developments by 15 October 1998 (UN 1998d). No information was forthcoming.

THE RESPONSIBILITY OF THE RWANDAN GOVERNMENT

The reports cited above demonstrate that *all* sides committed serious crimes during the conflict. As regards debates within Rwanda, the extent of involvement by the RPA is clearly of importance and constituted a key recommendation of the UNSG's team.

Early reports stated that attacks on Kibumba and Katale camps (25/26 October 1996) 'were instigated by Rwandan soldiers or elements supported by the [RPA]' (IRIN 1996v). On 30 October, Kagame denied RPA troops were fighting in Zaïre, but admitted that Banyamulenge who *had* been in the RPA, may have returned to defend their community (IRIN 1996vii). Although reports on 7 November stated that up to 50 per cent of the armed 'rebel' presence in Goma was RPA (IRIN 1996xvii), Kagame reiterated (on 13 November) that the conflict was an internal Zaïrian problem (IRIN 1996xxvi; see 1996xiii; xxix). On 2 December, Kagame stated that although he was not 'altogether unhappy' with what had happened in eastern Zaïre, 'we [the RPA] were not directly involved with what took place' (Braeckman 1996).

Seven months later, in an interview in the *Washington Post* (9 July 1997), Kagame stated that 'mid-level commanders' of the RPA had led the AFDL throughout the campaign (Pomfret 1997b). The Rwandan government had taken this decision because, despite persistent requests, the UN had failed to disarm the camps. According to Kagame, in early October 1996, Rwandan agents had learned of plans by the ex-FAR/*interahamwe* to attack Banyamulenge and invade Rwanda.[14] Weapons and troops had been sent to the Banyamulenge. Kagame maintained that the 'battle plan' (formulated by him and his advisers) was to 'dismantle the camps' and destroy the ex-FAR/*interahamwe*. Kagame stated that, although the bulk of the AFDL were Congolese, key units belonging to the RPA had been deployed 'when there was a need for precision' and that an RPA officer (considered the senior AFDL commander) had been 'assigned to help the army of Congo [AFDL]'. Kagame admitted that the RPA had played a role *throughout* the campaign to topple Mobutu ('We found the best way was to take it to the end').

On 27 October 1997, the Pan African News Agency (PANA) published an interview with Kagame in which he admitted that refugees had been *unintentionally* killed when the RPA fought ex-FAR/*interahamwe* mixed up with women and children, but that 'This cannot qualify their deaths as a massacre' (Kanhema 1997). Kagame described these deaths as 'a result of war' and that he had 'no apologies or regrets on the conduct of my soldiers' (ibid.). The South African *Sunday Independent* had carried the same interview on 26 October. Kagame's spokesperson denied that Kagame had said the RPA was implicated in the killing of civilians (IRIN 1997xvi) and, on 28 October, Kagame declared: 'I do not know that any refugees died at the hands of our forces or the forces of Kabila' (quoted in IRIN 1997xvii). In an interview on 24 October, however, an adviser to the Rwandan President stated: 'we had to kill those criminals, and if there were women and children in the way, we can't be naïve; this is war' (quoted in Jones 2001: 148). Likewise, the PANA article quoted an RPA colonel (speaking independently of Kagame): 'We are not doing police work here, we are fighting a war and we have no time to investigate who is a hostage on the other side of the line' (Kanhema 1997).

While the involvement of RPA soldiers in the *unintentional* killing of unarmed civilians remains unresolved, human rights reports suggest complicity in massacres (HRW & FIDH 1997: 14; AI 1997c: 8; IRIN 1997viii). Eyewitnesses described the perpetrators of massacres as Kinyarwanda-speakers (HRW & FIDH 1997: 14). This does not necessarily indicate that these soldiers were Rwandan. They could have been Banyarwanda, Banyamulenge (understood broadly) or Burundian (given that those not fluent in Kirundi and Kinyarwanda may confuse the two languages). Other witnesses, however, maintained that commanding officers and troops in areas where massacres took place were fluent in English, Kinyarwanda and Kiswahili, a characteristic of RPA soldiers who had grown up in southern Uganda (ibid.). Furthermore, witnesses maintained that the Kiswahili spoken was characteristic of Rwanda and not the Zaïre/DRC variant (ibid. n. 35). Witnesses told AI that, at the time of alleged massacres south of Kisangani (April 1997) most of the troops in the area were RPA (1997c: 17).

The October 1997 HRW and FIDH report contained a list of eight AFDL commanders who were either involved in, or must have been aware of, the massacre of civilians. At least four of the eight were confirmed members of the RPA and had been present in areas where massacres had taken place – three of them present at Mbandaka on 13 May 1997 (HRW & FIDH 1997: 29–31; see Pomfret 1997a; AI 1997c: 12).

The NGO Physicians for Human Rights (PHR) (instrumental in excavating mass graves of genocide victims in Rwanda on behalf of

ICTR prosecutors) also received 'reliable reports that Rwandan military have committed, and continue to commit, widespread atrocities against civilian populations in Eastern Congo' (PHR 1997). Again, the identification rested on language (English, Kinyarwanda and Kiswahili). Although the report speculated that other armed groups may have masqueraded as RPA, the team noted that eyewitness reports came from diverse sources; were marked by internal consistency; and withstood 'specific, intrusive, and repetitive questioning' (ibid.).

THE PROSPECTS FOR JUSTICE

The UNSG's team stated that as a 'successor government' the new DRC government was bound by international human rights treaties ratified by the former regime (the International Covenant of Civil and Political Rights, for example). It was under a legal obligation, therefore, to investigate alleged crimes committed on its territory and bring those responsible to trial (UN 1998a para 97). The report recognised, however, that the DRC government had neither begun this process 'nor did it show the slightest inclination' of doing so (ibid.). Under these conditions the report recommended that an international tribunal be given jurisdiction over these alleged crimes, as the only way to end the 'cycle of impunity' (ibid.). The report recommended that the jurisdiction of the ICTR be enlarged to cover 'genocide and other similar violations committed in the territory of neighbouring states [by anyone] whatever their nationality, between 1 January 1994 and 31 December 1997' (ibid. 'Recommendations' para 4). The report stated that if an international tribunal was *not* given jurisdiction over alleged crimes, this would

> encourage the feeling that the international community is not prepared to react impartially to grave violations of human rights and humanitarian law and, in the long term, would feed collective feelings of victimisation and denial of justice, contributing to the cycle of collective reprisals and encouraging a belief in impunity. (UN 1998a para 97)

The evidence gathered by the UNSG's team would remain 'in a secure place' until either a full, unobstructed investigation could take place, the DRC authorities demonstrated a determination to pursue those responsible, or, failing that, when the ICTR acquired jurisdiction ('Recommendations' para 5).

In 1998 Judge Laity Kama (President of the ICTR), referring to Zaïre/DRC in 1996–97, stated that she was 'uneasy' that while certain crimes are prosecuted 'other crimes, which take place as a repercussion, are not' and that this was a problem of 'equality' (quoted in Hazan 1998). She noted that despite the recommendation of the UNSG's team, the tribunal's mandate had not been extended even though this 'would only require a Security Council resolution' (ibid.).

Conflict has continued to ravage Eastern DRC from August 1998 until the time of writing, with Rwandan and Ugandan backed rebels fighting the Kinshasa government and one another. The Lusaka Peace Agreement (7 July 1999) between the various warring parties in DRC,[15] reaffirmed (in Article 8.2.2(e)) that *génocidaires* (those who had committed the 1994 genocide in Rwanda) should be handed over to the ICTR. In addition, Article 9.1 states that the 'Joint Military Commission', which was to oversee the cease-fire, should (with OAU/UN assistance) 'put in place measures for: (a) handing over to the UN International Tribunal and national courts, mass killers and perpetrators of crimes against humanity; and (b) handling of other war criminals'. Although this provision implies that an international tribunal should have jurisdiction over crimes committed in DRC between 1996 and 1999, these crimes do not come within the ICTR's current temporal jurisdiction. An HRW report (2000b) in May 2000 recommended that the UNSC establish an additional judicial chamber at the ICTR to prosecute violations of international humanitarian law committed by all parties to the DRC conflict.

The International Rescue Committee (2001) has estimated that in the period August 1998–April 2001, 3.5 million people had died as a result of the conflict (350,000 as a direct result of violence by all sides). Even if the fate of Rwandan refugees and Congolese civilians in 1993–97 is deemed insufficient to extend the jurisdiction of the ICTR, the scale of subsequent violence perhaps should.

Reports indicate that countless thousands of people were killed in Zaïre/DRC between 1993 and 1997. Victims included: Zaïrian Tutsi, Rwandan Tutsi refugees (of the 1960s/70s) and Tutsi Banyamulenge killed by the ex-FAR/*interahamwe*, 'autochthonous' militia and FAZ soldiers; Rwandan refugees (who wished to return to Rwanda) killed by ex-FAR/*interahamwe*; and Rwandan refugees killed by the AFDL (possibly with RPA complicity). Likewise, thousands of 'autochthonous' Zaïrians were killed by ex-FAR/*interahamwe* while Zaïrian Hutu were killed by 'autochthonous' militia and the AFDL. So far, no one has been held accountable for these crimes.

ENDING IMPUNITY

The Rwandan government has never denied that RPA soldiers committed serious human rights abuses in 1994. For example, Kagame told the UNCE (in 1994) that RPA soldiers had been arrested for human rights abuses and would be 'subject to heavy military discipline and punishment' (UN 1994s para 99). The apparent suppression of Gersony's preliminary findings, the small number of RPA courts martial and that (at the time of writing) the ICTR has not indicted any RPA soldiers, leaves this issue unnecessarily unresolved. HRW warns: 'Failing to provide [victims of RPA crimes with] justice … will feed resentment and desire for revenge, explosive sentiments in a region where armed groups continue to operate in opposition to recognised governments' (2002a).

As regards the question of the attack on Habyarimana's plane, available evidence indicates that those responsible for the genocide committed this act. And yet, Hourigan's memo and its apparent suppression raises unresolved questions. On its part, the Rwandan government has stated that in 'the interests of truth and to finally put the matter to rest, the government of Rwanda supports a full investigation conducted by the ICTR involving all political and military groups that were present in Rwanda in 1994' (IRIN 2000xiv). At the time of writing, it remains unclear whether the ICTR will initiate such an investigation.

As regards accusations of human rights abuses committed in Zaïre/DRC from 1993 onwards, one should recognise that it is the same bodies who were pro-active in having the 1994 genocide of Tutsi recognised (and provided the bulk of evidence against those responsible) who have published allegations of crimes in Zaïre/DRC. The UNCE's reports (October and December 1994) decisively recognised the 1994 genocide of Tutsi, drawing on evidence provided by the same bodies who have made allegations regarding Zaïre/DRC: UNHCHR, HRW, AI, FIDH, MSF, USCR and Oxfam (see UN 1994o paras 59–60; 1994s para 48). Accepting the allegations made by these bodies in one context and dismissing (or ignoring) them in another, may generate a perception that the international community does not respond impartially to all allegations of human rights abuses and violations of international humanitarian law, a perception that in the long term may 'feed collective feelings of victimisation and denial of justice, contributing to the cycle of collective reprisals and encouraging a belief in impunity' (UN 1998a para 97).

As the ICG observe, 'In the Hutu community [in Rwanda] today … the massacre of refugees in Eastern Congo in 1996 and 1997 has become the main source of ethnic conscious raising and justifies the latent or explicit denial of the genocide against the Tutsis' (2002b: 17). There is a pressing need for judicial investigation in order to disable 'the dangerous culture of collective guilt and retribution, which too often produces further cycles of violence' (Kritz 1996: 591; see Borneman 1997: 6).

In Rwanda, the need to end the 'culture of impunity' has been a constant theme since 1994. Following the UNSC resolution establishing the ICTR (November 1994), the Rwandan representative stated: 'The recent genocide in Rwanda … is the direct result of [the] culture of impunity'; that it would be 'impossible to build a state of law and arrive at true national reconciliation if we do not eradicate the culture of impunity which has characterised our society since 1959'; and that an international tribunal was needed to 'teach the Rwandese people a lesson, to fight against the impunity to which it had come accustomed since 1959' (UN 1994p).

Following the execution in April 1998 of 22 people convicted of genocide, the Rwandan foreign minister stated that the executions would help 'eradicate the culture of impunity which has been going on for more than three decades' (IRIN 1998ii). A Rwandan newspaper editorial stated: 'Though painful it might be to take someone's life … painful medicine was necessary to heal our sick society, an example to all, that the days of impunity are over and everyone must answer for his crimes' (New Times 1998c; see IRIN 2001iii). Paul Kagame (Rwandan President and head of the RPA) has consistently referred to the need to end impunity:

> We must also rise and fight against the culture of impunity that has been rampant in the country for a long time, culminating in the genocide. (Kagame 2000a)

> Key among … difficulties we face [is] justice that could not take root so as to do away with unfairness and the culture of impunity. (Kagame 2000b)

> In our various efforts to mend our social and economic fabric in the past six years, one may highlight the following accomplishments

> ... Rehabilitation of the justice sector with a goal of replacing the culture of impunity with rule of law. (Kagame 2001)

> The Government of National Unity ... has had the task of establishing law and order ... building a culture of tolerance to replace that of impunity that had characterised the colonial and post-colonial regimes in Rwanda. (Kagame 2002)

Ending impunity should not be confused with simply finding people guilty. Rather, it entails a consistent and coherent effort to respond to *all* allegations of human rights abuses in a dogmatic, tenacious and transparent way. Demonstrating that allegations are untrue is as a much a part of demonstrating that impunity has ended as convicting those found responsible. The true, perhaps unpalatable, nature of ending impunity is summed up by del Ponte:

> For me, a victim is a victim, a crime falling within my mandate as the prosecutor is a crime, irrespective of the identity or the ethnicity or the political ideas of the person who committed the said crime. Justice does not accommodate political opportunism. No one should remain immune from prosecutions for the worst crimes. (Quoted in Fondation Hirondelle 2002i)

6
Appealing to the Past: The Debate Over History

The preceding chapters have demonstrated that an appeal to 'history' was central to the colonial construction of racial distinction; establishing the 'Hutu Republic' and genocidal propaganda. Current efforts to account for the 1994 genocide continue to be framed by reference to 'history'. Consequently, the preceding exploration of contemporary debates has, to an extent, assumed the explanatory quality and truth claims of history. This chapter, however, takes a perspectival shift and problematises that persistent 'appeal to history'.

Problematising the 'appeal to history' should not be confused with problematising survivor memory. The survivors' experiences of death and loss must be gathered, preserved and, above all, acknowledged lest survivors be 'condemned to dwell alone and nameless in the ruins of memory' (Das 1996: 69). This chapter is written with a full appreciation of Elie Wiesel's statement regarding survivors of the Holocaust, that 'Any survivor has more to say than all the historians combined about what happened' (quoted in Cargas 1986; see Hirsch 1995: 79).

The 'history' considered here is not the personal experience or testimony of *rescapés*. Rather, it proceeds from a recognition of continuity in the role played by macro-narratives in intermittent violence and ultimately genocide. One must ask whether our faith in the 'other country' of the past as a repository of redemptive, explanatory truth is misplaced.

One could argue that these macro-narratives were simply fabrications and that we should seek to write a new 'authentic' history of Rwanda. Who is to write this 'new history'? Johan Pottier (1995) has demonstrated that one can choose 'one's historian' for whatever purpose; there is no single 'academic' version of Rwandan history, or, as Peter Uvin notes, 'All in all, one can argue almost any position ... and invoke a series of famous and not so famous social scientists to "prove" it' (1997: 93). C. Newbury makes a related point:

[E]xplaining how and why the uses and abuses of power led to violence in the past could serve as an important lesson to leaders who wish to build a different society in the future. Yet, not surprisingly in such a polarised atmosphere, historical reconstruction is itself highly contested. *Here, with an intensity that surpasses the normal clichés, there is no single history; rather there are competing 'histories'.* (1998: 8–9; emphasis added)

Which narrative should we accept, and how should we assign 'authority' among competing voices? Our response to such multiplicity could be dismissive – after all, there can be only one *true* history. We should remember, however, that genocidal propaganda took the same absolutist approach. Ultimately, it may be more apposite to reflect on the nature of historiography, to recognise that the *past* is a contested place and that different interpretations of it should be explored (rather than dismissed) because they reveal what actors hold to be *current* disparities. We may feel unease in surrendering our faith in history as 'realist transparency', but it is a challenge one must face given that 'the interpretation of history has been a recurrent poison in Rwanda's body politic' (Linden 1998: 1).

INTRODUCTION

The meaning of history is important to Rwandese. Power is history and history is power. If you are in a position of telling your history you are in a position of power. The structure of power is constructed on the construction of history. (Former Rwandan government minister, exile, Switzerland, May 1999)

The 1994 genocide was based on 'mental maps of history' (C. Newbury 1998: 7) presenting Tutsi as an 'alien race' who had ruled Rwanda oppressively prior to the 'social revolution' of 1959 and that the RPF was attempting to re-establish that regime (see des Forges 1995: 46; HRW & FIDH 1999: 72ff). It is, perhaps, 'not a coincidence that one of the main brains behind Hutu extremist ideology, Ferdinand Nahimana [RTLM Director of Programmes] was a historian' (Sibomana 1999: 81).

The central role of history in legitimising political authority in Rwanda was described by one exile as follows:

Each power writes its own history, to serve its political ambitions. Rwandese make a policy and afterwards massage history to make it coincide with their political ideas. (Rwandan NGO worker, exile, Belgium, March 1999)

Consequently, a singular, stable 'authentic' history is imbued with a redemptive quality:

> It is now time to sit down and see what from the past was good and proper and then make a common agreement of our history. It is clear that the history of Rwanda has yet to be written. (Rwandan Protestant Church official, Kigali, returnee, May 1998)

> The only real form of reconciliation is to tell people about history, so we know the truth. What was the real cause of the genocide? We need to know the truth. The genocide was a product of history. (Rwandan academic, exile, France, June 1999)

Such hopes are laudable, but do they place too much faith in historiography, failing to recognise the 'epistemological limits to social scientific (as to all) understanding' (Freeman 1991: 195)? Can such hopes be satisfied by historiography, which, at heart, is a selective interpretative exercise? Finally, do these statements, inadvertently, aspire to a singular, absolutist history, the same instrumental form of history as found in genocidal propaganda?

'APPEALING TO HISTORY': A COLONIAL LEGACY

The genealogy of contemporary narratives must be traced back to colonial rule and the introduction of unquestioned 'history as legitimation':

> In a great and unsung collaborative enterprise over a period of decades, Europeans and Rwandan intellectuals created a history of Rwanda that fitted European assumptions [*Seigneurs Tutsi* and *Serviteurs Hutu*] and accorded with Tutsi interests. The Europeans provided a theoretical, teleological framework and the Rwandans provided the supporting data to describe the progress of Rwanda to the height of its power at the end of the nineteenth century. [T]hese mutually supportive historians created a mythic history to buttress a colonial order .... The joint product was shaped in Rwanda and packaged in Europe, and then delivered back into the school-rooms of Rwanda by European or European-educated teachers. In addition, the results of the collaborative enterprise were accepted by intellectuals in the circles around the court, even those without European-style schooling – and integrated into their

oral histories. It was not surprising that Tutsi were pleased with this version of history. But even the majority of Hutu swallowed this distorted account of the past, so great was their respect for European-style education. (des Forges 1995: 45)

This is not to claim that there was no historical consciousness in Rwanda prior to the colonial period, but to recognise that the nature of historical narratives was transformed. In his study of the alleged Iraqi origins of the Iraqw (Tanzania), Ole Bjørn Rekdal (1998) makes relevant comments regarding the relationship between oral history and writing. The earliest Iraqw oral traditions do not mention an Asian provenance. Despite this, Rekdal's informants consistently referred to an exodus from Asia to East Africa. Rekdal concluded that this narrative was a new phenomenon. So where had it come from? For Rekdal, the recent widespread acceptance of the narrative strongly suggested a written source, and he identified two written works, both of which contained the Iraqi provenance of the Iraqw (1998: 19; Ramadhani 1955; Kamera 1978). Furthermore, the influence of Kamera's text was 'obviously enhanced by the fact that this was a real book, printed, published, and made readily available ... Moreover it was written by a scholar with a Ph.D. from abroad' (Rekdal 1998: 20). Such a 'concrete' text had important consequences for how history was being *re-oralised*. The introduction of written history, and reference to it, became a powerful means for attributing authority and authenticity.

Rekdal's findings suggest that written 'history' is perceived as possessing inherent authority, re-utilised by actors as they (re)construct oral narratives. In this way, 'orality and literacy, far from being mutually contradictory poles, can interact and support each other' (Finnegan 1988: 110). The introduction of written history changes the nature of oral narratives either explicitly (as particular written texts are referred to as 'authoritative'), or implicitly, as actors strive to emulate in their oral narratives a perception of 'objective', stabilised history analogous to that found in written accounts.

Stable, written histories were required by the Belgian authorities (and Roman Catholic Church) if their distorted image of Rwanda as a 'healthy hierarchy of races' (Chrétien 1985: 142) was to be internalised, because 'the development of literacy and the circulation of ideas through print [provides a] capacity to imagine identity in terms of a community larger than that of the immediate circle of fellows' (Fardon 1987: 177; see B. Anderson 1983: 66–79). Such a project also suited the ruling '*élite* Tutsi' both as a means to legitimate their position and find 'new sources of solidarity and unity' to counteract the accentuated stratification caused by colonial rule (Linden 1977: 4).

It is the *oeuvres* of the three main 'historians' of the colonial period (Albert Pagès, Louis de Lacger and Alexis Kagame) that mark the introduction of the appeal to 'history' as a central component of Rwandan political discourse. It is the continuous acceptance, reiteration, reinterpretation *and* refutation of these works that characterised the post-independence appeal to history. As Sibomana observes: 'In the wake of [Alexis] Kagame, all historians, whatever their ethnic origin or their political opinions, dressed up Rwanda's history and turned it into a tool for political propaganda' (1999: 80). The relationship between political 'legitimacy' and a desire to construct *a history* was introduced by a coloniser and 'internalised' by the colonised (see Comaroff & Comaroff 1992: 34; 43). As Jan Vansina observes:

> [A]ll sides in today's Central African crisis reinvent history. They use portions of the existing historiography written by respected authors, the most influential being Alexis Kagame or Louis de Lacger, to derive novel interpretations of supposedly well-established facts ... the politically active public relies on the accessible conclusions of a professional historian among their number – such as Alexis Kagame (a Tutsi in Rwanda), Ferdinand Nahimana (a Hutu extremist in Rwanda), and Emile Mworoha (a Tutsi in Burundi). (1998: 39)

The Belgians introduced a belief that a 'true', single history was attainable, and the Rwandese political class have continued to evoke a past that they believe is 'fair and impartial' (Malkki 1995: 73). The problem remains that although Rwanda may indeed have *one past*, there are *multiple histories*.

APPEALING TO 'HISTORY'

> Historical narratives are not portraits, mirror images or reports of what actually happened, but reconstructed interpretations. (Munz 1977: 217–18)

An assumption entrenched in the Western historical genre is that it is an 'objective' exercise – the historian is a neutral conduit revealing the *past* 'as it actually happened'. Consequently, there can be only one *true* history to be retold and, thus, beyond dispute. If one accepts such a belief, how does one react when confronted with multiple historical narratives? Does one choose one narrative over another, for after all only one can reveal 'what actually happened'? In doing this we would fail to investigate the relationship *between* Rwandan narratives and what they reveal about *current* perceptions of conflict in Rwanda.

At another level, if one assumes that a single, 'true' history is attainable, one misunderstands the nature and capacities of historiography. In writing a historical narrative, even the most disinterested historian, with no ulterior motive to distort, does not produce a simple transparent 'window on the past'. Her/his narrative is the result of *interpretation* and this differs among historians.

So how do we detect intentional distortion or negation of real events? Paradoxically, in order to steel history against manipulation, we must first surrender the claim that it is merely a transparent, neutral conduit.[1] The better we understand the nature and capacities of 'historians' history' the better placed we are to detect 'fictive history' (see Apter 1997: 20). For it is on this misplaced belief in the 'objective', absolute quality of history that those who would intentionally distort the past rely (Holocaust deniers, for example). We must recognise that writing history is an act of interpretation, but one constrained by *the chronicle of events* (see White 1973). Interpretations inevitably differ, but they must be consistent with the *chronicle of events* if they are to be accorded the quality of 'history'.[2] In other words: 'Scholars often arrive at different historical interpretations, but those who purposely distort the historical record and disregard vast amounts of historical documentation know exactly the game they play' (Totten & Parsons 1997: xxi). Historiography is more resilient to such abuses if we accept that is a product of interpretation (within limits set by the *chronicle of events*).

What is the *chronicle of events*? Christopher Browning wished to write a narrative of the mass murder of Jews by Reserve Police Battalion 101 at Jozefów (Poland) on 13 July 1942. Browning only had access to transcripts of 125 perpetrator interviews (there were no survivors and no contemporary documents regarding that specific event). Browning observes that each man played a different role on that day – saw and did different things. Each subsequently repressed or forgot certain aspects of the experience or reshaped his memory of it in a different way (Browning 1992b: 29). Despite this multiplicity of perspectives, there is sufficient corroboratory testimony to produce an 'event' beyond contention – that Reserve Police Battalion 101 arrived at Jozefów on the morning of 13 July 1942 and shot many hundreds of Jews. Despite the partiality and contradictions of the interviews, the corroboratory elements still push the balance of probabilities far beyond any reasonable doubt; there is no debate over the *existence or nature* of the event. We have, therefore, a time-and-place specific event (made up of a series of smaller events) of which we are certain and which can be placed in the *chronicle of events*. This entry in the *chronicle* 'is separable from the causal or other interpretative accounts that might elaborate it' (Lang 1992: 307). The sum of the interviews can be reduced to a single, basic statement, an entry in the *chronicle of events* ('On the 13 July 1942 ...').

So does the *chronicle of events* correspond to 'history'? No, because a discrete entry in the *chronicle* is different from the 'real-time' narrative of that day that Browning wished to construct. Browning was not concerned only with the *whether* (the existence of the event) but the *how*. If he was to communicate the horrors of that day in a *meaningful* way, a 'real-time' narrative was required (replicating the way in which the events actually unfolded). Without a synthesising narrative we would be left with only a set of discrete, atomised accounts in which the horror remains hidden rather than revealed. Synthesised, meaningful narrative is what we recognise as 'history', not the simple *chronicle of events*. The *chronicle* is a 'point zero' to which second-order elaboration ('history') must remain true.

So, why and how does narrativisation make an event(s) 'meaningful'? Above all, that is how it happened. Oral material available to a historian is often narrativised already ('I saw this, then I did that' or 'This happened, then that happened') (see White 1973: 6). This sense of *processual time* provides 'a unifying and organising principle, a means of imposing order' (Hirsch 1995: 19). This is how actors recount experience and must, if it is to be meaningful, be replicated in the historian's synthesising narrative. This replication ('reality effect') must demonstrate process, diachronic (unfolding) interconnectedness at whatever level of abstraction (hour, day, year, decade, century) along a 'causal-temporal-logical line' (see Errington 1979: 239). To make the past accessible, narratives must replicate how actors experience the world as *procession*.

To achieve this 'reality effect', the historian synthesises/integrates fragmented personal narratives in order to demonstrate how they interconnect in and over time (see Comaroff & Comaroff 1992: 16).

To do this, interpretation is unavoidable *for the individual narratives themselves do not tell us how they are interconnected* (see S. Friedlander 1992: 6).

Eye-witnesses to an event do not experience it in its entirety (see Jay 1992: 104).[3] As the 'Rashomon Effect' demonstrates, no single eyewitness experiences the whole of an event or series of events, only a particular perspective (see Scott 1985: xviii; Mazur 1998). For the historian to reconstruct a meaningful narrative of an event, or series of events, she/he must take a wider view than that accessible to any single eyewitness or participant (Passmore 1974: 148). Historical narratives assume a 'meanwhile': 'this eyewitness experienced this, meanwhile *at the same moment*, another experienced that' (see Errington 1979: 239).

The historian's narrative artificially integrates these multiple 'fields of vision'. A historical narrative is more than any one eyewitness could have experienced. Both synchronically (at a moment in time) and diachronically (over time) the historian has access to a wider field of vision than the eyewitness. This wider field of view determines *how* the historian integrates multiple fields of vision. By occupying an artificial, all-seeing position that no single eyewitness could have occupied (acting as an 'omniscient' observer) the historian is able to 'detect' structures and trends that were hidden from those who were 'actually there'. Thus, 'events seem more logical in hindsight than when the observer is caught in the middle of the confusion' (Hirsch 1995: 19). The *post facto* detection of 'structures and trends' is possible because the historian can take a wider view than those 'actually there' and because (unlike eyewitnesses) the historian *knows how the narrative ends*.

In synthesising extant narratives, the historian has already committed an act of interpretation. She/he has already generated a surplus of all that could *possibly* be said about an event.

No historian can write a full account that would do justice to all that could possibly be said about an event or series of events, but must choose to ask a particular *question* regarding an event or series of events (see Eaglestone 2001: 28; Hirsch 1995: 18). In the context of the Holocaust, historians may choose to focus on the victims as a whole (Hilberg 1985[1961]); a set of victims (Gross 2001); a single victim (Baker 1980); a group of perpetrators (Browning 1992a; Lifton 1986); a single perpetrator (Arendt 1963; Breitman 1991). All draw on the same *chronicle of events*, but ask different questions of it:

It is the concerns and unanswered questions of historians that from the beginning will cause them to screen out some testimony as irrelevant, ponder and weigh other testimony for its importance, and immediately seize upon yet other testimony as obviously crucial. These questions will set the parameters within which any ... narrative can be constructed. (Browning 1992b: 31)

Given the determining influence of the question asked, historians will produce different narrative interpretations of the same, specific event. Regarding his narrative of events at Jozefów on 13 July 1942, Browning states:

Even if different historians did agree on a long list of basic facts or particular events [the *chronicle of events*] which occurred that day in Jozefów, they would produce neither the same narrative nor the same interpretation ... If other kinds of questions had been asked, other aspects of the testimony would have seemed more important and been selected instead; a different story would have been told ... the *questions* being posed shape the plot and narrative together. (1992b: 30–1; emphasis added)

Two qualitatively different narratives of the same event or event-sequence are not necessarily in conflict. Rather, *different questions* are asked of the same *chronicle of events* and generate different interpretations. Other residual possibilities, which would remain true to the *chronicle*, could be written.

Such selectivity is not suspect, but necessary if a meaningful, *accessible* narrative is to be written. Every form of inquiry is selective and determined by *a priori* 'concerns and unanswered questions'. In focusing on a specific question she or he wishes to answer, the historian strips away what (in her or his opinion) is 'unnecessary detail' (see Stanford 1994: 120; Passmore 1974: 153; Errington 1979: 239). An historical narrative, therefore, is 'a selective account of the actual sequence of events, but it is no random selection' (Hastrup 1992: 9). Historians select only what (in their opinion) is relevant to the questions they seek to answer.

Even if historians ask essentially the same question of an event or series of events, there is no guarantee that this will generate identical narratives. Each historian interprets the *chronicle of events* by means of underlying concepts or 'extra-historical' ideas and categorisations not found in the *chronicle* itself. These ideas/categorisations vary from historian to historian. Even if 'Historians seek to be detached, impassionate, impartial, no historian starts out with his mind a blank, to be gradually filled in by the evidence' (A. J. P. Taylor 1956, cited in Passmore 1974: 146).

In order to reveal what they consider to be underlying structures and trends (beyond eyewitness testimony) historians use *figurations* that are not necessarily present in the *chronicle of events*, because discrete testimony 'cannot order the past into those convenient distinctions that we wish to draw in retrospect' (Bartov 1998: 811; see Rosenberg 1987: 149). Figurations include archetypes, generalisations, paradigms and analogies, all of which are designed to categorise people and events as 'one of a type' in order that their interconnectedness may be more clearly demonstrated. For example, a complex series of events is categorised by the (polyvalent) term 'revolution'. It is only 'by gathering into meaningful clusters the apparently separate and unrelated facts of historical happenings [as found in the *chronicle of events*] that we are able to form coherent concepts of what has happened in the past' (Rosenberg 1987: 148). These figurations must be 'conceptually and perceptually cut out of the flux of experience' (Clifford 1988: 38). Such figurations (or 'typifications' [see Filmer 1972: 213]) are necessary if the historian is to enable the reader to think about newly encountered persons or event(s) *in terms that are familiar*.

Such second-order categorisations are the interpretative choice of the historian, and are not, necessarily, found in the experience of those who 'were there'. In choosing to categorise an event or person in a particular way (from a surplus of possibilities) the historian consciously rejects other available categorisations (see Laclau & Mouffe 1985: 108). An event or series of events is categorised as 'one of a type' according to value-laden terms not, necessarily, used at the time or by all 'eyewitnesses' ('The American *War of Independence*' vs. 'The American *Revolution*'). Historians differ not only in how they categorise the same event or series of events, but also in what *kinds* of categorisation they consider to have utility. There is also a danger that interpretative categorisation may slide into projection (*Seigneurs Tutsi* and *Serviteurs Hutu* [see Chrétien 1985: 130]). But categorisation is essential. If the historian is to demonstrate how interconnected events unfolded, the reader must be able to 'connect' with people and events in a familiar, meaningful and accessible way through categories with which they are pre-acquainted. Such categorisation is not, however, predetermined by the *chronicle*:

Historic events possess only the kind of meaning which historians assign to them. Since there is no objective meaning inherent in any historic event that awaits discovery, meaning is not given but is created. The meaning of any particular event is not a function of its objective properties but hinges upon the choices of categories selected by a given subject [the historian] for its interpretation. (Wurzburger 1980: 15; quoted in Rosenberg 1987: 149)

This implies that different interpretative narratives – using different categorisations – will emerge.

Another reason why interpretative narratives that ask the same question will not necessarily be identical is that historians construct narratives for different (imagined) audiences and are written on 'different scales' (see Eaglestone 2001: 38; Ricouer 1976: 31). School history books are written differently from those intended for an adult audience (see Passmore 1974: 158), and while some history is written purely for pleasure (see Carpenter 1995: 1) other narratives are intended to be instructive. History is never history *per se*, but 'history-for' (Lévi-Strauss 1966: 260).

Even where there is no intention to distort the past for ulterior motives, historiography generates different interpretations (see A. Cohen 1985: 101). Historical narratives, therefore, are not 'realist transparencies' even if they may claim (or are assumed) to be (see Comaroff & Comaroff 1992: 13). Interpretation is necessary. If one just wants unmediated 'facts' (as they have survived) then all you will have is a multifarious set of narratives that indicate an entry in the *chronicle*. But to understand the interconnectedness of events, then synthesised narratives and multiple interpretation(s) are inevitable. Ultimately, there can be no single correct narrative of the past but only a 'multiplicity of interpretations' (Bond & Gilliam 1994: 2).

And yet, any reliable interpretation is constrained by *exterior* limits. Unlike fiction, historical narratives are made up of events *outside* the imagination of the writer (see White 1973: 2 n. 5). The *chronicle of events*, therefore, establishes the parameters within which any interpretation *must* fall (Stanford 1994: 129). In the case of Browning's narrative, any denial of the events of 13 July 1942 at Jozefów would immediately be confronted not with the 125 interviews *per se*, but with the corroboratory elements contained in those interviews that push the balance of probabilities far beyond any reasonable doubt (entry of those events in the *chronicle*). Narrative interpretations, to be credible, must always operate within *exterior* limits of this kind (P. Anderson 1992: 64), but a 'consensus at the level of *chronicle* leaves the way open to divergence at the levels beyond it' (Lang 1992: 307). There is an important distinction between interpretations that deny the very existence of events and those that draw different conclusions from events whose existence is incontestable (Browning 1992b: 32).

There is a further level of interpretation beyond that of the historian: the consumer. There is always a 'gulf of uncertainty' (Parkin 1984: 355) between the historian's intended meaning and the interpretation(s) of the consumer. Actors rarely approach history with an 'open mind', but often as a way of corroborating existing assumptions and beliefs, as a depersonalised form of 'opinion leadership' (see Klapper 1960; Carpenter 1995: 7–8) to which people turn to confirm views they *already* hold. Ultimately, 'history teaches only the lessons that people choose to learn' (Wurzburger 1980: 15). Consumers may selectively infer from historical narratives that which reinforces beliefs that exist outside historiography (see Neustadt & May 1986).

HOW THE PRESENT 'CREATES' THE PAST

The discussion here has a precursor in Liisa Malkki's (1995) study of historical narratives conveyed by Burundian Hutu refugees in Tanzania in the mid-1980s. For Malkki, these narratives were driven by an urgent preoccupation with rendering a 'history' that will explain a single cataclysmic event, the massacre of Hutu in Burundi in 1972 (1995: 53). In this sense historical narratives appear propelled by the question 'how-did-the-past-create-the-present?' (Chapman et al. 1989: 5). And yet, the content of narratives is determined by 'concerns and unanswered questions' asked in the *present*. We should, therefore, ask 'how-did-the-present-create-the-past?' (ibid.).

The content of historical narratives is determined by the *present* social and political needs of the historian and her/his imagined audience (see S. Friedlander 1992: 1; Santer 1992: 143). Thus, 'images of the past commonly legitimate a present social order' (Connerton 1989: 3). In order to account for the *present* – to justify, understand or criticise it – *particular questions* are asked of the past. In a sense, 'all history is contemporary history: our contemporary interests determine what we select for consideration from the past' (Passmore 1974: 159). Conversely, any conscious attempt to talk only 'in the present' will inevitably refer to the *past* (see Haidu 1992: 279) because 'Past, present, and future are tied into one another in the human imagination far too tightly for it to be worth our while arguing about the relative importance of one or the other' (Chapman et al. 1989: 6).

Maurice Halbwachs argued that 'even at the moment of reproducing the past our imagination remains under the influence of the present social milieu' (quoted in Coser 1992: 49). The questions by which we interpret the past are determined by what our present perception considers important. When confronted with the past, with the 'continuous mass of mere happenings' (Hastrup 1992: 8) we 'notice only those things that are important for our immediate purposes. The rest we ignore' (Berger 1984 [1963]: 71). As 'the present' is ephemeral, the questions we ask of the past constantly change.

There is a also the practice of 'periodisation' of the past ('Pre-colonial', 'Colonial', 'Post-independence', 'Pre-genocide', 'Post-genocide'). In order to demarcate 'a period', 'turning points' must be identified (Berger 1984 [1963]: 69). Such 'turning points' are only detectable, however, because of the hindsight of the present – that we know the final outcome. We detect 'turning points' that may not have been apparent at the time or, if they were, held different significance(s) from what they now hold (see Fardon 1987: 177). With the benefit of present hindsight, everything that came before a 'turning point' is now interpreted as a period of 'preparation', one with *inevitable* consequences. This determinacy was, of course, hidden from those who 'were there'. We may, therefore, isolate a series of 'turning points' not because they were significant at the time, but that they appear to answer the pressing questions we ask in the present. Past events may then come to appear 'more predictable and controllable than they actually are, which leads historians and non-historians alike, to perceive some kind of order in the past, the present and the future' (Hirsch 1995: 19).

This sense of control and prediction means that historical narratives always involve moralisation regarding the future (White 1987: 21–5). Nancy Struever (1970) argues that in fourteenth-century Florence, history was written with a moral purpose: to map out the course of action the city should take in the future (see Errington 1979: 238). The events of the *past* were mapped out in causal chains that showed the consequences of having a particular kind of city-state, ruler, policy and so on. Such narratives implicitly clarify what has (and has not) 'worked' and thus what *will* work in the future. Historical narratives can take the form of 'an argument with respect to the evaluation of present conditions and the possibility and desir-ability of changing them' (Fardon 1987: 178; see Carpenter 1995: 1).

Constructed according to contemporary concerns, historical narratives enable actors to map not only the past, but also the future (see A. Cohen 1985: 99).

HISTORICAL NARRATIVES AS SHARED PRACTICE

Burundian narratives conveyed to Malkki were 'constructed in opposition to other versions of what was ostensibly the same world, or the same past' (1995: 55). Burundian refugees in Tanzania were continually engaged in constructing narratives that were 'oppositional' – their content determined by opposing narratives (1996: 380). Michel Pêcheux (1982) argues that statements (including historical narratives) never occur in isolation, but in (implicit or explicit) dialogue with alternative positions. Given this imperative of competitive dialogue, a degree of shared practice is required if opposing narratives are to compete, rather than 'talk past' each other. In this way, despite their substantive differences, the Rwandan historical narratives considered below, share not only the generic characteristics of any historical narrative (see above), but also an implicit consensus on what is *worthy* of contestation in Rwanda's past.

In his analysis of politics in a South Indian temple, Arjun Appadurai argues that different interpretations of the past are inevitable (1981: 201). Competing narratives must, however, operate within a shared framework – they must, to a degree, 'share a past' (ibid. 216). Appadurai proposes that a shared framework must exist to allow *debate* over the past to take place. While narratives vary substantively, their construction operates within a minimal set of formal constraints (ibid. 203). Two of Appadurai's constraints are of particular importance. First, 'depth': there must be consensus on the relative value of different time-depths in the mutual evaluation of the *past*. As will become clear, Rwandan narratives agree on periodisation, determined by 'turning points' or 'defining moments' (see Malkki 1995: 54; J. Comaroff 1985: 17ff). Narratives share a 'time-depth framework', clustering around particular events and periods. Appadurai also suggests that to ensure credibility competing narratives must be interdependent. Again, Rwandan narratives refer to competing narratives either explicitly (introducing and rejecting alternative interpretations) or implicitly (one interpretation is emphasised in the full knowledge that it implicitly rejects an alternative). Discerning implicit interdependence depends, of course, on a consumer's knowledge of possible alternatives (see Billig 1987: 91).

If competing narratives are to fulfil their function – to modify or dismiss competing narratives – they must share not only the belief that history is 'absolute' rather than interpretative, but must also be constructed around 'a shared constellation of meaningful objects [persons and events]' (Bond & Gilliam 1994: 17). Fundamental agreement and implicit co-operation is a prerequisite for any substantive disagreement (see Chilton 1997: 184). Competing narratives may not share substance, but they must agree on what is considered worthy of contest.

There is a further shared practice: isolating a meta-narrative of Rwandan history, a proposition that overarches the narrative, proceeding from the perception of 'some kind of order in the past, the present and the future' (Hirsch 1995: 19; see Lyotard 1997). This competition over a meta-narrative is a consequence of the basic question that Rwandese ask of the past: 'How did we get to a situation in which at least 800,000 people were brutally murdered and was this the consequence of an inveterate continuity?' This question is asked in the present, its answer(s) lies in the past and the resulting meta-narratives point to possible futures.

At many points Rwandan historical narratives refer to the same entry in the *chronicle*, but how they interpret it (demonstrate how it interconnects with other entries in the *chronicle*) and how they categorise it, differ (see Appadurai 1981: 217). Rwandese also choose to emphasise certain entries in the *chronicle* and ignore others. It is not so much a question of fabricated material, but that certain events are intentionally omitted, downplayed or given different comparative weight, what Lemarchand (1996: 19) calls 'cognitive dissonance'.[4]

HOW TO REPRESENT HISTORICAL NARRATIVES?

The narratives used below were drawn from interviews conducted in 1997–99 in Rwanda (among government officials, pro-government journalists and civil society leaders; henceforth 'Rwanda') and in Europe (among exiled Rwandan academics, former government officials, and civil society leaders; henceforth 'Europe').

As mentioned above, this chapter has a precedent in the work of Malkki (1995). Both Malkki and myself encountered narratives that were told (and retold) in such a similar manner that they were almost formulaic. Individual narratives coalesced into a 'collective narrative' (Malkki 1995: 56). This raises the methodological issue of how this powerful sense of 'repetition and thematic unity' (ibid.) can be conveyed.

There are a number of options. One could adopt the 'conventional' (and *unquestioned* style) by which an author simply recounts 'the history of Rwanda'. Such a strategy assumes there is one *history* of Rwanda (rather than one *past*) and fails to investigate the relationship *between* narratives. One could choose short, 'exemplary quotations' from interviews in order to illustrate 'general narrative themes'. Fragmented quotations do not, however, correspond to how historical narratives are experienced by the listener/reader, the fact that their impact relies on replicating the manner in which actors experience the world (as procession).

Malkki encountered the same challenge regarding a representational strategy that would capture the repetitive character of oral historical narratives. Her solution was to use 'panels': narrative passages set apart from the rest of the text. These panels contained 'chapters' of an artificial, standardised narrative whose parameters were determined thematically or by periodisation/turning points as employed by actors. Panels are not simply quotations, but composites of several persons' accounts on the same theme or period in which the clauses and sentences of the original interview are left intact.

There are numerous drawbacks to this strategy. Panels present material as if there was total standardisation among those interviewed and privilege certain statements over others. Any sense of the particular context in which interviews took place or the identity of the informant is lost.

Editing narratives may be considered suspect. And yet, as we saw above, the selective use of narratives *already constituted* is intrinsic to any historical narrative. The narratives conveyed to me were already selective and contained edited versions of earlier narratives. There is no 'pure', pristine, primary narrative that demands preservation and unflinching adherence. I am merely continuing an existing process of selection and reconstruction. Furthermore, the 'history' chapters of realist books on Rwanda are far more brutal in their editing. They take multiple narratives from individuals, integrate them and re-present them in a sanitised form. Such a representational strategy is not considered suspect, but perfectly legitimate. While I may edit and integrate the narratives in an artificial way, I at least try to retain a sense of their original character even if the panels are my own construction.

THE NARRATIVES

The following narratives are arranged under the headings of 'Europe' and 'Rwanda'. Such unity is not merely a reflection of their geographic provenance. Placing narrative extracts together reflects their substantive consistency. I have resisted the temptation to arrange them under the headings of 'Hutu' and 'Tutsi'. All those interviewed hold an ascribed ethno-racial identity according to their pre-1997 ID card. And yet, Hutu in the present Rwandan government and Hutu exiles in Europe interpret certain aspects of the Rwandan past differently. Likewise, these narratives are only attributable to a certain élite group and do not cover all potential 'ethnic' narratives. For example, 'Hutu' resident in Europe, accused of participation in the genocide – and who were not prepared to be interviewed – would, one assumes, express very different narratives from those 'Hutu' whose opinions are expressed here. In other words, there is no *empirical* correspondence between ethno-racial identity (irrespective of the degree of self-ascription) and the content of historical narratives.

Although it would be easy to annotate the narratives with references to 'professional history' – in order to confirm or deny the validity of what is being asserted – our concern here is the function of the narratives. In light of this, endnotes should be considered only as 'points of information' and not as value judgements. As regards the central role of the 'consumer' of historical narratives (see above), the 'reflections' that appear after each set of panels should not be read as definitive or binding. Depending on the reader's prior knowledge of Rwanda, the narratives below may suggest (multiple) alternative readings. Whatever I may write, it is the reader who 'becomes the final arbiter measuring history against history and interpretation against interpretation' (Bond & Gilliam 1994: 11).

FIRST CLUSTER: PRE-COLONIAL RWANDA

Panel One: Ethnicity in pre-colonial Rwanda

'Europe' (drawing on five interviews)

The Belgians did not create ethnicity. At the end of the nineteenth century, King Rwabugiri [1860–95] launched a campaign against a neighbouring state with an army of Hutu, Tutsi and Twa soldiers. The Hutu had to work for the Tutsi. You cannot, therefore, deny that ethnicity – Hutu and Tutsi – existed before the colonists arrived. Westerners did not invent Hutu, Tutsi and Twa – these terms have their own meaning in our language. They are not equivalents.

'Rwanda' (drawing on eight interviews)

Some say 1994 was the logical consequence, the summit, of what had been going on for centuries. But, you wouldn't find evidence of inter-ethnic violence before the twentieth century or even before 1959. The Government's position is that 1994 does not, in fact, have much to do with age-old hatred between Hutu and Tutsi. In a way differences did exist before colonisation, but nowhere in our history was there a civil war between Hutu and Tutsi. This was a nation – the three groups were social economic categories and were not ethnic groups. This did not prevent social mobility up and down.[5] A Hutu could become a Tutsi and then join the royal group – a clan. Before the colonialists arrived the country was peaceful. Hutu and Tutsi were fighting together and conquering new territories in Rwanda. This was total integration – these titles had no ethnic value at all.

Regarding the relevant 'time-depths' with which Rwandese are concerned, it is significant that none of my respondents made any reference to what Malkki (1995: 59) calls the 'myths of foundation and precedence': the 'Hamitic Hypothesis'. It would be an under-statement to state that the existence of 'ethnicity' in pre-colonial Rwanda has become a matter of intense debate since 1994 (see Pottier 1995; C. Newbury 1998: 9–10). This question marked the start of all the historical narratives of Rwandese interviewed. What is striking about the above, is that the two narratives are not diametrically opposed, that 'ethnic groups' did or did not exist. Rather the debate is more nuanced, concerning the relationship between – *rather than the existence of* – the two (three) categories and whether they should be considered as 'ethnic' or 'socio-economic'. This echoes the question above regarding figuration/categorisation as central to inter-pretation of the past.

Both panels contain a shared desire to clarify a duality perceived to be central to the Rwandan conflict (and by which the 1994 genocide is understood) 'the Hutu vs the Tutsi'. As will become apparent in the following panels, the real debate concerns the *degree* to which colonisation accentuated and distorted existing social distinction. In this sense, the statements above should be read as laying foundations for an evaluation of colonial influence.

For those in Europe, colonialism built upon existing 'ethnic' division, while for those in Rwanda, colonialism distorted an egalitarian 'economic' division of labour, one in which '<u>the</u> Tutsi' were not oppressors. In this sense, the narratives are 'preparation' for claims and counter-claims that Tutsi were co-responsible for 'ethnically based' oppression in the colonial period. In other words, if colonialism *wholly* distorted social relations by introducing fixed ethnic distinction, '*the* Tutsi' cannot be held responsible for the oppression of '*the* Hutu' during colonial rule.

Panel Two: Ethnic conflict in pre-colonial Rwanda

Bearing in mind the disadvantage of using standardising panels, it is necessary to present two different, but interrelated 'Europe' opinions regarding pre-colonial conflict:

'Europe' #1 (drawing on three interviews)

Tutsi extremists claim that before the arrival of the Europeans, traditional society was an 'ideal society', a paradise without any conflict. This is not true. There were conflicts at the level of power, but they were not ethnic, but between strong and weak clans. For example, the *coup d'état* of Rucunshu [1896] had taken place before the arrival of the whites.[6] These massacres were not committed by Tutsi against Hutu, but between Tutsi clans. One could even talk of genocide. In fact, the Tutsi Banyiginya clan was eliminated. There was, therefore, a feudal system in which two Tutsi clans, each with their own Hutu supporters, fought each other. Ethnic groups, therefore, had existed for a long time and there were Hutu who supported one Tutsi clan and other Hutu who supported the other Tutsi clan. Before colonisation, therefore, there were conflicts and struggles for power, but these were not ethnic conflicts. This was not a struggle between Hutu and Tutsi. Rather, this was a feudal society where the majority of the population, Hutu and 'les petits Tutsi', were peasants, living in a situation resembling Europe in the fifteenth century.

'Europe' #2 (drawing on four interviews)

From the seventeenth to the twentieth century Hutu suffered. The history of Rwanda in the sixteenth and seventeenth centuries was characterised by an inter-ethnic conflict as Tutsi sought to capture power from the Hutu kings. History reports that the Hutu kingdoms were conquered. So, there was an ethnic conflict before the Belgians arrived. By the end of the nineteenth century, King Rwabugiri was still waging a war of conquest – to capture territories in the north and the north-west of Rwanda. When the Germans and then the Belgians arrived,[7] Rwanda was not yet united under a single monarch. In the north and the west there were still autonomous, Hutu entities. Once they had been conquered, was there any resistance? We don't know. But even if the rivalry between ethnic groups was not expressed it certainly existed. The Hutu suffered so much under the Tutsi monarchy.

'Rwanda' (drawing on eight interviews)

There was no ethnic conflict before colonisation, although Hutu, Tutsi and Twa existed. Like all the countries of the world, Rwanda was not a paradise. There was a complicated system. There was a system of three chiefs that maintained a balance, an equilibrium. Not all Tutsi were masters. In fact, the ruling class was harsher on ordinary Tutsis or on those who did not agree with them. These Tutsi were dispossessed of their cattle and land. The Hutu majority were in servant positions, but there were also Hutu in the ruling class. Hutu were the head of some regions, and in the army, although they were not the majority. At the same time Hutu and Tutsi were united when they wanted to attack. Then they didn't talk about Hutu and Tutsi; instead everybody was behind the king. A person's position depended on the social class of an individual, not ethnicity. More cattle meant more power, and Tutsi had more, Hutu had less.

In the 'Europe#1' panel, the 'well-integrated, peaceful nation' as found in the previous 'Rwanda' panel ('Panel One: Ethnicity in pre-colonial Rwanda') is refuted. And yet, 'Europe#1' does not suggest that there was an 'inter-ethnic' conflict between 'Hutu' and 'Tutsi', but an '*intra*-ethnic' conflict among a *minority* of 'Tutsi'.[8] Although implicit in this is that 'ethnic groups' existed, and were not solely 'created' by the colonial authorities, the emphasis is placed on conflicts among a 'Tutsi élite' and not '<u>the</u> Hutu vs <u>the</u> Tutsi'.

In contrast, the 'Europe#2' panel does talk of '*inter*-ethnic' conflict in terms of the conquest of 'autonomous Hutu entities' by the 'Tutsi king', the *mwami* of the central kingdom. This assertion negates the previous 'Rwanda' panel, which claimed that the territory that constitutes *contemporary* Rwanda was a 'well-integrated nation' prior to colonisation. And yet, interpreting the conflict *between* kingdoms as an 'ethnic conflict' is substantively different from the assertion in the 'Rwanda' panel that *within* the central kingdom there was no 'ethnic conflict'. Phrases in the 'Rwanda' panel, such as 'Hutu and Tutsi were fighting together and conquering new territories' and 'Hutu and Tutsi were united when they wanted to attack' demonstrate an awareness of the conflict between kingdoms, but it is not interpreted 'ethnically'. These conflicts are interpreted in terms of 'conquest' and 'conflict between kingdoms', not as conflict between 'ethnic groups'. By not interpreting this conflict through an 'ethnic lens' the 'Rwanda' panel is able to claim that there was no 'inter-ethnic' conflict between 'the Hutu' and 'the Tutsi'. The panel concedes there was conflict, but it was between 'non-ethnic' kingdoms. In this way, the 'Europe#2' and the 'Rwanda' panels are concerned with the same events (entries in the *chronicle of events*), but the former interprets them through an 'ethnic lens', the latter through a 'national lens'.

While the 'Rwanda' panel seeks to maintain an image of an 'integrated, peaceful society' disturbed by colonialism, both 'Europe' panels emphasise conflict: the first '*intra*-ethnic' conflict, the second '*inter*-ethnic' conflict. All three positions should be understood as 'preparation' for a discussion of colonial influence on Rwanda. They prepare the way for a consideration of the fundamental question: 'did the Tutsi élite rule Rwanda oppressively prior to colonisation, or was this a consequence of colonial rule?'

SECOND CLUSTER: COLONIAL RWANDA

For Rwandese, it is the colonial period (c1922–61) around which most discussion of the *past* takes place. This 'cluster' is separated in to two sections. The first concerns the general influence of colonisation on Rwanda. The second concerns the *Pères Blancs*[9] ('White Fathers') who, for both Rwandese in Europe and Rwanda, are considered the 'true' colonisers.

Panel One: The colonial influence on ethnicity

'Europe' (drawing on ten interviews)

Colonisation crystallised, structured and heightened ethnic hatred – but it did not create ethnic distinction. The Belgians constructed distinction upon existing ethnic identities, exploited them, exacerbating social differences. It is one thing to say ethnicity didn't exist, but it is another to say the Belgians accentuated division to facilitate their administration. Tutsi were privileged in education and in access to administrative posts and Hutu were excluded from power. The colonisers and missionaries formalised what already existed. They said, 'those that are poor farmers are all Hutu, and those Tutsi who don't own cows will become Hutu'. Meanwhile, the Tutsi aristocratic class – the chiefs and the king – maintained their privileges. These were strengthened because forced labour was imposed on the peasants. Colonisation accentuated identities and reinforced conflict. During the colonial period there was 'indirect rule'. In this way, the king and the feudal system benefited. The Tutsi élite took what they could and profited, above all by closing access to power. Furthermore, it was the Belgians who helped the Tutsi élite to conquer the smaller Hutu kingdoms. In this way, the Tutsi élite benefited from the presence of the Germans and then the Belgians by increasing their power and centralising their kingdom. For 50 years, Rwandese accepted this power and collaborated with it. In governing Rwanda through an intermediary – the Tutsi élite – the Belgians favoured ethnic exclusion in Rwanda – an exclusion that became a political reflex.

'Rwanda' (drawing on eleven interviews)

Division came with colonialism. For the purposes of divide and rule the colonialists deformed history and decided who was Hutu and Tutsi. Between 1931 and 1935 there was a census. The Belgians handed out identity cards on which was written the 'tribe' of each Rwandese. Because the Belgians couldn't find objective criteria they just said, 'the one with more than ten cows is a Tutsi, and Hutu are those with less than ten cows', or 'You're short; therefore you're a Hutu. You're tall; therefore you're a Tutsi.' They even used people's features; the shape of your nose, whether your face was straight. The Belgians showed favouritism, reinforcing what they chose to call 'Tutsi'. They established a school in Butare only for children of Tutsi administrators. Colonialism stratified and polarised society. In reality, the majority were not 'Hutu' and 'Tutsi', just neighbours, who shared day-to-day life in peaceful co-existence. There were intermarriages; they helped each other build houses and so on. In reality, there was no hatred, no conflict between two groups. But the Belgians and missionaries came and divided people; saying, 'you are a Hutu'. Furthermore, Europeans could not accept that black people could create such a civilisation. Therefore, they said that Tutsi were Ethiopians. But, it was the Belgians were who ruling and who told the Tutsi to oppress. Therefore, it was the Belgians who were responsible for oppression. If the master came from outside, you can't talk of Tutsi oppressing others.

Both the 'Europe' and the 'Rwanda' panels agree on the 'core proposition' that Belgian colonisation distorted existing social distinction. There is consensus regarding not only the preservation of a 'Tutsi élite' as rulers, but that colonisation strengthened their position. This point, however, is made in two distinct ways. Although the 'Europe' panel distinguishes among 'the Tutsi' by referring to 'the Tutsi aristocratic class' and 'the Tutsi élite', they portray this élite class as 'willing accomplices' of colonial rule, consolidating their existing authority and extending it to the detriment of 'smaller Hutu kingdoms'. In contrast, the 'Rwanda' panel refers to the 'stupid' Hamitic myth, implying that the Tutsi élite were *unwilling* victims of absurd racial fantasies, thus denying any voluntary collusion with the Belgians.

In summary, both narratives agree that colonisation distorted pre-colonial social distinction. The sticking point, however, and significant when seeking to confirm or deny 'Tutsi co-responsibility' for later 'ethnic' conflict, concerns whether the 'Tutsi élite' *voluntarily* collaborated with the Belgian rulers. For, if this were the case, then the 'Tutsi élite' can be portrayed as having benefited from the policies of ethnic discrimination that would lead, ultimately, to the 1994 genocide. While on the surface blame and responsibility is directed at the Belgians the underlying question is 'who was the victim?' Were Tutsi unwilling victims of Belgian colonialism? Were 'Hutu' the victims of the 'Tutsi élite'? Or, were Rwandese victims of Belgian colonialism?

Panel Two: The 'White Fathers' (*Pères Blancs*)

'Europe' (drawing on eleven interviews)

In a way the impact of the *Pères Blancs* is more important than that of the Belgians. The RPF try to demonise the *Pères Blancs* and say that they created the ethnic divide in the country. That is not true. The RPF resent the *Pères Blancs*, because they worked for the masses, for the Hutu, the 'petits Tutsi' and Twa. It was the Catholic Church that evangelised and civilised the country, built schools, hospitals, trained the population and emancipated all people – without distinction. At least this is what they tried to do, but they made mistakes. They strengthened the Tutsi élite – insulating them in power and fuelling the ethnic conflict. The strategy of the *Pères Blancs* was to convert Tutsi chiefs in order to achieve a massive conversion of the population (in accordance with the instructions of their founder, Cardinal Lavigerie). Mgr Léon Classe [Vicar Apostolic from 1927] favoured maintaining the privileges of the aristocratic Tutsi, reinforcing their feeling of superiority over the Hutu. He said Tutsi were born to rule and govern, while the Hutu were to be their servants. The Hutu masses and Tutsis in lower clans remained in poverty and misery. Classe made arrangements with the Belgians to admit the children of Tutsi chiefs to education from which Hutu were excluded. In this way the Church created a Tutsi élite to the detriment of the Hutu people. So, what did the *Pères Blancs* not do for the Tutsi? They gave them education and presented them as a Hamitic regime. Classe also persuaded the Belgians to introduce the bogeyman of Communism and to present the Catholic Church as a shield against Communism.[10] After World War II, a new generation of missionaries arrived with a new language. Mgr André Perraudin [Apostolic Vicar of Kabgayi from 1956] spoke of social rights, justice and equality. The *Pères Blancs* tried to put Hutu in seminaries and reveal their situation to them. They were taught about the French Revolution, about humanity, fraternity and so on – a form of consciousness raising. On 11 February 1959 Perraudin said, 'you are equal brothers, love each other'.[11] Contrary to Classe, Perraudin preached the equality of races and a respect for social justice. After Classe left, the *Pères Blancs* followed a spirit of justice, love and reconciliation.

'Rwanda' (drawing on five interviews)

The *Pères Blancs* were a political and economic power. The King was chased out in the name of the Church because he would not be baptised.[12] Only the Tutsi élite were educated in preparation for leadership. At the *Groupe Scolaire* in Butare there were only Tutsi. By excluding the Hutu the *Pères Blancs* made the division very deep. Classe said that only the Tutsi should rule and therefore the Belgians made 95 per cent of chiefs Tutsi. Classe used the same language as the Nazis, calling Tutsi 'Supermen'. The *Pères Blancs* reinforced ignorance. Their strategy was first to confuse the king, who induced others to convert out of fear ('the king is afraid, so we should be'). But ethnicity was the Church's biggest lie and helped to elaborate this ideology. Mgr Classe chose the Tutsi, because they were leaders; Perraudin switched back to the Hutus, leading to the first genocide in 1959. Colonialists declared that the Hutu should be the oppressed class, but there were still a lot of poor Tutsi. From the death of Mgr Classe in 1945 the Catholic Church supported the Hutu to make up for its crimes of the past. They tried to do this by preaching hatred against the Tutsi. The word 'enemy' was used to talk about Tutsis in *Kinyamateka*[13] and by others. In Rwanda Mgr Perraudin is considered to be the author of the 1994 genocide.

Although the 'Europe' panel suggests the *Pères Blancs* had some positive effect on Rwanda, they, like the 'Rwanda' narrative, consider the missionaries as key agents in exacerbating ethnic division. In both narratives a single actor, Mgr Classe, personifies this process.[14] There is, however, a subtle difference in interpretation. Again, in the 'Europe' narrative, the 'Tutsi élite' are presented as having *voluntarily* benefited from colonial rule. In contrast, the 'Rwanda' narrative portrays the 'Tutsi élite' as *involuntary* 'victims' of the *Pères Blancs*: a *mwami* is presented as having been 'confused' by the *Pères Blancs* and another is ousted because he refuses baptism. Again, the real issue is whether the 'Tutsi élite' were 'victims' or 'collaborative beneficiaries' of the *Pères Blancs*. Consequently, were the 'Tutsi élite' innocent victims of the 1959 'genocide' or responsible for the 1959 'revolution'?

THIRD CLUSTER: THE 'REVOLUTION'/'GENOCIDE' OF 1959

'Europe' (drawing on ten interviews)

In 1959 the Hutu realised their legitimate aspirations for change and put an end to a long period of social injustice of which they had been victims before and during colonisation. Influenced by Western culture in the seminaries, Hutu saw that the Tutsi élite and the colonial administration were unjust. They published the Bahutu Manifesto that spoke of rights for Hutu and Tutsi. The people aspired to democracy and the end of social injustice. The

Hutu asked to share power but were pushed away. The king and his entourage wanted to maintain the *status quo* and resorted to repressive means, killing Hutu leaders. The 1959 revolution would have been peaceful had the traditional power not introduced violence into the inevitable process of change. In the 1950s, the whole of Africa was moving towards independence and the Tutsi élite were part of that movement. But the Belgians did not want to leave. So they introduced democracy and encouraged the revolution – 'you are like the Tutsi, but you need a revolution'. The Belgians made the revolution. So, the Belgians had a double language. First they were pro-hierarchy and then pro-democracy. For the regimes of the first and second Republics, 1959 was a revolution, but for the RPF it is genocide. But, they forget the other elements of that revolution. The Revolution took place in the context of independence and only those in power were targeted, and even they were not killed. For example, Kigeli V, the *mwami*, was well treated, and now lives in the US. Both Hutu and Tutsi were massacred. The attacks on Tutsi followed the killing of Hutu leaders. The events of 1959 were, incontestably, a revolution and one cannot compare 1959 with 1994, because the violence affected only Tutsi in power. Furthermore, the fighting stopped quickly, and the Tutsi who remained were no longer maltreated. This was a social revolution – a demand for democracy, social justice, equality and access to property. The RPF say we're a threatened minority, we were killed in 1959, 1960, 1973. This is excellent propaganda, but dangerous, because Hutu will not accept they did not liberate themselves in 1959. The RPF say, 'Hutu killed because the white men told them to, not knowing that they committed genocide'. It suggests that Hutu did not achieve the revolution, that Hutu are stupid, that they can only be killers.

'Rwanda' (drawing on nine interviews)

The first acts of genocide were committed in 1959 while Rwanda was still under Belgian rule. Belgian army helicopters were used to bomb villages, Belgian army trucks transported Tutsi to the border with Burundi. This was deliberate ethnic cleansing co-ordinated by the Belgian administration. The Belgians facilitated the revolution. It was the era of independence in Africa. The *mwami* started travelling to Germany and Belgium and he came back with new ideas and started fighting for independence and democracy. The Belgians denounced him and other Tutsi as communists. In a Christian country this was enough to qualify someone as a criminal who should die.[15] For the masses there was no more convincing a slogan than to denounce Tutsi as communists. The Belgians assassinated the King in Bujumbura on 29 July 1959.[16] The Belgians wanted to remain in Rwanda because they were losing Congo and in Burundi UPRONA [*Parti de l'Unité et du Progrès National*] were winning. They needed Rwanda to control Congo, so they mobilised Hutu against Tutsi and created Parmehutu. They thought, 'If we ride with the Hutu élite this will guarantee a place in Rwanda for Belgians'. This was an 'assisted revolution' by the Roman Catholic Church and the Belgians – and they killed influential Tutsi to clear the way.[17] It was not just against chiefs and the king and the government that came to power at independence was a government of the Belgians' own making. The 'Revolution' equalled killing people; Tutsis, their cows, burning their houses, chasing them away. Therefore, the Belgians created what happened in 1994 by teaching that whoever is a stumbling block, just eliminate them.

For both narratives, 1959 is a 'turning point', a demarcation between the past prior to and during colonisation and 'modern' Rwanda in which the 1994 genocide was to take place. It is a 'summing up' of all that occurred prior to independence, delineating the processes of colonisation; a 'setting of lines' for what would lead to the 1994 genocide. For the 'Europe' narrative, 1959 was an end to the dual oppression ('double colonialism') of the colonist and the 'Tutsi élite', a result of the 'consciousness raising' of '<u>the</u> Hutu' and the legitimate aspiration of social justice for all Rwandese.

What is striking is that the 'Rwanda' panel does not suggest that '<u>the</u> Hutu' were wholly responsible. Rather, as the 'Tutsi élite' had been before them, the emerging 'Hutu élite' are portrayed as dupes of colonial machination. Both narratives share two 'core propositions': that the events of 1959 were instigated by the Belgian administration and that they must be understood in the context of pan-African independence. Both narratives also agree that the Belgians demonised the 'Tutsi élite' because the latter demanded immediate independence. And yet, Rwandese in Europe are keen to argue that despite the 'assisted' nature of the 'revolution' its outcome was coterminous with genuine 'Hutu aspirations'.

The previous narratives merely prepare the ground for 1959. Although primary responsibility is placed on the Belgians, the real issue is whether the 'Tutsi élite' were legitimately removed from power according to 'democratic' principles (thus confirming the part they played in 'ethnic oppression') or whether they were violently removed as part of a Belgian plan to obstruct true democratisation; a plan in which a 'Hutu élite' played an active part.

In the 'Rwanda' narratives, 1959 marks incipient genocide and the indiscriminate targeting of all 'Tutsi'. In contrast, the 'Europe' narratives maintain that only a minority of those designated as 'Tutsi' were targeted, categorised according to 'democratic', rather than ethnic, reasons. This dichotomy is explicit in the use of two alternate categories: 'revolution' (in which a political group is targeted) and 'genocide' (targeting a whole group, irrespective of social position). Furthermore, the reasons given for violence differ. In the 'Europe' narratives, the violence was owing to the provocation of the 'Tutsi élite', while in the 'Rwanda' narratives, it is the Belgians who instigate violence. Despite this, the point is clear. In the 'Europe' narratives, 1959 was a peak of violence, justified in the context of 'social justice' and 'pan-African independence', a legitimate response to an 'oppressive regime' that 'collaborated' with the Belgians. In contrast, the 'Rwanda' narratives suggest 1959 marked the beginning of a consistent project of violence – a 'genocidal philosophy' – that was to culminate in 1994.

FOURTH CLUSTER: 1959–90

'Europe' (drawing on four interviews)

In 1959, those born to power with huge pastoral lands were targeted and suffered heavily. But ordinary Tutsi remained and even took part in the revolution. The ordinary Tutsi stayed while the aristocracy went into exile. When those outside saw that the others were not following, there was a rift among Tutsi. They denounced those who stayed as collaborators of Kayibanda. During the early years of independence there was a multiparty system. There were UNAR members of Parliament and until 1963 two UNAR ministers. But, this ended with the attacks of the *inyenzi*. When the *inyenzi* attacked, Hutu extremists wrongly reacted against Tutsi who stayed, believing there was an alliance with those Tutsi in exile. They used this to unify Hutu. But, after 1967, and until 1994, no one was killed because they were Tutsi – Tutsi were not persecuted. During the Second Republic [1973–94] Hutu shared power with the Tutsi, proportional to the number of Tutsi in Rwanda.[18] In a letter in 1964, President Kayibanda asked the Tutsi refugees to return to Rwanda. He warned the exiles that when they attack, the Tutsi inside are in trouble.[19] He invited them to come back as ordinary people, not as nobles, but to work as ordinary people. Kayibanda never took money and was convinced he had a mission to protect the weak people. But he was also weak and manipulated the constitution so he could remain in power. Before the 1994 genocide there were many mixed marriages, the ethnic question had completely disappeared. There was only the regional question, of north vs south. The conflict of north vs south was a major problem that was overstepped by the Hutu vs Tutsi conflict in 1991. In fact, the Abakiga [Hutu] from the north were more violent against the Tutsi than ordinary Hutu. The Abakiga had always been excluded from power, so they violently took power in 1973. In 1973 there was a problem between north vs south. Hutu in the army and politicians from Gisenyi and parts of Ruhengeri were claiming the regime wanted to marginalise and eliminate them. Following Habyarimana's military coup in 1973 about 50 Hutu politicians from the south disappeared.[20] So, when multi-partism was introduced [in March 1991], some Hutu took the opportunity to oppose Habyarimana's regime. After 1991 the problem was more and more ethnic rather than regional.

'Rwanda' (drawing on 13 interviews)

After independence genocide continued, in 1963, 1967, and the last one in 1994. Parmehutu took the teachings of the missionaries and inverted them, saying that Hutu suffered under Tutsi colonisers. It was taught in schools that Tutsi are bad people; don't let them come back. Tutsi were second-class citizens – no Tutsi was a *préfet* or a *bourgmestre*, no Tutsi held a job in the government or army, and they could be no more than 10 per cent in schools.[21] The top government civil servants and high-ranking military officers were not allowed to marry Tutsi (not a law, but told to people in groups). Rather than addressing the problems of the past, the post-independence governments exacerbated them. From 1962 the government took 'ethnic' differences seriously and preached an ethnic vision based on minor issues such as height, complexion and other aspects of physical appearance. They knew the only way they could stay in power was through these politics of exclusion – Tutsi were scapegoats. In 1959, 1960 and 1964 there were attacks by Tutsi exiles. This was an opportunity to kill all Tutsi who lived in Rwanda because they were Tutsi. The idea of exterminating the Tutsi was not a real project, but it was something considered possible. It was just like European anti-Semitism, not always a question of extermination, but the basis for extermination had existed for a long time. After 1973, if there were economic problems they would blame the Tutsi. Even in the mid-1980s the poor economy was blamed on Tutsi, because some Tutsi were strong in business. Habyarimana wanted to continue the values of the 'social revolution', but the only value of that revolution was that Tutsi were not citizens. After 1973, Tutsi were not much of an issue. Deprived of education and social benefits, but not considered a threat. Rather, Hutu were concerned with regionalism. There was internal division in Rwanda. Among the Hutu, there are the 'Banyanduga' from the south and the 'Bakiga' from the north. The northern Hutu consider the Hutu from the south to be just as bad as Tutsi. There was a single party, the MRND, but in the early 1990s (following the attack of the RPF in October 1990) there was pressure for multipartyism. When Habyarimana saw there was an external threat, he tried to unite Hutu against the RPF by attacking Tutsi. Before then, Tutsi were downtrodden, but not considered a threat. But Habyarimana looked for supremacy and made a 'common cause against an external enemy'. While 1959 was genocide it is was an ongoing operation, with further massacres in 1963 and 1973. What happened in 1994 came as no surprise – there has been a philosophy for 35 years, the 1994 genocide was planned since 1959.

This cluster marks the consolidation of the consequences, the cause-and-effect, of pre-colonial and colonial Rwanda. In the 'Europe' narrative, 1959 is interpreted as a 'flash in the pan', in the 'Rwanda' panel as the beginning of a persistent 'genocidal philosophy'. The 'Europe' panel states that post-independence Rwanda was marked by integration of 'Tutsi' who remained. Violence is not denied (1963), but again a *minority* of 'Tutsi' (*inyenzi*) are presented as having provoked violence (as in 1959). Both the 'Europe' and 'Rwanda' panels make reference to internal, *intra*-ethnic conflict between 'Hutu' of the north and south.

While the 'Rwanda' narratives consider the years 1959–90 to be marked by a persistent, if sometimes dormant, genocidal project, the 'Europe' narratives explicitly dismiss the opposing narrative, the claim to constant persecution and attack. In this cluster, unlike those preceding, there is no longer a third, intermediary party upon which some blame may be placed (Belgium, the *Pères Blancs*).

SUMMARY

Both sets of narratives ask a processual question of the past – 'How did we get to a situation in which up to 1 million people were brutally murdered? Who was/is responsible?' There is consensus on those points in time that are considered worthy of contention, and at certain points the narratives are in substantive agreement. The conflict over the past is less dichotomous and more elusive than one may have expected. So can we, tentatively, identify meta-narratives, given that the past is used to demonstrate 'systems of causation' (Hastrup 1992: 9)?

The 'pre-colonial' and 'colonial clusters' appear to be 'preparation' for the real 'turning point' – the 1959 genocide/revolution. The interpretation of this event and its aftermath hinges on whether the 'Tutsi élite' were 'unwilling victims' of colonial oppression or 'willing beneficiaries'.

For Rwandese in Europe, the 1959 revolution was a legitimate response to the oppression of a 'Tutsi élite' who had 'collaborated' with the Belgians. According to such an interpretation, the 'Tutsi élite' must share co-responsibility for 1959 with the Belgians. While these narratives admit there were moments of violence in 1959 – that Tutsi were killed and many fled into exile – they insist that this was a 'revolution' based upon a genuine demand for democracy and social justice. These panels argue that not all Tutsi were targeted and that those who were attacked were defined in political/class terms, not ethnic. The assertion is that the events of 1959 were not a precursor of 1994, but an attack on a minority ruling élite that brought it upon itself. And yet, although the 'Europe' meta-narrative maintains that the 1959 'revolution' was an 'egalitarian' project, it was quickly destroyed by events: by the attack of the *inyenzi* and by the partisan coup of a 'Hutu élite' – Habyarimana and his 'northern faction' – *not all Hutu*.

A tentative meta-narrative: 'a Tutsi élite was co-responsible for crystallising ethnic division – the revolution was a legitimate attempt to reverse this – again the Tutsi élite are co-responsible for derailing this project with their attack in 1963 – this division was exploited by a minority of Hutu – a minority that would eventually commit the 1994 genocide'.

This processual narrative, this interpretation of the *chronicle*, contains an argument; that a minority of Tutsi must share co-responsibility in creating ethnic division, and that not all Hutu should be held responsible for 1994. Thus, the contemporary globalisation of guilt to '<u>the</u> Hutu' is *illegitimate*.

The 'Rwanda' narrative suggests that the 'Tutsi élite' were double victims of the colonial authorities. They were used as an instrument of indirect rule, forced to oppress Rwandese on behalf of the colonist. When this élite tried to break free from their own subjugation (and the subjugation of Rwanda) the Belgian authorities destroyed them. A 'Hutu élite' were accomplices in this destruction, and it was a pattern of destruction that would be perpetuated up to 1994.

A tentative meta-narrative: 'Tutsi are victims: of Belgian indirect rule; of Belgian opposition to independence; and of violence orchestrated by a Hutu élite. Thus, the contemporary globalisation of victimhood to "<u>the</u> Tutsi" is *legitimate*.'

In a sense, the meta-narratives are not in a straightforward opposition to one another. Rather than being 'outward looking' and assigning responsibility to an opposing collectivity, they are 'inward looking' and seek to communicate qualities about the two groups: that guilt *should not* be assigned to '<u>the</u> Hutu' and that victimhood *should* be assigned to '<u>the</u> Tutsi'.

Although there is a profound truth in the axiom that 'Those who cannot remember the past are condemned to repeat it' (Santayana 1905: 284), a persistent appeal to absolute history (one that misconstrues the nature and capacities of historiography) has been a central element in instigating violence and ultimately genocide in Rwanda. Given the overwhelming nature of 1994, reflection on the past is inevitable and necessary. As Dominick LaCapra warns, 'What is not confronted critically does not disappear; it tends to return as the repressed' (1992: 126). Such a 'critical reflection' will, however, generate different interpretations. We should not allow our faith in a single, 'real' history to prevent us from accepting and exploring competing narratives that reflect contemporary concerns in Rwanda. If we strive to isolate one version of Rwandan history such concerns will remain hidden. Finally, if the 'appeal to history' is not to play a destructive role in the future an appreciation of the interpretative basis of historiography and a recognition of the limits to its claim to truth must be encouraged.

Afterword

Given that the debates reviewed above are ongoing and contain elements that have constantly reproduced themselves over decades, a 'conclusion' seems inappropriate. The best one can do is draw some tentative lessons.

Chapter 1 demonstrated that when the assumption that a universal 'ethnic quality' exists is combined with a failure to understand the racial construction of social distinction in Rwanda, we may project on to Rwandan society an image of distinction more concrete than is warranted, an image that resonates with that found in genocidal propaganda. In a sense, external commentators attempt to counter the perpetrator's claim to possess 'objective' schema of social distinction by deploying their own 'objective' schema. Both seek to impose 'objective' clarity. The assertion and condemnation both depend on similar epistemological assumptions. By responding with their own claims to 'objectivity', external commentators give inadvertent credence to the 'objective' claims of perpetrators. Such an approach always runs the risk of appearing as inadvertent corroboration. External commentators on genocide must disjoin themselves from arguments regarding 'objective' social distinction and place the full focus on the *subjective*, groundless constructions deployed by perpetrators to delineate targets.

Chapter 2 demonstrated that the phrase 'social revolution of 1959' does not correspond to the actual events of November 1959, but is a metonym for the broader triumph of a divisive, racial understanding of Rwandan society. It is natural, therefore, that the post-genocide government has focused its denunciation on 1959. In a sense, however, this denunciation inadvertently rests upon accepting the distorted representation found in genocidal propaganda of 1959 as *'le moment fondateur'*. More regrettably, this focus has distracted attention from the horrifying events of late 1963/early 1964, which must be seen as the true precursor to the genocide of 1994. Reorienting the debate around the events of 1963/64 would be more apposite.

Chapter 3 demonstrated how the Holocaust has played a central role as comparator in discussions of the 1994 genocide. Although this is natural and there are significant comparisons to be made, making the Holocaust preponderant not only obscures significant

180

divergent characteristics of the Rwandan genocide, but may undermine our ability to detect, prevent and/or swiftly stop future genocides that do not adequately resemble the Holocaust. At the same time, however, the use of the Holocaust as comparator must be understood as a legitimate counter to Western caricatures of the Rwandan genocide as 'tribal bloodlust', 'tribal carnage' and 'tribal slaughter' in the 'Dark Heart of Africa'. Rwandese are forced to draw analogies with the Holocaust in order to counteract the racist, ethnocentric distortion found in Western media coverage. Strengthening an appreciation of the UNGC as a generic model of genocide and challenging the Conradian perspectives of (some) Western journalists should be a priority.

Chapter 4 demonstrated that although infrequent statements by members of the post-genocide Rwandan government imply collective guilt (contrary to the individual criminal responsibility intrinsic to the crime of genocide), a more pressing issue is the subliminal impact of the term 'Hutu moderate'. Although ubiquitous, it is never defined. From the skein of Rwandan politics in the period 1990–94, one can tentatively isolate to whom the term refers. The contemporary term 'Hutu moderate' appears to be a *post facto* delineation of a group that was bracketed with Tutsi by the perpetrators of the genocide. Furthermore, the wholly retrospective use of the term prevents this group from acting as a guard against the perpetrator's binary construction of Rwandan society being given contemporary salience. Renaming this group 'Hutu opposing Habyarimana and his power' (as suggested by one *rescapé*) and recognising that their very existence demonstrates the absurdity of dualistic genocidal propaganda would offset the role that the current term 'Hutu moderate' may play in implicit globalisation of guilt.

Chapter 5 demonstrated that if an end to the 'culture of impunity' is to be realised, then the investigation of all allegations of human rights abuses must be dogmatic, tenacious and transparent. Allowing certain allegations to circulate without judicial investigation (while it is being applied in other cases) unnecessarily transforms unproven allegations into divisive resources. Ending the culture of impunity must be understood to be as much about disproving allegations as convicting those found responsible. If the application of justice is perceived to be selective (in a region saturated by calls for justice) then a belief in impunity may return with even greater vigour.

Chapter 6 demonstrated that the appeal to history was a central component in constructing and maintaining division in Rwanda and was intrinsic to genocidal propaganda. There is a danger that actors continue to appeal to history in this absolutist fashion. The instrumental power inherent in a belief that a single, absolute history is attainable (and preferable) has not only proved to be deadly, but overestimates the capacities and misunderstands the nature of historiography. While there may be a non-negotiable *chronicle of events*, the narratives that actors recognise (and value) as history are the product of an interpretative exercise that inevitably generates different narratives. While Rwanda has a single past, a single, definitive history is unattainable. Given the role played by history in Rwanda's past, a recognition of the limits of historiography should be encouraged.

The prescriptions above are made with a full appreciation of the enormous challenge faced by all who wish to account for the 1994 genocide. Ultimately, we may have to accept that although our condemnation of it is absolute, the Rwandan genocide will always resist being reduced to a single, absolute 'account'. Then again, if we self-consciously recognise the limits of our own words and refuse to claim absolute clarity we enact a final rejection of the absolutist basis of the genocidal mentality. This would surely be the most fitting memorial to the victims.

Endnotes

CHAPTER 1

1. René Degni-Ségni estimated that 500,000 to 1 million Tutsi were killed in the genocide, but concluded that the *exact* number would never be known (UN 1994k para 24). In August 2001, the Rwandan government conducted a census, the preliminary report of which stated that 1,074,017 people had been killed between 1 October 1991 and 31 December 1994; 66 per cent of genocide victims were male; and those aged one to 21 years had been the most affected age group of both genders (IRIN 2001iv). The report stated that, of those killed, 97.3 per cent were Tutsi, although 'it was unclear if this figure refers to those aged between one and 21 years old or to all people killed during the period reviewed' (ibid.). Given that this figure covers a period time *out with* the genocide itself (including casualties in the preceding civil war), the figure of 500,000–800,000 Tutsi killed during the 1994 genocide remains that most commonly used.
2. Organic Law No. 08/96 of August 30, 1996 on the Organisation of Prosecutions for Offences constituting the Crime of Genocide or Crimes against Humanity committed since October 1, 1990 (Article Ia) states 'genocide ... as defined in the [UNGC] of 9 December 1948'.
3. According to genocide scholars, the UNGC has three key weaknesses. First, although commonly perceived as referring only to 'mass killing', it co-mingles lethal and non-lethal acts. Second, is the ambiguity of 'destruction in whole or in part' (Fein 1993: 10). The lack of quantitative criteria leaves the threshold between one or two massacres and an episode of genocide 'inherently indeterminate' (Harff & Gurr 1988: 366). Third, the Convention excludes the annihilation of political groups (see Chalk 1989: 151; Du Preez 1994: 48ff; Drost 1959: 122–3; Harff & Gurr 1988).
4. The same can be said of anthropology. A review of 65 studies of 'ethnicity' in sociological and anthropological literature found that only 13 actually defined the term (see Isajiw 1974).
5. Ethnic classification is 'frequently mapped according to a series of binary discriminations which oppose an "us" to a "them"' (Fardon 1987: 170: see Boas 1943; Staub 1989: 58).
6. The Lue (Thailand) spoke no exclusive language, had no particular dress, architecture or religion. When individual Lue were asked what made them distinctive, they would cite 'cultural traits' that they shared with neighbouring groups. Moerman concluded that 'someone is Lue by virtue of believing and calling himself Lue and acting in ways that validate his Lueness' (1965: 1222). Being Lue was a self-assigned (or self-ascribed) identity, not an observable, behavioural phenomena. In this way, 'Relations of similarity and difference are not given in the empirical phenomena themselves but are generated by people who act on them

and decide, using criteria of their own choosing, to which class, category or concept they conform' (Holy 1987: 16).

7. Ethnic labels, therefore, 'function in a recursive way, since the labels used by colonisers, missionaries and foreign scholars were returned to and appropriated by the people in question' (Eriksen 1993: 90).

8. '[O]nce ethnicity has been "objectified" as a basis for social classification, [it] becomes ... a pragmatic basis for the formation of interest groups and networks, social resources for pursuing individual and communal utilities' (J. L. Comaroff 1987: 311–12).

9. Fardon demonstrates that 'the Chamba' did not exist in the nineteenth century. The contemporary term 'Chamba' 'describes people whose origins, languages and practices are diverse [and the] ethnic entities which have the form of the modern Chamba ethnicity are modern inventions. This invention did not take place in a vacuum ... the term Chamba has historical precedents – but [modern "Chamba"] resulted in a form different from those before' (1987: 182).

10. A lineage is patrilineal group that can 'trace its [male descent] ties to a common ancestor, usually three to six generations in the past' (C. Newbury 1988: 95). Lineages held independent rights over land and cattle in common. The head of the lineage (chosen by the previous lineage head) had the right to distribute lands to both lineage members and clients who would provide gifts of food and beer in return for the use of land (*ubukonde*) (ibid. 97). Although lineages were classed as either 'Tutsi' or 'non-Tutsi', this did not prevent intermarriage, although the offspring of a male 'non-Tutsi' member of the lineage and a Tutsi women would produce 'non-Tutsi' children (C. Newbury 1983: 258). Although C. Taylor (1999: 167) indicates that children would become 'Tutsi', it is unclear whether only the children became 'Tutsi', or the 'non-Tutsi' man was *kwihutura* ('cease being Hutu and become Tutsi').

11. Clans contain(ed) Hutu, Tutsi and Twa members. It was assumed that membership in these units was, like lineages, determined by patrilineal descent. If, however, 'clans were originally subsections of a single ethnic group [owing to being patrilineal, how] would they have come to contain ... members of other ethnic groups?' (D. Newbury 1980: 39). Although clients may have adopted the clan identity of their patrons, D. Newbury suggests that although there were clan identities prior to the penetration of the central kingdom, in the absence of the later rigidity of 'Hutu' and 'Tutsi', they were not 'multi-ethnic', just clans. With the expansion of the central kingdom, however, clans were amalgamated and transformed into 18 *supra-clans* as an expression of *Nyiginya* centralisation. It was according to this gradual process, occurring in tandem with the rigidifying of ethnic distinction, that the *clans* took on their current character of being 'multi-ethnic' (ibid.).

12. As C. Newbury writes: 'Clientship in Rwanda was not a static social "given" it was a dynamic phenomena' (1998: 17), with forms of clientship changing 'from ties of alliance to instruments of exploitation' (ibid. 209). At different times and in different places, clientship involved differentiation and/or cohesion; protection and/or oppression, deference and/or resentment (Lemarchand 1996: 12). For example, in its original

form *umuheto* clientage involved more powerful lineages giving cattle to less powerful lineages in return for protection of their herds (des Forges 1972: 5–6). Thus, *umuheto* was 'a bond of elites, rather than the arbiter of hierarchical status differences' (C. Newbury 1978: 19). From the time of Rwabugiri, *umuheto* (linking lineage with lineage) was gradually replaced by *ubuhake*, 'Whereby Tutsi pastoralist patrons granted the use of cattle to particular Hutu who were their clients' (C. Newbury 1988: 4). In contrast to *umuheto*, *ubuhake* was an individual linkage between client and patron in which the patron gave a cow to the client, thereby extending clientship to families who did not possess cattle themselves, exposing clients to 'more arbitrary forms of exploitation' (Mamdani 2001: 65; see Prunier 1995: 13). *Ubuhake* clientship, however, involved less than 17 per cent of the population and a significantly higher proportion of Tutsi than Hutu (C. Newbury 1980: 106).

13. *Akazi* (unpaid labour) added eleven days per adult member per year for the construction of public buildings, drainage projects, anti-erosion projects, reforestation and the cultivation of cash crops (see C. Newbury 1980: 104; 1988: 153ff). Traditional obligations (*prestations coutumières*) included tribute in kind (*ikoro*) owed by chiefs/subchiefs to the *mwami* and collected from the population. During the colonial period, however, the expression *prestations coutumières* came to serve as 'a magic label under which a multitude of additional *corvées* [were] thrust upon the peasantry under the pretext that custom somehow conferred automatic legitimacy upon all forms of work' (Lemarchand 1970b: 889).

14. In the nineteenth century, *uburetwa* consisted of two days of unpaid work out of every five for each *family*, performed by a single member, although Hutu in *ubuhake* clientship were not required to perform *uburetwa* (C. Newbury 1980: 101). In 1916, *uburetwa* was increased to two or three days in every six (Lemarchand 1970b: 888). In 1927 it was modified to one day out of every seven for *all adult men* rather than *a family* (C. Newbury 1978: 23), although 'it was imposed specifically on Hutu', colonial administrators arguing it was a symbol of 'Hutu submission' (C. Newbury 1988: 112; 141–2). The labour service required of *petits Tutsi* consisted only of seasonal work on chiefly residences (ibid. 140). The application of *uburetwa* to individuals further undermined the corporate role of the lineages, weakening the ability of local corporate groups to resist exploitation by chiefs (C. Newbury 1978: 23). The colonial codification meant that it was expanded to areas where it had not previously been present.

15. Before this 'reform', there had been three types of chieftancy. First, there was a Hutu 'land chief' who acted as arbitrator in land disputes and organised agricultural tribute (*ikoro*) and labour dues (*uburetwa*) (Pottier 2002: 14). Parallel to the 'land chief' was a Tutsi 'cattle chief' responsible for collecting taxes on cattle and an 'army chief'. The 1926 reforms abolished this system and replaced it with a single chief with sub-chiefs under his authority (C. Newbury 1978: 22). The 'checks and balances' by which clients could play co-territorial chiefs off one another were dismantled (see Lemarchand 1970b: 88; Chrétien 1985: 143).

16. By 1959, 43 chiefs out of 45 and 549 sub-chiefs out of 559 were Tutsi (Chrétien 1985: 145)

17. There was also the sense that the chiefs were told 'You whip the Hutu or we will whip you' (Watson 1991: 4; see Prunier 1995: 27 n. 68).

18. The 'Hamitic' hypothesis emerged in the nineteenth century, according to which 'higher political forms of African civilisation – in particular tribal monarchies – had been introduced to the Dark Continent by pastoralists ... from Egypt and the Nile valley. Centralised, "higher" order peoples and polities in the heart of Africa were not, therefore, indigenously African. Africanised Hamites were dark in colour ... but racially distinguishable from their "truly" African neighbours by their greater height, finer lips, and narrower noses. Primordial Africans were now referred to as "Bantus": squat in body form, agriculturists by occupation, and more "primitive" in intellectual and political sophistication' (Miles 2000: 108–9).

19. Although the term 'Bantu' was only coined in the nineteenth century by the German linguist Whilhelm Bleek, in 1993 the pro-genocidal newspaper *Kamarampaka* called for the creation of a pan-African *Coalition bantou pour la démocratie* (see Chrétien et al. 1995: 170).

20. Kagame's history consists of a cultural and historical justification for the future independence of church and state under the control of a Tutsi élite (Linden 1977: 5). According to Lemarchand, Kagame's 1952 book was 'avidly read by Tutsi intellectuals, some of whom found in it justification of their supremacist claims' (1970a: 137; see Sibomana 1999: 80).

21. Although it is stated that the census identified 'Tutsi' if a person possessed ten or more cows (see, for example, AR 1995: 11–12), Mamdani (2001: 98) demonstrates that estimates of the number of cows in Rwanda at the time does not correspond with the number of 'Tutsi' designated as such by the census. In addition, the vast majority of *petits Tutsi* did not possess any cattle. Drawing on the work of Tharcisse Gatwa (1998: 84), Mamdani suggests that three criteria were in operation: local information from church sources regarding the 'identity' of those in a given locality; physical measurements; *and* the ownership of cows (2001: 99). Similarly, HRW and FIDH (1999: 37 n. 8) state that 'the procedure for population registration took no account of ownership of cattle' and that identity was based on what people *said* they were (self-ascription).

22. Until 1997, the ID card read '*Ubwoko* (*Hutu, Tutsi, Twa, Naturalisé*)' and the French '*Ethnie*'. In July 1991, consultants advised international donors that aid should be made conditional on the removal of ethnic identity from ID cards (HRW & FIDH 1999: 92). Article 16 of the Arusha Protocol of 3 August 1993 stated that the BBTG would remove 'ethnic origin' from all official documents (see Schabas & Imbleau 1997: 301).

23. The concept of 'double colonialism' appeared in genocidal propaganda. On 15 April 1994, Donat Murego (speaking on *Radio Rwanda*) stated that in 1959 *le menu peuple* (the 'common folk') had 'thrown off the feudal yolk, of the Tutsi regime, and the Colonial yolk, of the white regime ... otherwise called double colonialism' (see Chrétien et al. 1995: 126).

24. Recently elected communal councillors and *bourgmestres* formed themselves into a Legislative Assembly; appointed Dominique

Mbonyumutwa as President and Grégoire Kayibanda as Prime Minister; and abolished the monarchy.

25. In 1957, Grégoire Kayibanda formed *Mouvement Sociale Muhutu* which became *Parti du Mouvement de l'Émancipation Hutu* (Parmehutu) on 18 October 1959, with the addition of the prefix MDR (*Mouvement Démocratique Républicain*) in May 1960.

26. Those who changed their stated *ethnie/ubwoko* (the *abaguze ubwoko*) illegally were subject to imprisonment or a fine (Prunier 1995: 76 n. 62).

27. *Mouvement Révolutionnaire National pour le Développement*, the single party formed in 1975 by Juvénal Habyarimana.

28. Falashas: a Jewish sect in Ethiopia of whom c30,000 were evacuated by the Israeli government between 1984 and 1991.

29. The *Parti Libéral*'s emphasis on liberal politics and economics attracted Tutsi businessmen and became known as the 'Tutsi party', even though only one of its executive committee (Landoald Ndasingwa) was Tutsi (see Bertrand 2000: 111).

30. Despite this, many of Habyarimana's associates had Tutsi mistresses, while his personal doctor had a Tutsi wife (see C. Taylor 1999: 170).

31. As Prunier puts it, 'an evil that was both facelessly abstract and embodied in the most ordinary person living next door' (1995: 170).

32. These were not, however, discrete factors and 'each operated in a climate created by the intersection of multiple pressures which were experienced differently in their kaleidoscopic combination for different classes, genders, generations, and individuals' (C. Newbury & D. Newbury 1999: 296).

33. Article 57 of the Civil Code of 1988 stated that a person would be identified by 'sex, ethnic group, name, residence and domicile'. Article 118 stated that birth certificates would include 'the year, month, date and place of birth, the sex, the ethnic group, the first and last name of the infant'.

34. 'On reading through the *travaux préparatoires* of the [UNGC] [Sixth Committee discussions 21 September–10 December 1948] it appears that the crime of genocide was allegedly perceived as targeting only "stable" groups, constituted in a permanent fashion and membership of which is determined by birth, with the exclusion of the more "mobile" groups which one joins through individual voluntary commitment, such as political and economic groups. Therefore, a common criterion in the four types of groups protected by the [UNGC] is that membership in such groups would seem to be normally not challengeable by its members, who belong to it automatically, by birth, in a continuous and often irremediable manner' (ICTR 1998 para 511).

CHAPTER 2

1. For a reference to the attack on Mbonyumutwa in genocidal propaganda, see Chrétien et al. 1995: 115–16.

2. 'In genocides the victimised groups are defined primarily in terms of their communal characteristics, i.e. ethnicity, religion or nationality. In

politicides the victim groups are defined primarily in terms of their hierarchical position or political opposition to the regime and dominant groups' (Harff & Gurr 1988: 362).

3. The 'Hutu' parties (MDR-Parmehutu and Aprosoma) won 84 per cent of votes while the two 'Tutsi' parties (UNAR and RADER, the former having called on Rwandans to boycott the election) won less than 9 per cent (Lemarchand 1970b: 911). As a consequence, MDR-Parmehutu won 160 *bourgmestres* out of 229 (Chrétien 1985: 158). Many of the new Hutu *bourgmestres* merely took over the patron status of Tutsi chiefs they replaced, using violence against Tutsi as a means of consolidating their position (see Lemarchand 1970b: 912–14; Gravel 1968: 192–5).

4. The 'Coup of Gitarama' – 28 January 1961 (see Chapter 1 n. 24). A UNGA resolution (20 December 1960) recommended postponing legislative elections until 1961, to provide a period to promote 'national reconciliation' (Lemarchand 1970b: 915). The Belgian colonial authorities initially agreed to respect this request, but then prepared the way for the '*coup*'. As Lemarchand notes, 'It is hard to believe that the [*coup*] could have taken place without the knowledge of the Belgian authorities [and] without certain European members of the administration taking part in it' (ibid. 919). Indeed, the Belgian Special Resident convened the Gitarama meeting on the same day the UN Commission for Ruanda-Urundi arrived in Bujumbira (de Heusch 1995: 5).

5. Harroy states that on 10 November 1959, the *gendarmerie* (under Belgian command) was deployed to prevent a 'counter revolution' by the '*Ingabo z'umwami*', the *mwami*'s army (1984: 292). In Harroy's words, 1959 was an 'assisted revolution' (ibid.).

6. Between 15 and 20 Tutsi officials were executed (on the orders of Belgian officers, according to de Heusch 1995: 5; see Reyntjens 1985: 463). These included Etienne Afrika (UNAR 'Minister of Cattle Raising'); Joseph Rutsindintwarane (President of UNAR); Michel Rwagasana (Secretary-General of UNAR); Prosper Bwanakweri (President and founder of RADER); and Lazare Ndazaro (co-founder and vice-president of RADER) (Lemarchand 1970a: 223). This marked the end of the presence of UNAR or RADER inside Rwanda.

7. For accusations of 'treachery' among the Tutsi inside the country, see a declaration by Anastase Makuza, President of the National Assembly in 1964 (Chrétien et al. 1995: 123–4).

8. Lemarchand argues that this particular report was false and would not correspond to the geographical location of the massacres (1970a: 225; see Reyntjens 1985: 466). It is, however, possible that the names of the rivers were misreported.

9. In May 1994, Augustin Bizimungu (FAR Commander-in-Chief) described as 'excesses' the massacres committed 'by forces linked to the Government' (quoted in UN 1994g para 21).

10. In January 1960, Guy Logiest (Belgian Special Resident) declared '[W]e must take action in favour of the Hutu ... we are led to take sides. We cannot stay neutral' (quoted in Lemarchand 1970b: 909). In late 1960, a semi-official memo submitted by Belgium to the UN proposed a '*protectionism éducateur*' whose aim was 'the progressive elimination of the

Tutsi elite from the political scene [and to] facilitate the entry of Hutu elements into the political arena' (ibid. 907). Thus, 'one can hardly exaggerate the part played by Belgian officials in accelerating and extending the revolutionary process, in structuring its development along coherent political lines, and facilitating the seizure of power from above' (ibid. 923).

11. The New York Agreements (1962) gave UNAR two ministerial posts, two secretariats of state, two *préfets* (of ten), two *sous-préfets* and a senior post in the 'Commissariat for Refugees' (Lemarchand 1970a: 197). On 17 May 1962, Michel Rwagasana (in a statement to the Legislative Assembly) committed the UNAR to working with Kayibanda's government, stating that his party 'can no longer be considered an opposition, but rather a partner ... My party will therefore give its support to the government' (ibid. 203). Despite this, between 1962 and 1963, UNAR members were forbidden from holding public meetings, harassed, arrested and 'disappeared'. By May 1962, four of UNAR's seven deputies in the National Assembly had fled the country and in February 1963 the two UNAR ministers were dismissed (Reyntjens 1985: 449–52).

12. The UNAR newspaper in Rwanda – *L'Unité* – declared (in July 1962) that 'UNAR assures the government of its total support in the fight against terrorism'. The party expelled the *inyenzi* leaders and called on surrounding countries not to allow 'terrorist' bases (Reyntjens 1985: 462).

13. Following Kabera's assassination, his brother, Joseph Kayijaho, vice-president of Ibuka ('Remember'), the umbrella association of genocide survivor organisations, left Rwanda having been assaulted by soldiers on two occasions. The executive secretary of Ibuka, Anastase Murumba, also left the country having been publicly berated by politicians close to the government (see HRW 2000a), as did Jean Bosco Rutagengwa, the founding president of the association.

14. For additional examples of genocidal propaganda presenting the RPF as *inyenzi*, see Chrétien et al. 1995: 100; 113; 119; 129–31; 134; 139; 156; 193; 235; 243; 265.

CHAPTER 3

1. More than 1.5 million Armenians were murdered between 1915 and 1923 (see Melson 1992; Hovannisian 1999; Dadrian 1995).

2. Rwanda's domestic genocide law of August 1996 provides the death penalty for: 'a) persons whose criminal acts or whose acts of criminal participation place them among the planners, organisers, instigators, supervisors and leaders of the crime of genocide or of a crime against humanity; b) persons who acted in positions of authority at the national, prefectorial, communal, sector or cell level, or in a political party, or fostered such crimes; c) notorious murderers who by virtue of the zeal or excessive malice with which they committed atrocities, distinguished themselves in their areas of residence or where they passed; d) persons who committed acts of sexual torture'.

3. The RPF entered Rwanda from Uganda on 1 October 1990. Despite initial success, the front was then forced to conduct a guerrilla war. In May 1992 an RPF offensive resulted in 350,000 people being internally displaced, with a further 800,000 being displaced following the RPF offensive of February 1993. In August 1993, with the signing of the Arusha Peace Accords, the fighting ended (see HRW & FIDH 1999: 48ff for details).

4. Rwandese are aware of Russell's statement (see UN 1994p; Mikekemo 1998).

5. See Freeman (1991: 187) and his reference to Wiesel's (1968) argument that the Holocaust is inexplicable (see Chalk 1989: 149; Bauer 1987: 215).

6. Alan Rosenberg (1987: 155) notes that in an earlier work Bauer (1973: 11–12) conceded that the Nazis sought to annihilate the Gypsies.

7. As Fein notes: 'Although most contemporary genocides take place in the Third World, much of the theory about genocide is derived from a dominant or exclusive focus on the Holocaust, which occurred in a modern, Western, Christian and post-Christian Society' (1993: xv; see Du Preez 1994: ii).

8. 'One major difference between the Holocaust and other forms of genocide is that pragmatic considerations were central with all other genocides, abstract ideological motivations less so' (Bauer 2001: 47).

9. 'The perpetrators represent an elite or segment of the dominant ethnic group that felt threatened by the imposition of a new structure in which their ethnic group's interests could be subordinated' (Fein 1998: 160).

10. As Degni-Ségui observed in June 1994: 'The reason for what is taking place in Rwanda is not ethnic as such, but rather political, the aim being the seizure of political power, or rather the retention of power, by the representatives of one ethnic group ... who are using every means, principally the elimination of the opposing ethnic group, but also the elimination of political opponents within their own group' (UN 1994k para 56).

11. '[The genocide] was, among other things, largely a fight for good jobs, administrative control and economic advantage' (Prunier 1995: 227).

12. Du Preez (1994: 68) gives the German killing of Herero (1904, in what is now Namibia) and the killing of Ibo (1966–67 in Nigeria/Biafra) as examples of pragmatic genocides.

13. Du Preez (1994: 68) gives the Nazi killing of Jews and Roma / 'Gypsies'; the Stalinist killing of Kulaks; the Khmer Rouge killing of bourgeoisie and the Turkish killing of Armenians as examples of transcendent genocide.

14. '[T]he assault on the Jews was purely ideological; that is, it had no *a priori* pragmatic elements, as in the case of literally all genocidal attempts we know of' (Bauer 1998: 39).

15. 'The wanton killing of Tutsi civilians ... became the quickest and most "rational" way of eliminating all basis of agreement with the RPF' (Lemarchand 1995: 9–10). Bauer considers Rwanda to have been 'a pragmatically motivated genocide' (2001: 46).

16. 'The Protocols of the Elders of Zion': a forgery made in Russia for the Okhrana (secret police) in 1897, which blamed 'the Jews' for the

country's ills and claimed that a secret Jewish cabal was plotting to take over the world.

17. In a speech on 5 May 1944, Himmler stated: 'In my view, we as Germans, however deeply we may feel in our hearts, are not entitled to allow a generation of avengers filled with hatred to grow up with whom our children and grandchildren will have to deal because we, too weak and cowardly, left it to them' (quoted in Bartov 1998: 785 n. 22). A leaflet distributed in Ruhengeri *préfecture* in early 1991 stated: 'Go do a special *umuganda*. Destroy all the bushes and the *Inkotanyi* who are hiding there. And don't forget that those who are destroying the weeds must also get rid of the roots [women and children]' (quoted in Article XIX 1996: 34).

18. As des Forges notes: 'In October 1993 there were 50,000 people killed in Burundi and no one [internationally] did anything and this encouraged extremists [in Rwanda] to argue ... "Look we can get away with it"' (quoted in Fein 1998: 161).

19. Having returned from Rwanda on 4 April 1994, Roger Winter, the director of USCR, wrote an article in which he stated that to present Rwanda as an other case of 'African tribal bloodletting [was a] fatalistically superficial interpretation' (Winter 1994). His piece was turned down by several US papers until the *Toronto Globe* finally published it on 14 April (JEEAR 1996b).

20. For a critique of Kaplan's article and Malthusian approaches to Rwanda, see D. Newbury 1999.

21. 'Having created a reality beyond its wildest fantasies, humanity cannot imagine what it created ... human agency becomes tenuous, the disaster being ascribed either to insane genius or to anonymous forces' (Bartov 1998: 799).

22. The requirement that every Rwandan perform one day of unpaid collective work each week (repairing roads, digging anti-erosion ditches, clearing the brush).

23. See the 1964 law, *Loi postant résidence, recensement et cartes d'identité des Rwandais*.

24. Akhavan suggests that had massive human rights abuses not occurred in Yugoslavia (resulting in the ICTY), it is unlikely that an international tribunal would have been established to try those responsible for genocide in Rwanda because 'the plight of African victims would not generate the same outcry as the suffering of Europeans' (1996: 501).

CHAPTER 4

1. 'The issue is about being Rwandese, not being a Hutu or a Tutsi' (Kagame, quoted in Gaye 2000).

2. The statute of the ICTR defines 'crimes against humanity' as crimes committed as part of a widespread or systematic attack against any civilian population on national, political, ethnic, racial or religious grounds and includes murder and persecution on political, racial and religious grounds (Art. III Statute of the ICTR). Rwanda's domestic law regarding the genocide (August 1996) refers to the Convention on the

Non-Applicability of Statutory Limitations to War Crimes and Crimes Against Humanity of [1968] to define 'crimes against humanity' (Art. I). The 1968 Convention, in turn, refers to the Charter of the International Military Tribunal (Nuremberg), which states that 'crimes against humanity' include murder and extermination, against any civilian population or persecution on political grounds (Art. VI para c).

3. The full title of the ICTR is the 'International Criminal Tribunal for the Prosecution of Persons Responsible for Genocide and Other Serious Violations of International Humanitarian Law Committed in the Territory of Rwanda and Rwandan Citizens responsible for genocide and other such violations committed in the territory of neighbouring States, between 1 January 1994 and 31 December 1994' (UN 1994q).

4. Citizens would be free to join the political party of their choice; Habyarimana would resign from being president of the MRND; the current 'Parliament' (100 per cent MRND) would be replaced with a National Conference; there would be freedom of action for all political parties, negotiations with the RPF and a solution to the refugee question; and equal access for all parties to the media (especially the radio) (see Bertrand 2000: 102ff). The same demands appeared in a joint MDR, PSD, PL *communiqué* on 17 November 1991 (see Prunier 1995: 134).

5. Twagiramungu had suggested that *Mouvement Démocratique Républicain* become *Mouvement Démocratique Rwandais* (Bertrand 2000: 88).

6. Thus, 'The announcement of potential massacres designed to justify actual massacres, supposedly to anticipate the enemy' (Chrétien et al. 1995: 321; see Lemarchand 1996: 29–30; Bringa 2002: 202–3).

7. Although the MDR received the Foreign Ministry (important given the imminent start of negotiations with the RPF) and the Ministry of Information (important given the previous use of the media to incite violence against Tutsi), the MRND(D) held on to the Interior and Defence ministries, thereby maintaining control of the military, *gendarmerie* and local administration – all essential to carrying out the genocide.

8. Of which the significant points were: (1) negotiate peace with the RPF; (2) strengthen the judicial system and respect for human rights; (3) reform the civil service so that it was neutral vis-à-vis political parties; (4) find a political solution to the refugee problem; (5) arrange elections in twelve months' time (see Bertrand 2000: 176–8).

9. This policy was introduced by Agathe Uwilingiyimana, MDR Minister for Education, and made her very popular among the population. After she was attacked in her home on 8 May 1992 (probably by MRND(D) militants) demonstrations took place in her support (Bertrand 2000: 195). Having become Prime Minister in July 1993, she continued to be denounced (see Article XIX 1996: 93) and was killed in the first hours of the genocide.

10. All were killed by the Presidential Guard: Agathe Uwilingiyimana, MDR Prime Minister; Frédéric Nzamurambaho, PSD Minister of Agriculture; Boniface Ngulinzira, MDR Foreign Minister.

11. 'The N'sele Cease-fire Agreement between the Government of the Rwandese Republic and the Rwandese Patriotic Front, as amended at

Gbadolite, 16 September 1991, and at Arusha, 12 July 1992' (see Schabas & Imbleau 1997: 247–52).

12. 'Protocol of Agreement between the Government of the Republic of Rwanda and the Rwandese Patriotic Front on the rule of law, signed 18 August 1992' (see Schabas & Imbleau 1997: 253–8).

13. 'Protocol of Agreement on Power-Sharing within the Framework of a Broad-Based Transitional Government between the Government of the Republic of Rwanda and the Rwandese Patriotic Front, signed 30 October 1992' (see Schabas & Imbleau 1997: 259–78).

14. 'Protocol of Agreement Between the Government of the Republic of Rwanda and the Rwandese Patriotic Front on Power-Sharing within the Framework of a Broad-Based Transitional Government (Continuation of the Protocol of Agreement signed on 30 October, 1992)', signed 9 January 1993. The Presidency would remain in the hands of the MRND(D). Cabinet: MRND(D) (5 posts, including Ministry of Defence); RPF (5 posts, including Ministry of the Interior); MDR (4 posts, including Prime Minister and Foreign Minister); PSD (3 posts); PL (3 posts); PDC (1 post). Transitional Assembly: MRND(D) (11 seats); RPF (11 seats); MDR (11 seats); PSD (11 seats); PL (11 seats); PDC (4 seats). In addition, other 'registered parties will have one seat each' (see Schabas & Imbleau 1997: 279–92).

15. 'The Supreme Court [whose Presiding Judge would be selected by the National Assembly] shall ... have criminal jurisdiction over the President of the Republic' (Art. 27j, October 1992 agreement). In addition, the August 1992 agreement stated a 'National Commission on Human Rights' would be established to 'investigate human rights violations committed by anybody ... in particular, by organs of the State and individuals in their capacity as agents of the State' (Art. 15).

16. The youth wings of the MDR *Inkuba* ('Thunder') and of the PSD *Abakombozi* ('The Liberators') both attacked MRND(D) supporters (HRW & FIDH 1999: 55).

17. Although the RPF claimed it had attacked to stop the massacres (see Bertrand 2000: 218), the massacres had by then ceased. It has been argued that the offensive was designed to strengthen the Front's negotiating position at Arusha (Jones 2001: 82–3). It should be recalled that Article VII(2) of the cease-fire agreement (12 July 1992) defined 'cessation of hostilities' not only in terms of military operations and 'harmful civilian operations' (massacres), but also 'denigrating and unfounded propaganda through the mass media' (see Schabas & Imbleau 1997: 251). The latter had continued, even if the other two conditions had effectively ceased by the time of the offensive.

18. MDR: Murego (Executive Secretary) was a personal enemy of Twagiramungu (President). PL: Stanislas Mbonampeka was a rival of the party president Mugenzi. PDC: Gaspard Ruhumuliza (Minister for Tourism) was a challenger of the party's founder, Jean-Népomucène Nayinzira (Prunier 1995: 181).

19. Twagiramungu (MDR), Mugenzi (PL), Frédéric Nzamurambaho (PSD), Jean-Népomuscène Nayinzira (PDC).

20. At the end of November 1993, Nsengiyaremye and Twagiramungu signed a declaration reaffirming the party's de-ethnicised position, stating that the party was called MDR, not 'MDR-Power' or 'MDR-Parmehutu' (Bertrand 2000: 252).

21. In June 1993, Ndadaye was elected by 64.8 per cent of the vote in a free and fair election. The former Tutsi President, Pierre Buyoya, accepted the result, followed by a smooth transfer of power (see Prunier 1995: 199).

22. RTLM claimed that 'After the coup in Burundi, all the Tutsi in Rwanda danced for joy, the Hutu of Rwanda were saddened' (quoted in Article XIX 1996: 90; see Chrétien et al. 1995: 198; 293–4; 322).

23. JDR, *Jeunesse Démocrate Républicaine*, youth wing/militia of the MDR.

24. What Prunier calls the 'CDR constellation' (1995: 182). In May 1992 the Central Committee of the MRND formed the *interahamwe* militia. Initially, the *interahamwe* was used to destabilise Nsengiyaremye's government, later undergoing military training and becoming a 'parallel army'. The CDR formed its own militia, *Impuzamugambi*, in 1993. Both underwent training by the Presidential Guard during 1993. Meanwhile, community-based 'self defence units' were being armed and trained (HRW & FIDH 1999: 106ff) while the *Service Central de Rensignements* (dismantled by Nsengiyaremye's government) had reformed itself into the *Réseau zéro* ('Zero Network') death squads (see Reyntjens 1995b; HRW et al. 1993: 43). All of these groups were provided with arms by a group of FAR officers: *Amasasu*.

25. Interim government formed on 8 April 1994: MDR (3 posts), PSD (3 posts), PL (3 posts), PDC (1 post) (see Guichaoua 1995: 758).

26. For references to *ibyitso* in genocidal propaganda, see Chrétien et al. 1995: 150; 155; 159; 169; 197; 203–5; 230; 292ff; 300; 323; 336.

27. This fictitious plan disseminated in genocidal propaganda (named after Artémon Simbananiye – the Burundian Foreign Minister at the time of the 1972 massacres) claimed that 'Tutsi' intended to 'equalise' the relative size of the ethnic groups by killing Hutu (see Chrétien et al. 1995: 133).

28. Two days after the opposition parties met the RPF delegation in Brussels, the RPA attacked and briefly held the town of Byumba.

29. Kayenzi, a commune in Gitarama *préfecture* where Nsengiyaremye was born.

30. *Amasasu* ('bullets' in Kinyarwanda): 'Alliance of Soldiers Provoked by the Age-old Deceitful Acts of the Unarists', a pro-genocide faction within the army, which, in a letter to Habyarimana in January 1993, called for a 'popular army' of 'robust youth' (the *interahamwe*) (Reyntjens 1994: 118; see Prunier 1995: 169; HRW & FIDH 1999: 103ff).

31. Nkubito had frequently defended Tutsi in court and founded the first Rwandan human rights organisation in September 1990 (ARDHO). As Public Prosecutor, in July 1990 he charged Hassan Ngeze (editor of *Kangura*) with inciting racial hatred. Having refused to prosecute those arrested in October, Nkubito was replaced by Révérien Mukama in November 1990. Denounced in *Kangura* as *ibyitso* (see Chrétien et al. 1995: 290; Article XIX 1996: 66), he was the victim of a grenade attack in November 1993 and was targeted in the genocide, escaping to the French embassy and eventually evacuated to Bujumbura.

CHAPTER 5

1. For a discussion of the Rwandan government's objections to the ICTR, see Dubois 1997; Akhavan 1996; UN 1994p.
2. Although Article I of the 1996 law states that it covers crimes 'since 1 October 1990', Article II categorises crimes committed during the period 'between 1 October 1990 and 31 December 1994'.
3. Jacky Héraud (pilot), Jean-Pierre Minoberry (co-pilot) and Jean-Michel Perrine (engineering officer).
4. Mohamed Othman (acting Chief of Prosecutions February–May 1997) maintains that such a rating system is not used by ICTR investigators (see Cruvellier 2000a).
5. Othman has stated: 'There was never any investigative line on the plane crash' (quoted in Cruvellier 2000a).
6. In April 2000, a Belgian court issued an international arrest warrant against the DRC Minister for Foreign Affairs, Yérodia Abdoulaye Ndombasi, accusing him of 'grave violations of international humanitarian law', especially inciting racial hatred against Tutsi refugees in a speech in August 1998. The arrest warrant was issued in accordance with the Belgian law of 1993 regarding violations of international humanitarian law that gives Belgian courts universal jurisdiction to prosecute suspects for war crimes, regardless of their nationality or where the crimes were committed. In February 2002, the International Court of Justice ordered Belgium to remove the international arrest warrant, arguing that it 'failed to respect the immunity from criminal jurisdiction and the inviolability which [Yérodia] enjoyed under international law' (IRIN 2002i).
7. Until mid-2003, del Ponte acted as chief prosecutor for both the ICTR and the ICTY. In August 2003, the UNSC amended Article 15 of the ICTR's statute so that the ICTR would have its own prosecutor, independent from the ICTY. Consequently, in September 2003, del Ponte was reappointed as prosecutor for the ICTY, while The Gambia's former attorney-general and justice minister, Hassan Bubacar Jallow, was appointed ICTR chief prosecutor for a four-year term.
8. The terms *Bangirima* and Mai Mai refer to militias drawn from the 'autochthonous' groups. Although the two terms are used interchangeably by the population, Mai Mai generally recruit from among Hunde and Nyanga around Masisi and Walikale, while *Bangirima* recruit Hunde, Nyanga and Nande from Rutshuru and Lubero (HRW 1996: 1 n. 2).
9. c719,000 in five camps around Goma (North Kivu); c307,000 in 22 camps around Bukavu (South Kivu); c219,000 (of whom c143,000 were Burundian) in twelve camps around Uvira (UNHCR 1996).
10. According to the charter of the AFDL (dated 18 October 1996), the alliance contained: *Parti de la Révolution Populaire* led by Laurent Kabila; *Conseil National de Résistance pour la Démocratie* led by André Kisase Ngandu; *Alliance Démocratique du Peuple* led by Déogratias Bugera; *Mouvement Révolutionnaire pour la Libération du Zaire* led by Masasu Nindaga (see Emizet 2000: 169 n. 11).
11. 'Article I(f)a. The provisions of this Convention shall not apply to any person with respect to whom there are serious reasons for considering

that: (a) He has committed a crime against peace, a war crime, or a crime against humanity.'

12. Article II common to the four Geneva Conventions of 1949: 'the present Convention shall apply to all cases of declared war or of any other armed conflict which may arise between two or more of the High Contracting parties, *even if the state of war is not recognised by one of them*. The Convention shall apply to all cases of partial or total occupation of the territory of a High Contracting Party' (emphasis added).

13. All quotations from the UNSG's team report (UN 1998a) are my own translations from a French version of the document.

14. Invasion plans were found at Mugunga camp after it was deserted, detailing a plan to invade Rwanda (CNN 1996).

15. Governments of Angola, DRC, Namibia, Rwanda, Uganda, Zimbabwe and the Congolese Rally for Democracy (RCD), Movement for the Liberation of the Congo (MLC).

CHAPTER 6

1. 'The more we can circumscribe what is meant by "objective history" – the more we can reveal what history claims for itself – the easier and clearer it will be to decide what is not history' (Eaglestone 2001: 63).

2. 'Holocaust denial isn't bad history: it isn't history at all' (Eaglestone 2001: 57).

3. 'We cannot know the narrative directly, nor can we know it totally: even the direct survivors can know only one part of what a historian will constitute as [the Holocaust]' (Haidu 1992: 294).

4. The intentional omission of certain events from historical narratives 'inevitably brings to mind the familiar notion of "cognitive dissonance": the perceptual screening of dissonant facts omits critically important bits of evidence from the picture, making it consistent with one's normative assumptions' (Lemarchand 1996: 19; see P. Anderson 1992: 64).

5. According to C. Newbury, 'A Tuutsi [*sic*] man who lost his cattle and was therefore "poor" could come to be considered a Hutu (although this process of declassification often encompassed two or three generations). Similarly, wealthy Hutu who acquired large numbers of cattle and formed linkages with powerful authorities could come to be considered Tuutsi' (1983: 275).

6. *Mwami* Mibambwe Rutarindwa (enthroned in 1865), was killed along with his ritual supporters, protectors, his wife and three children in November 1896 (C. Newbury 1998: 23). The conspirators were led by Kanjogera, Mibambwe's adoptive queen mother and two of her brothers. The '*coup*' took place in the context of a political struggle between the Bega and Banyiginya clans. Following the '*coup*' the Banyiginya clan was systematically purged of its most influential elements (see Lemarchand 1970a: 57ff). For reference to the '*coup*' in genocidal propaganda, see Chrétien et al. 1995: 157.

7. German explorers 'discovered' Rwanda in 1894. Following World War I, Belgium took over the administration of Rwanda. In 1922, the League of Nations put the kingdom of Ruanda-Urundi under the trusteeship of Belgium.

8. C. Newbury makes the same point: 'Before the mid-twentieth century, crises of governance in Rwanda often had violent consequences, but the violence was limited to a relatively small group of key participants in the competition, often members of the same ethnic group. The losers – usually highly placed political actors – often faced death or exile. Political violence was more often intra-ethnic than inter-ethnic ... In light of recent tendencies to see all conflict in Rwanda as tribal warfare, it is important to note that these were not ethnic conflicts; rather, they were conflicts among competing Tutsi lineages for control of the state' (1998: 17).

9. The *Société des Missionaires d'Afrique* founded in 1868 by Mgr Lavigerie.

10. Classe (1930) wrote: 'The greatest harm the government could possibly inflict on itself and on the country would be to do away with the Mututsi caste. Such a revolution would lead the country straight into anarchy and towards a viciously anti-European communism.'

11. Referring to a pastoral letter, 11 February 1959, 'Charity before all things' (Perraudin 1959).

12. Referring to the forced abdication of *mwami* Musinga in 1931.

13. The official newspaper of the Roman Catholic Church in Rwanda founded in 1933.

14. Individuals become 'metonyms of history' (Sahlins 1985: 35) that 'embody and motivate processes whose origins we, from our standpoint, ascribe to more dispersed causes' (Comaroff & Comaroff 1992: 38).

15. Before independence, UNAR's anti-colonial stance had been supported by socialist/communist countries at the UN (Reyntjens 1985: 448; 459). After independence, the Republic of China, the USSR, Eastern *bloc* countries and Cuba provided funds for military purposes (ibid. 459). Paradoxically, in a letter in September 1959, the Roman Catholic bishops not only accused UNAR of being under 'communist influence' but that the UNAR resembled 'national socialism' and was under the influence of 'Islamic fundamentalism' (see Linden 1977: 266).

16. *Mwami* Mutara Rudahigwa died (officially of a cerebral haemorrhage) after seeing a Belgian doctor in Bujumbura (Linden 1977: 262; see Lemarchand 1970b: 900). Paradoxically, genocidal propaganda blamed his death on *'the* Tutsi' (see Chrétien et al. 1995: 129; 335).

17. According to Harroy, 1959 was an 'assisted revolution' (1984: 292).

18. Officially, 10 per cent of secondary schools places and administrative posts were reserved for Tutsi.

19. See Kayibanda (1964). For a discussion of how this letter was distorted by genocidal propaganda, see HRW & FIDH 1999: 106; Chrétien et al. 1995: 122.

20. Kayibanda died in detention in 1976, 'most likely starved to death by his gaolers' (Prunier 1995: 82). The former Minister for International Co-operation, Augustin Muyaneza also died (or was killed) in detention sometime between 1974 and 1977 (ibid.).

21. During the rule of Habyarimana, there were no Tutsi *préfets* or *bourgmestres*. There was one Tutsi officer in the FAR, two Tutsi members of Parliament (out of 70) and only one Tutsi minister out of a cabinet of 25–30 persons (Prunier 1995: 75).

Bibliography

Achebe, C. (1988) 'An image of Africa' in Achebe, C. *Hopes and Impediments* (London: Doubleday)

African Rights (AR) (1995) *Rwanda. Dearth Despair and Defiance.* Revised edn (London: African Rights)

—— (1996) *Rwanda: Killing the Evidence, Murder, Attacks, Arrests and Intimidation of Survivors and Witnesses* (London: African Rights)

—— (2001) *Colonel Tharcisse Renzaho: A Soldier in the DRC* (London: African Rights)

—— (2002) *Tribute to Courage* (Kigali: African Rights)

Afrik'Netpress (2000) 'Un rapport confidentiel explosif sur la mort d'Habyarimana', 21 June

Akhavan, P. (1996) 'The International Criminal Tribunal for Rwanda: The Politics and Pragmatics of Punishment', *American Journal of International Law*, Vol. 90, No. 3

Allen, T. (1996) 'A flight from refuge' in Allen, T. (ed.) *In Search of Cool Ground: War, Flight and Homecoming in Northeast Africa* (Oxford: James Currey)

Alvarez, A. (2001) 'Justifying Genocide: The Role of Professionals in Legitimizing Mass Killing', *Idea: A Journal of Social Issues*, Vol. 6, No. 1

Amnesty International (AI) (1992) *Rwanda: Persecution of Tutsi Minority and Repression of Government Critics 1990–1992.* May 1992. AI Index AFR 47/002/1992 (London: Amnesty International)

—— (1993) *Zaïre: Violence Against Democracy.* September 1993. AI Index AFR/61/11/63 (London: Amnesty International)

—— (1994) *Rwanda: Reports of Killings and Abductions by the Rwandese Patriotic Army, April–August 1994.* October 1994. AI Index AFR47/16/94. <www. amnesty.org/ailib/aipub/1994/AFR/471694.AFR.txt> (London: Amnesty International)

—— (1995a) *Rwanda: Crying Out for Justice.* April 1995. AI Index AFR47/05/95. <www.amnesty.org/ailib/aipub/1995/AFR/470595.AFR.txt> (London: Amnesty International)

—— (1995b) *Rwanda: Arming the Perpetrators of the Genocide.* June 1995. AI Index AFR02/14/95 (London: Amnesty International)

—— (1996a) *Rwanda and Burundi: The Return Home: Rumours and Realities.* April 1996. AI Index AFR02/01/96. <www.web.amnesty.org/ai.nsf/index/ AFR020011996#TRR> (London: Amnesty International)

—— (1996b) *Rwanda: Alarming Resurgence of Killings.* August 1996. AI Index AFR47/13/96. <www.web.amnesty.org/ai.nsf/index/AFR470131996> (London: Amnesty International)

—— (1996c) *Zaïre: Amnesty International Condemns Human Rights Violations Against Tutsi.* September 1996. AI Index AFR62/13/96. <www.amnesty.it/ news/1996/16201396.htm> (London: Amnesty International)

—— (1996d) *Zaïre: Lawlessness and Insecurity in North and South-Kivu.* November 1996. AI Index AFR62/14/96. <www.web.amnesty.org/ai.nsf/ index/AFR620141996> (London: Amnesty International)

—— (1996e) *Great Lakes: Amnesty International Condemns Massacre of Around 500 Refugees In Eastern Zaïre*. 26 November 1996. AI Index AFR02/29/96. <www.amnesty.it/news/1996/10202996.htm> (London: Amnesty International)

—— (1997a) *Zaïre: Rape, Killings and Other Human Rights Violations by the Security Forces*. 19 February 1997. AI Index AFR62/006/1997. <www. web.amnesty.org/ai.nsf/index/AFR620061997> (London: Amnesty International)

—— (1997b) Amnesty International's Memorandum to the UN Security Council: Appeal for a Commission of Inquiry to Investigate Reports of Atrocities in Eastern Zaïre. AI Index AFR6/11/97 (London: Amnesty International)

—— (1997c) *DRC: Deadly Alliances in Congolese Forests*. 3 December 1997. AI Index AFR62/033/1997. <www.web.amnesty.org/ai.nsf/index/AFR 620331997> (London: Amnesty International)

Anderson, B. (1983) *Imagined Communities: Reflections on the Origin and Spread of Nationalism* (London: Verso)

Anderson, P. (1992) 'On Emplotment: Two Kinds of Ruin' in Friedlander, S. (ed.) *Probing the Limits of Representation: Nazism and the 'Final Solution'* (Cambridge MA: Harvard University Press)

Appadurai, A. (1981) 'The Past as a Scarce Resource', *Man*, Vol. 16, No. 2

—— (1996) *Modernity at Large: Cultural Dimensions of Globalization* (Minneapolis: University of Minnesota Press)

—— (1998) 'Dead Certainty: Ethnic Violence in the Era of Globalization', *Development and Change*, Vol. 29, No. 4

Apter, D. E. (1997) 'Political Violence in Analytical Perspective' in Apter, D. E. (ed.) *The Legitimization of Violence* (London: Macmillan)

Ardener, E. (1989a) 'Language, ethnicity and population' in Chapman, M. (ed.) *The Voice of Prophesy and Other Essays* (Oxford: Blackwell)

—— (1989b) 'Social anthropology and population' in Chapman, M. (ed.) *The Voice of Prophesy and Other Essays* (Oxford: Blackwell)

Arendt, H. (1963) *Eichmann in Jerusalem: A Report on the Banality of Evil* (New York: Viking Press)

Argyrou, V. (2002) *Anthropology and the Will to Meaning: A Postcolonial Critique* (London: Pluto)

Article XIX (1996) *Broadcasting Genocide: Censorship, Propaganda and State-Sponsored Violence in Rwanda 1990–1994* (London: Article XIX)

Australian Broadcasting Corporation (ABC) (1999) 'Chris Masters interviews former Australian war crimes investigator Michael Hourigan', *Four Corners*, broadcast 1 March 1999. <www.abc.net.au/4corners/stories/s20012.htm>

Baker, L. (1980) *Days of Sorrow and Pain: Leo Baeck and the Berlin Jews* (Oxford: Oxford University Press)

Bardakjian, K. (1985) *Hitler and the Armenian Genocide* (Cambridge MA: Zoryan Institute)

Barth, F. (1969) 'Introduction' in Barth, F. (ed.) *Ethnic Groups and Boundaries: The Social Organisation of Culture Difference* (London: Allen & Unwin)

Bartov, O. (1998) 'Defining Enemies, Making Victims: Germans, Jews, and the Holocaust', *American Historical Review*, Vol. 103, No. 3

Bauer, Y. (1973) *They Chose Life: Jewish Resistance in the Holocaust* (New York: The American Jewish Committee)

—— (1978) *The Holocaust in Historical Perspective* (Seattle: University of Washington Press)

—— (1979) 'Right and Wrong Teaching of the Holocaust' in Knopp, J. Z. (ed.) *The International Conference on Lessons of the Holocaust* (Philadelphia: National Institute on the Holocaust)

—— (1984) 'The Place of the Holocaust in Contemporary History' in Frankel, J. (ed.) *Studies in Contemporary Jewry, Volume I* (Bloomington: Indiana University Press)

—— (1987) 'On the Place of the Holocaust in History: In Honour of Franklin H. Littell', *Holocaust and Genocide Studies*, Vol. 2, No. 8

—— (1998) 'Comparison of Genocides' in Chorbajian, L. and G. Shirinian (eds) *Studies in Comparative Genocide* (Basingstoke: Macmillan Press)

—— (2001) *Rethinking Genocide* (London: Yale University Press)

Berger, P. L. (1984 [1963]) *Invitation to Sociology: A Humanistic Perspective* (Harmondsworth: Penguin)

Berkeley, B. (2001) *The Graves Are Not Yet Full: Race, Tribe and Power in the Heart of Africa* (New York: Basic Books)

Bertrand, J. (2000) *Le Rwanda, le piège de l'histoire. L'échec de l'opposition démocratique (1990–1994)* (Paris: Karthala)

Bideri, J. (2000) 'Press statement: Response to the National Post article of 1 March 2000 "Explosive leak on Rwanda genocide"'. Office Rwandais d'Information (ORINFOR), 6 March

Billig, M. (1987) *Arguing and Thinking – A Rhetorical Approach to Social Psychology* (Cambridge: Cambridge University Press)

Boas, F. (1943) 'Individual, Family, Population and Race', *Proceedings of the American Philosophical Society*, Vol. 87, No. 2

Bock, K. (1979) 'Theories of Progress, Development and Evolution' in Bottomore, T. and R. Nisbet (eds) *A History of Sociological Analysis* (London: Heinemann)

Bond, C. (1996) 'UN officials locate throngs of missing Rwandans', CNN, 21 November. <www.cnn.com/WORLD/9611/21/zaire>

Bond, G. and A. Gilliam (1994) *Social Construction of the Past: Representations as Power* (London: Routledge)

Borneman, J. (1997) *Settling Accounts: Violence, Justice and Accountability in Postsocialist Europe* (Princeton: Princeton University Press)

Bourdieu, P. (1977) *Outline of a Theory of Practice* (Cambridge: Cambridge University Press)

Bourdieu, P. and J.-C. Passeron (1977) *Reproduction in Education Society and Culture*. Trans. R. Nice (London: Sage)

Bowen, M., G. Freeman and K. Miller (1973) *Passing By: The United States and Genocide in Burundi, 1972* (New York: Carnegie Endowment for International Peace)

Braeckman, C. (1994) *Rwanda, Histoire d'un génocide* (Paris: Fayard)

—— (1996) 'Paul Kagame: A propos du retour des réfugiés et de la situation dans l'est du Zaïre' *Le Soir* 2 December

Brauman R., S. Smith and C. Vidal (2000) 'Rwanda: Politique de terreur, privilège d'impunité', *La Revue Esprit*, August/September. <http://membres.lycos.fr/obsac/OBSV3N30-Rwanda_terreur.html>

Breitman, R. (1991) *The Architect of Genocide: Himmler and the Final Solution* (New York: Alfred A. Knopf)

Bringa, T. (2002) 'Averted Gaze: Genocide in Bosnia-Herzegovina, 1992–1995' in Hinton, A. L. (ed.) *Annihilating Difference: The Anthropology of Genocide* (Berkeley: University of California Press)

Browning, C. R. (1992a) *Ordinary Men: Reserve Police Battalion 101 and The Final Solution in Poland* (New York: HarperCollins)

—— (1992b) 'German Memory, Judicial Interrogation, and Historical Reconstruction: Writing Perpetrator History from Postwar Testimony' in Friedlander, S. (ed.) *Probing the Limits of Representation: Nazism and the 'Final Solution'* (Cambridge MA: Harvard University Press)

Cargas, H. (1986) 'An Interview with Elie Wiesel', *Holocaust and Genocide Studies*, Vol. 5

Carlsson, I., H. Sung-Joo and R. Kupolati (1999) *Report of the Independent Inquiry into the Actions of the United Nations During the 1994 Genocide in Rwanda* (New York: United Nations)

Carpenter, R. H. (1995) *History as Rhetoric: Style, Narrative, and Persuasion* (Columbia SC: University of South Carolina Press)

Chalk, F. (1989) 'Genocide in the 20th Century: Definitions of Genocide and their Implications for Predication and Prevention', *Holocaust and Genocide Studies*, Vol. 4, No. 2

Chalk, F. and K. Jonassohn (1990) 'The Conceptual Framework' in Chalk, F. and K. Jonassohn (eds) *The History and Sociology of Genocide: Analyses and Case Studies* (London: Yale University Press)

Chapman, M., E. Tonkin and M. McDonald (1989) 'Introduction' in Tonkin, E., M. McDonald and M. Chapman (eds) *History and Ethnicity* (London: Routledge)

Chilton, P. A. (1997) 'The Role of Language in Human Conflict: Prolegomena to the Investigation of Language as a Factor in Conflict Causation and Resolution', *Current Issues in Language and Society*, Vol. 4, No. 3

Chrétien, J.-P. (1980) 'Vocabulaire et concepts tirés de la féodalité occidentale et administration indirect en Afrique Orientale' in Nordman, D. and J.-P. Raison (eds) *Sciences de l'Homme et conquête coloniale: Constitution et usage des Sciences Humaines en Afrique* (Paris: Presses de l'Ecole Normale Supérieure)

—— (1985) 'Hutu et Tutsi au Rwanda et au Burundi' in Amselle, J.-L. and E. M'Bokolo (eds) *Au Coeur de l'Ethnie: ethnies, tribalisme et état en Afrique* (Paris: Éditions la Découverte)

—— (1991) '"Presse libre" et propaganda raciste au Rwanda', *Politique Africaine*, Vol. 42

—— (1997) *Le défi de l'ethnisme; Rwanda et Burundi, 1990–1996* (Paris: Éditions Karthala)

Chrétien, J.-P., J.-F. Dupaquier, M. Kabanda and J. Ngarambe (eds) (1995) *Rwanda: Les Médias du génocide* (Paris: Éditions Karthala with Reporters sans frontières)

Classe, L. (1930) 'Pour moderniser le Ruanda', *L'Essor colonial et maritime*, Vol. 489

Clifford, J. (1986) 'Introduction: Partial Truths' in Clifford, J. and G. Marcus (eds) *Writing Culture: The Poetics and Politics of Ethnography* (Cambridge MA: Harvard University Press)

—— (1988) *The Predicament of Culture: Twentieth Century Ethnography, Literature and Art* (Cambridge MA: Harvard University Press)

Clinton, W. J. (1998) 'Speech at Kanombe airport, Kigali, 25 March 1998', *New Times* 23–31 March

CNN (1996) 'Zaïre humanitarian mission to go on. Officials say more refugees need help', CNN, 19 November. <www.cnn.com/WORLD/9611/19/zaire/index.html>

Codere, H. (1973) *The Biography of an African Society, Rwanda 1900–1960: Based on Forty-Eight Rwandan Autobiographies* (Tervuren: Musée de l'Afrique Centrale)

Cohen, A. P. (1985) *The Symbolic Construction of Community* (London: Routledge)

Cohen, R. (1978) 'Ethnicity: Problem and Focus in Anthropology', *Annual Review of Anthropology*, Vol. 7

Cohn, N. (1980) *Warrant for Genocide: The Myth of the Jewish World Conspiracy and the Protocols of the Elders of Zion* (New York: Scholars Press)

Comaroff, J. (1985) *Body of Power, Spirit of Resistance: The Culture and History of a South African People* (Chicago: University of Chicago Press)

Comaroff, J. and J. L. Comaroff (1992) *Ethnography and the Historical Imagination* (Boulder: Westview Press)

Comaroff, J. L. (1987) 'Of Totemism and Ethnicity: Consciousness, Practice and the Signs of Inequality', *Ethnos*, Vol. 52

Connerton, P. (1989) *How Societies Remember* (Cambridge: Cambridge University Press)

Conrad, J. (2000 [1899]) *Heart of Darkness* (London: Penguin)

Coser, L. (ed.) (1992) *Maurice Halbwachs on Collective Memory* (Chicago: University of Chicago Press)

Cros, M.-F. (1992) 'Témoignage: Une vie de Hutu-Tutsi', *Libre Belgique*, 11 March

Cruvellier, T. (2000a) '"Explosive Leak" or Wet Firecracker?', *Diplomatie Judiciaire*, 9 May. <www.diplomatiejudiciaire.com/UK/Tpiruk/TPIRUK14.htm>

—— (2000b) 'L'enquête sur l'attentat hante le TPIR', *Diplomatie Judiciaire*, 19 May. <www.diplomatiejudiciaire.com/Tpir/Parquet30.htm>

—— (2001) 'Carla del Ponte sur l'offensive', *Diplomatie Judiciaire*, 8 April. <www.diplomatiejudiciaire.com/Tpir/Parquet36.htm>

Cyrus-Reed, W. (1996) 'Exile, Reform, and the Rise of the Rwandan Patriotic Front', *The Journal of Modern African Studies*, Vol. 34, No. 3

d'Hertefelt, M. (1971) *Les clans du Rwanda ancien: éléments d'ethnosociologie et d'ethnohistoire* (Tervuren: Musée Royal de l'Afrique Centrale)

Dadrian, V. N (1995) *The History of the Armenian Genocide: Ethnic Conflict from the Balkans to Anatolia to the Caucasus* (Oxford: Berghahn Books)

Das, V. (1996) 'Language and Body: Transactions in the Construction of Pain', *Daedalus*, Vol. 125, No. 1

de Heusch, L. (1995) 'Rwanda: Responsibilities for Genocide', *Anthropology Today*, Vol. 11, No. 4

De Lacger, L. (1939a) *Ruanda. Vol.1, Le Ruanda ancien* (Namur: Grand Lacs)

—— (1939b) *Ruanda. Vol.2, Le Ruanda moderne* (Namur: Grand Lacs)

—— (1959) *Le Ruanda: Aperçu historique* (Kabgayi: Imprimérie de Kabgayi)

De Sousa Santos, B. (1987) 'Law: a map of misreading: towards a postmodern conception of law', *Journal of Law and Society*, Vol. 14

des Forges, A. (1972) 'Defeat is the Only Bad News: Rwanda under Musinga, 1896–1931', Yale University: Ph.D. Thesis

—— (1995) 'The Ideology of Genocide', *Issue: Journal of Opinion*, Vol. 23, No. 2

—— (2003) 'Will the RPF be tried for alleged atrocities?' Presentation at *Transitional Justice in Rwanda: Lessons and Challenges*, 23 May 2003, British Institute of International and Comparative Law

Dorsey, M. (2000) 'Violence and Power-Building in Post Genocide Rwanda' in Doom, R. and J. Gorus (eds) *Politics of Identity and Economics of Conflict in the Great Lakes Region* (Brussels: VUB University Press)

Drogin, R. (1996) 'Debate continues on number of refugees remaining in Zaïre', *Los Angeles Times*, 22 November

Drost, P. N. (1959) *The Crime of State, Vol. 2. Genocide* (Leyden: A. W. Sythoff)

Du Preez, P. (1994) *Genocide: The Psychology of Mass Murder* (London: Bowerdean)

Dubois, O. (1997) 'Rwanda's national criminal courts and the International Tribunal', *International Review of the Red Cross*, Vol. 321

Eaglestone, R. (2001) *Postmodernism and Holocaust Denial* (Cambridge: Icon Books)

The Economist (2000) 'Editorial: Hopeless Africa' *The Economist*, 13 May

Edwards, S. (2000a) 'UN probes leading Rwandan officials – Investigators "scared stiff": Tutsi suspects hold most senior government posts', *National Post*, 21 February

—— (2000b) '"Explosive" leak on Rwanda genocide Informants told UN investigators they were on squad that killed Rwanda's president – and a foreign government helped', *National Post*, 1 March

Eltringham, N. P. (2000) 'Institutions and individuals: The Rwandan Church and the discourse of guilt' in Goyvaerts, D. (ed.) *Conflict and Ethnicity in Central Africa* (Tokyo: University of Foreign Studies)

Emizet, K. N. F. (2000) 'The massacre of refugees in Congo: a case of UN peacekeeping failure and international law', *Journal of Modern African Studies*, Vol. 38, No. 2

Eriksen, T. H. (1993) *Ethnicity and Nationalism: Anthropological Perspectives* (London: Pluto Press)

—— (1996) 'The epistemological status of the concept of ethnicity'. <http://folk.uio.no/geirthe/Status_of_ethnicity.html>

Errington, S. (1979) 'Some comments on style in the meaning of the past', *Journal of Asian Studies*, Vol. 38, No. 2

Evans, R. (1997) *In Defence of History* (London: Granta)

Evans, W. (1980) 'From the land of Canaan to the land of Guinea', *American Historical Review*, Vol. 85, No. 1

Evans-Pritchard, E. E. (1940) *The Nuer: A Description of the Modes of Livelihood and Political Institutions of a Nilotic People* (Oxford: Oxford University Press)

Fairhead, J. (1989) *Food Security in North and South Kivu (Zaïre): Final Consultancy Report* (Oxford: Oxfam)

Fardon, R. (1987) '"African Ethnogenesis": Limits to the Comparability of Ethnic Phenomena' in Holy, L. (ed.) *Comparative Anthropology* (Oxford: Blackwell)

—— (1999) 'Ethnic Pervasion' in Allen, T. and J. Seaton (eds) *The Media of Conflict: War Reporting and Representations of Ethnic Violence* (London: Zed Books)

Fein, H. (1993) *Genocide: A Sociological Perspective* (London: Sage)

—— (1994) 'Genocide, Terror, Life Integrity, and War Crimes' in Andreopoulos, G. J. (ed.) *Genocide, Conceptual and Historical Dimensions* (Philadelphia: University of Pennsylvania Press)

—— (1998) 'Testing Theories Brutally: Armenia (1915), Bosnia (1992) and Rwanda (1994)' in Chorbajian, L. and G. Shirinian (eds) *Studies in Comparative Genocide* (Basingstoke: Macmillan Press)

Filmer, P. (1972) 'On Harold Garfinkel's Ethnomethodology' in Filmer, P., M. Phillipson, D. Silverman, and D. Walsh (eds) *New Directions in Sociological Theory* (London: Collier Macmillan)

Finnegan, R. (1988) *Literacy and Orality: Studies in the Technology of Communication* (Oxford: Blackwell)

Fondation Hirondelle (2002i) 'UN Prosecutor Rallies UK Support to Investigate Rwandan Army', *Hirondelle News Agency*, 3 December. <www.globalpolicy.org/security/issues/rwanda/2002/1204coop.htm>

—— (2002ii) 'Exclusive Interview with Carla del Ponte', *Hirondelle News Agency*, 19 December. <http://allafrica.com/stories/200212190040.html>

Fowler, R. (1991) *Language in the News: Discourse and Ideology in the Press* (London: Routledge)

Freeman, M. (1991) 'The Theory and Prevention of Genocide', *Holocaust and Genocide Studies*, Vol. 6, No. 2

French, H. W. (1998) 'Reports point to mass killings of refugees in Congo', *New York Times*, 27 May

Friedlander, H. (1980) 'The Manipulation of Language' in Friedlander, H. and S. Milton (eds) *The Holocaust, Ideology, Bureaucracy and Genocide* (New York: Kraus International)

Friedlander, S. (1992) 'Introduction' in Friedlander, S. (ed.) *Probing the Limits of Representation: Nazism and the 'Final Solution'* (Cambridge MA: Harvard University Press)

Gachinya, F. (1996a) 'The Tutsi Republic: Will it do Better?', *New Times*, July

—— (1996b) 'Let Our People Go!', *New Times*, October

Gahama, J. (1983) *Le Burundi sous administration belge: La période du mandat, 1919–1939* (Paris: Khartala)

Gatwa, T. (1998) 'The Churches and Ethnic Ideology in the Rwandan Crisis (1900–1994)', University of Edinburgh: PhD Thesis

Gaye, A. (2000) 'Paul Kagame: My Side of the Story', *West Africa Magazine*. <www.rwanda1.com/government/interviews_my_side.htm>

Geertz, C. (1983) *Local Knowledge* (New York: Basic Books)

Gibney, M. (1999) 'Kosovo and beyond: popular and unpopular refugees', *Forced Migration Review* 5. <www.fmreview.org/FMRpdfs/FMR05/fmr510.pdf>

Goldhagen, D. (1996) *Hitler's Willing Executioners: Ordinary Germans and the Holocaust* (London: Vintage)

Gourevitch, P. (2000 [1998]) *We Wish to Inform You that Tomorrow We Will be Killed With our Families: Stories from Rwanda.* Paperback edn. (London: Picador)

Gowing, N. (1998) 'New Challenges and Problems for Information Management in Complex Emergencies: Ominous Lessons from the Great Lakes and Eastern Zaïre in Late 1996 and Early 1997'. Draft paper presented at *Dispatches from Disaster Zones: The Reporting of Humanitarian Emergencies* London, 27–28 May 1998

Gravel, P. (1968) *Remera: A Community in Eastern Rwanda* (The Hague: Mouton)

Greenberg, S. B. (1980) *Race and State in Capitalist Development* (New Haven: Yale University Press)

Grellier, A. (2002) 'Interview with Carla del Ponte', *Diplomatie Judiciaire*, 4 December. <www.diplomatiejudiciaire.com/UK/Tpiruk/TPIRUK23.htm>

Gross, J. T. (2001) *Neighbors: The Destruction of The Jewish Community in Jedwabne, Poland* (Princeton: Princeton University Press)

Guichaoua, A. (1992) *The Problem of the Rwandese Refugees and the Banyarwanda Populations in the Great Lakes Region* (Geneva: ILO-UNHCR)

—— (ed.) (1995) *Les crises politiques au Burundi et au Rwanda (1993–1994): Analyses, faits, et documents* (Paris: Éditions Karthala)

Haidu, P. (1992) 'The Dialectics of Unspeakability: Language, Silence, and the Narratives of Desubjectification' in Friedlander, S. (ed.) *Probing the Limits of Representation: Nazism and the 'Final Solution'* (Cambridge MA: Harvard University Press)

Hajer, M. (1995) *The Politics of Environmental Discourse: Ecological Modernisation and the Policy Process* (Oxford: Clarendon Press)

Harff, B. (1987) 'The Etiology of Genocide' in Wallimann, I. and N. Dobkowski (eds) *Genocide and the Modern Age: Etiology and Case Studies of Mass Death* (New York: Greenwood)

Harff, B. and Gurr, T. (1988) 'Research Note: "Toward Empirical Theory of Genocides and Politicides: Identification and Measurement of Cases since 1945"', *International Studies Quarterly*, Vol. 32

Harroy, J.-P. (1984) *Rwanda: De la féodalité à la démocratie (Souvenir d'un compagnon de la marche du Rwanda vers la démocratie et l'independance)* (Brussels: Hayez)

Hastrup, K. (1992) 'Introduction' in Hastrup, K. (ed.) *Other Histories* (London: Routledge)

Hawk, B. (ed.) (1992) *Africa's Media Image* (Westport: Praeger)

Hayden, R. M. (1996) 'Imagined communities and real victims: Self-determination and ethnic cleansing in Yugoslavia', American Ethnologist, Vol. 23, No. 4

Hazan, P. (1998) 'Les crimes commis contre les Hutus ne doivent pas demeurer impunis', *Le Temps*, 18 September

Hilberg, R. (1985 [1961]) *The Destruction of the European Jews* (New York: Holmes & Meier)

Hinton, A. L. (1998) 'Why did the Nazis kill? Anthropology, genocide and the Goldhagen Controversy', *Anthropology Today*, Vol. 14, No. 5

—— (2002) 'Introduction: Genocide and Anthropology' in A. L. Hinton (ed.) *Genocide: An Anthropological Reader* (Oxford: Blackwell)

Hirsch, H. (1995) *Genocide and the Politics of Memory: Studying Death to Preserve Life* (Chapel Hill and London: The University of North Carolina Press)

Holy, L. (1987) 'Introduction: Description, Generalisation and Comparison: Two Paradigms' in Holy, L. (ed.) *Comparative Anthropology* (Oxford: Blackwell)

Holy, L. and M. Stuchlik (1983) *Actions, Norms and Representations: Foundations of Anthropological Inquiry* (Cambridge: Cambridge University Press)

Horowitz, D. (1991) *A Democratic South Africa?: Constitutional Engineering in a Divided Society* (Berkeley: University of California Press)

Hovannisian, R. G. (ed.) (1999) *Remembrance and Denial: The Case of the Armenian Genocide* (Detroit: Wayne State University Press)

Human Rights Watch (HRW) (1993) *Beyond the Rhetoric: Continuing Human Rights Abuses in Rwanda*. June 1993 (New York: Human Rights Watch)

—— (1994) *The Aftermath of Genocide in Rwanda: Absence of Prosecution, Continued Killings*. September 1994 (New York: Human Rights Watch)

—— (1995) *Rwanda/Zaïre: Rearming with Impunity. International Support for the Perpetrators of the Rwandan Genocide*. May 1995 (New York: Human Rights Watch)

—— (1996) *Forced to Flee, Violence Against the Tutsi in Zaïre*. July 1996. <www.hrw.org/reports/1996/Zaire.htm> (New York: Human Rights Watch)

—— (2000a) *Rwanda: The Search for Security and Human Rights Abuses*. April 2000. <www.hrw.org/reports/2000/rwanda> (New York: Human Rights Watch)

—— (2000b) *Democratic Republic of Congo: Eastern Congo Ravaged: Killing Civilians and Silencing Protest*. May 2000. <www.hrw.org/reports/2000/drc/Drc005.htm> (New York: Human Rights Watch)

—— (2002a) Letter sent to US Ambassador John Negroponte, President of UN Security Council. 9 August 2002 (New York: Human Rights Watch)

—— (2002b) *Action Urged Regarding Non-Co-Operation with ICTR and ICTY: Letter to Security Council Members*. 25 October 2002 (New York: Human Rights Watch)

Human Rights Watch (HRW) and Fédération Internationale des Ligues des Droits de l'Homme (FIDH) (1996) *Shattered Lives, Sexual Violence during the Rwandan Genocide and Its Aftermath*. <www.hrw.org/reports/1996/Rwanda.htm> (New York: Human Rights Watch)

—— (1997) *Democratic Republic of the Congo, what Kabila is Hiding: Civilian Killings and Impunity in Congo*. October 1997. <www.hrw.org/reports97/congo/> (New York: Human Rights Watch)

—— (1999) *'Leave None to Tell the Story': Genocide in Rwanda* (New York: Human Rights Watch)

Human Rights Watch (HRW), Fédération Internationale des Ligues des Droits de l'Homme (FIDH), Interafrican Union for Human and People's Rights and The International Center for Human Rights and Democratic Development (1993). *Report of the International Commission of Investigation on Human Rights Violations in Rwanda since October 1, 1990*. March 1993. (New York: Human Rights Watch)

Human Rights Watch (HRW), Fédération Internationale des Ligues des Droits de l'Homme (FIDH), Ligue des Droits de la Personne dans la Region des Grands Lacs (LDGL), Organisation Mondiale Contre la Torture (OMCT), Centre National pour la Cooperation au Développement (CNCD), Nationaal Centrum Voor Ontwikkelingssamenwerking (NCOS) and Novib (1994). *Rapport Final de la Commission Internationale d'Enquête sur les Violations des Droits de l'Homme au Burundi depuis le 21 Octobre 1993*. 5 July 1994. (New York: Human Rights Watch)

Integrated Regional Information Network (IRIN): *see* separate list at the end of this Bibliography

International Criminal Tribunal for Rwanda (ICTR) (1998) The Prosecutor vs. Jean-Paul Akayesu: Judgement. 2 September 1998 (Arusha: ICTR)

—— (1999) The Prosecutor vs. Clément Kayishema and Obed Ruzindana: Judgement. 21 May 1999 (Arusha: ICTR)

—— (2002) Prosecution Opening Statement. Prosecutor vs. Bagasora, Nsengiyumva, Kabiligi, Ntabakuze. 2 April 2002. <www.ictr.org/wwwroot/ENGLISH/PRESSREL/2002/312chile&delponte.htm#_Toc5768077>

International Crisis Group (ICG) (1999) *Five Years After the Genocide in Rwanda: Justice in Question* (Brussels: International Crisis Group)

—— (2001) *The International Criminal Tribunal for Rwanda: Justice Delayed* (Brussels: International Crisis Group)

—— (2002a) *Tribunal Pénal International Pour le Rwanda: Le Compte à Rebours* (Brussels: International Crisis Group)

—— (2002b) *Rwanda at the End of Transition: A Necessary Political Liberalisation* (Brussels: International Crisis Group)

International Rescue Committee (IRC) (2001) *Mortality in Eastern Democratic Republic of Congo*. <http: //intranet.theirc.org/docs/mortII_report.pdf>

Isajiw, W. W. (1974) 'Definitions of ethnicity', *Ethnicity*, Vol. 1

Jacob, I. (1984) *Dictionnaire Rwandais–Français: Extrait du dictionnaire de l'Institut National de Recherche Scientifique* (Kigali: L'Imprimerie Scolaire)

James, W. (1996) 'Uduk Resettlement' in Allen, T. (ed.) *In Search of Cool Ground: War, Flight and Homecoming in Northeast Africa* (Oxford: James Currey)

Jay, M. (1992) 'Of Plots, Witnesses, and Judgements' in Friedlander, S. (ed.) *Probing the Limits of Representation: Nazism and the 'Final Solution'* (Cambridge MA: Harvard University Press)

Jefremovas, V. (1991) 'Petty Commodity Production and Capitalist Enterprise: Brick and Roof Tile Making in Rwanda', University of Toronto: Ph.D. Thesis

—— (1995) 'Acts of Human Kindness: Tutsi, Hutu and the Genocide', *Issue: Journal of Opinion*, Vol. 23, No. 2

Jennings, C. (1998) *Across the Red River: Rwanda, Burundi and the Heart of Darkness* (London: Weidenfeld & Nicolson)

Jere-Malanda, R. (2000) Interview with Paul Kagame, *New African Magazine*, July 2000. <www.rwanda1.com/government/interviews_newafricanmag.htm>

Joint Evaluation of Emergency Assistance to Rwanda (JEEAR) (1996a) 'Chapter 3: Humanitarian Aid and Effects' in Eriksson, J. (ed.) *The International Response to Conflict and Genocide: Lessons from the Rwanda Experience: Synthesis Report*. <www.reliefweb.int/library/nordic/book5/pb025e.html> (Copenhagen: Ministry of Foreign Affairs)

—— (1996b) 'Chapter 4: Crisis and Withdrawal (6 April 1994–21 April 1994)' in Adelman, H. and A. Suhrke (eds) *The International Response to Conflict and Genocide: Lessons from the Rwanda Experience: Study 2: Early Warning and Conflict Management*. <www.reliefweb.int/library/nordic/book2/pb021h. html> (Copenhagen: Ministry of Foreign Affairs)

Jones, B. D. (2001) *Peacemaking in Rwanda: The Dynamics of Failure* (London: Lynne Rienner)

Kagabo, J. and V. Mudandagizi (1974) 'Complainte des gens de l'argile', *Cahiers d'Études Africaines*, Vol. 14, No. 53

Kagabo, J. and C. Vidal (1994) 'L'extermination des Rwandais tutsi', *Cahiers d'Études Africaines*, Vol. 34, No. 4

Kagame, A. (1952) *Le Code des Institutions Politiques du Rwanda Précolonial* (Brussels: IRCB)

—— (1954) *Les organisations socio-familiales de l'ancien Rwanda* (Brussels: Académie Royale des Sciences Coloniales)

—— (1958) *L'Histoire du Rwanda* (Leverville: Bibliothèque de l'Étoile)

—— (1959) *Inganji Karinga*. 2 Vols (Kabgayi)

Kagame, P. (2000a) Address to the nation by H.E. Paul Kagame, on his inauguration as President of the Republic of Rwanda. 22 April 2000. <www.rwanda1.com/government/president/speeches/2000/speech_PRINT. html>

—— (2000b) H.E. Paul Kagame, President of the Republic of Rwanda, On the occasion of the official opening of The National Summit on Unity and Reconciliation. 18 October 2000. <www.rwanda1.com/government/ president/speeches/2000/10_18_00_speech_URC_summit_PRINT.html>

—— (2001) Address at Harvard University: Accomplishments and Challenges in Reconciliation and Reconstruction in Rwanda. 5 February 2001. <www.rwanda1.com/government/president/speeches/2001/02_05_01_ken nedy_school_PRINT.html>

—— (2002) Remarks by H.E Paul Kagame, President of the Republic of Rwanda at a State Banquet in Honour of H.E Joachim Chissano, President of the Republic of Mozambique. Kigali, 26 October 2002 <www.rwanda1.com/ government/president/speeches/2001/10_27_02_chissbanq.html>

Kamasa, E. (1998) 'Rwanda–United Nations Relations on the Mend', *New Times*, 11–18 May

Kamera, W. (1978) *Hadithi za Wairaqw* (Dar es Salaam)

Kanhema, N. (1997) 'Rwanda Admits Role in Killing of Hutu Refugees in Ex-Zaïre', *Pan African News Agency*, 27 October. Africanews online, www. africanews.org

Kaplan, R. D. (1994a) 'The Coming Anarchy: how scarcity, crime, overpopulation and disease are rapidly destroying the social fabric of our planet', *Atlantic Monthly*, February 1994 <www.theatlantic.com/election/ connection/foreign/anarcf.htm>

—— (1994b) 'Into the bloody new world: a moral pragmatism for America in an age of mini-holocausts', *Washington Post*, 17 April 1994

Karasira, P. (1996) 'ICTR Kigali Office in Disarray', *New Times*, October 1996

Kayibanda, G. (1964) 'Adresse du Président Kayibanda au Rwandais émigrés ou réfugiés à l'étranger', *Rwanda, Carrefour d'Afrique*, Vol. 31

Khan, S. M. (2000) *The Shallow Graves of Rwanda* (London: I.B. Tauris)

Kigeli, J.-B. (1999) 'Rwandan Monarchy Makes a Firm Statement of Position', Statement Released by the International Strategic Studies Association and *Defense and Foreign Affairs*, 1. October 1999. <www.strategicstudies.org/crisis/rwanda.htm>

Kiley, S. (1994a) 'I saw hills covered with bodies resembling lawns of flesh', *The Times*, 14 May

—— (1994b) 'Tutsi refugees face choice of starvation or being murdered', *The Times*, 14 May

Klapper, J. T. (1960) *The Effects of Mass Communication* (New York: Free Press)

Kritz, N. (1996) 'The rule of law in the post-conflict phase: Building a stable peace' in Crocker, C. A. and F. O. Hampson (eds) *Managing Global Chaos: Sources of and Responses to International Conflict* (Washington DC: US Institute of Peace Press)

Kuper, A. (1988) *The Invention of Primitive Society* (London: Routledge)

LaCapra, D. (1992) 'Representing the Holocaust: Reflections on the Historians' Debate' in Friedlander, S. (ed.) *Probing the Limits of Representation: Nazism and the 'Final Solution'* (Cambridge MA: Harvard University Press)

Laclau, E. and C. Mouffe (1985) *Hegemony and Socialist Strategy: Towards a Radical Democratic Politics* (London: Verso)

Lang, B. (1992) 'The Representation of Limits' in Friedlander, S. (ed.) *Probing the Limits of Representation: Nazism and the 'Final Solution'* (Cambridge MA: Harvard University Press)

Le Monde (1964) 'L'extermination des Tutsis: Les Massacres du Ruanda sont le manifestation d'une haine raciale soigneusement entretenue', *Le Monde*, 4 February

—— (1997) 'Des réfugiés hutu rwandais ont été massacrés dans l'est du Zaire', *Le Monde*, 26 February

Leach, E. (1954) *Political Systems of Highland Burma* (London: G. Bell & Sons)

Lemarchand, R. (1970a) *Rwanda and Burundi* (London: Pall Mall Press)

—— (1970b) 'The coup in Rwanda' in Rothberg, R. I. and A. A. Mazrui (eds) *Protest and Power in Black Africa* (Oxford: Oxford University Press)

—— (1977) 'Rwanda' in Lemarchand, R. (ed.) *African Kingships in Perspective* (London: Frank Cass)

—— (1995) 'Rwanda: The Rationality of Genocide', *Issue: Journal of Opinion*, Vol. 23, No. 2

—— (1996) *Burundi: Ethnic Conflict and Genocide* (Cambridge: Cambridge University Press)

—— (2000) 'Coming to Terms with the Past: The Politics of Memory in Post-Genocide Rwanda', *L'Observatoire de l'Afrique Centrale*, Vol. 3, No. 27. <http://membres.lycos.fr/obsac/OBSV3N27-TermswithPast.html>

—— (2001) 'Disconnecting the Threads: Rwanda and the Holocaust Reconsidered', *Idea: A Journal of Social Issues*, Vol. 7, No. 1. <www.ideajournal.com/genocide-2001-lemarchand.html>

Lemarchand, R. and D. Martin (1974) *Selective Genocide in Burundi* (London: Minority Rights Group)

Levene, M. (1999) 'Connecting Threads: Rwanda, the Holocaust and the Pattern of Contemporary Genocide' in Smith, R. (ed.) *Genocide: Essays Toward Understanding, Early-Warning and Prevention* (Williamsburg VA: Association of Genocide Scholars)

Lévi-Strauss, C. (1966) *The Savage Mind* (Chicago: University of Chicago Press)

Lienhardt, R. G. (1961) *Divinity and Experience: The Religion of the Dinka* (Oxford : Clarendon Press)

Lifton, R. J. (1986) *The Nazi Doctors: Medical Killings and the Psychology of Genocide* (New York: Basic Books)

Linden, I. (1977) *Church and Revolution in Rwanda* (Manchester: Manchester University Press)

—— (1997) 'The Church and Genocide: Lessons from the Rwandan Tragedy' in Baum, G. and H. Wells (eds) *The Reconciliation of Peoples: Challenge to the Churches* (Geneva: WCC Publications)

—— (1998) 'The Role of INGOs in Rwanda: 1990–1998', Paper presented at the *Regional Consultative Workshop on Comprehending and Mastering African Conflicts*, Bamaki, Mali, 1998

Linke, U. (1997) 'Gendered difference, violent imagination: Blood, race, nation', *American Anthropologist*, Vol. 99, No. 3

Little, F. H. (1991) 'Early Warning: Detecting Potentially Genocidal Movements' in Hayes, P. (ed.) *Lessons and Legacies: The Meaning of the Holocaust in a Changing World* (Evanston: Northwestern University Press)

Longman, T. (1998) 'Empowering the Weak and Protecting the Powerful: The Contradictory Nature of Churches in Central Africa', *African Studies Review*, Vol. 41, No. 1

—— (2001) 'Identity Cards, Ethnic Self-Perception, and Genocide in Rwanda' in Caplan, J. and J. Torpey (eds) *Documenting Individual Identity: The Development of State Practices in the Modern World* (Princeton: Princeton University Press)

Loos, B. (1997) 'Moreels accuse les rebelles zaïrois de génocide: La secrétaire d'État à la Coopération persiste et signe. Il s'explique', *Le Soir*, 25 February

Lowe, C. (1997) 'Talking about "Tribe": Moving from stereotypes to analysis', *Africa Policy Information Center* <www.africaaction.org/docs97/eth9711. 1.htm> (Washington DC: APIC)

Lynch, C. (2002) 'U.N. Official Criticises Rwanda', *Washington Post*, 25 July

Lyons, J. (2001) Prepared statement of Mr. James R. Lyons regarding the April 6, 1994 assassination of the Presidents of Rwanda and Burundi in addition to all others on board the Presidential Aircraft. 16 April 2001. <www.truthout.org/docs_01/0180.McKinney.Africa-P.htm>

Lyotard, J.-F. (1997) *The Postmodern Condition: A Report on Knowledge* (Minneapolis: University of Minnesota Press)

Malkki, L. (1995) *Purity and Exile: Violence, Memory and National Cosmology Among Hutu Refugees in Tanzania* (Chicago: University of Chicago Press)

—— (1996) 'Speechless Emissaries: Refugees, Humanitarianism, and Dehistoricization', *Cultural Anthropology*, Vol. 11, No. 3

Mamdani, M. (2001) *When Victims Become Killers: Colonialism, Nativism, and the Genocide in Rwanda* (Oxford: James Currey)

Maquet, J.-J. (1950) 'L'IRSAC au Rwanda', *Grands Lacs*, Vol. 1

—— (1961) *The Premise of Inequality in Ruanda: A Study of Political Relations in Central African Kingdom* (Oxford: Oxford University Press)

Maupas, S. (2000) 'Interview avec Carla del Ponte, procureur général des tribunaux internationaux', *Diplomatie Judiciaire*, 9 June. </www.diplomatie judiciaire.com/Tpir/Parquet31.htm>

Mazur, A. (1998) *A Hazardous Inquiry: The Rashomon Effect at Love Canal* (Cambridge MA: Harvard University Press)

Medécins Sans Frontières (MSF) (1997) *Forced Flight: A Brutal Strategy of Elimination in Eastern Zaïre.* 16 May 1997 (Brussels: MSF)

Meisler, S. (1976) 'Holocaust in Burundi: 1972' in Veehoven, W. (ed.) *Case Studies on Human Rights and Fundamental Freedoms: A World Survey* (The Hague: Nijhoff)

Melson, R. (1992) *Revolution and Genocide: On the Origins of the Armenian Genocide and the Holocaust* (Cambridge: Cambridge University Press)

Melvern, L. R. (2000) *A People Betrayed: The Role of the West in Rwanda's Genocide* (London: Zed)

Michaels, M. (1994a) 'Descent into Mayhem', *Time Magazine*, 18 April

—— (1994b) 'Streets of Slaughter', *Time Magazine*, 25 April

Mikekemo, K. (1996) 'The Conspiracy of Silence', *New Times*, October

—— (1998) 'Capital Punishment Deserving for Rwandan Genocide Perpetrators', *New Times*, 27 April–3 May

Miles, W. (2000) 'Hamites and Hebrews: Problems in "Judaizing" the Rwandan Genocide', *Journal of Genocide Research*, Vol. 2, No. 1

Modood, T. (1997) 'Introduction: The Politics of Multiculturalism in the New Europe' in Modood, T. and P. Werbner (eds) *The Politics of Multiculturalism in the New Europe: Racism, Identity and Community* (London: Zed)

Moerman, M. (1965) 'Ethnic identity in a complex civilization: Who are the Lue?', *American Anthropologist*, Vol. 67

Mucyo, J. (1998) 'Clinton's Historic Visit to Rwanda', *New Times*, 14–21 March

Mukandoli, U. (1998) 'Reflection on Genocide', *New Times*, 17–24 April

Munyaneza, C. (1996) 'Could Genocide Have Been Avoided?', *New Times*, January–February

Munz, P. (1977) *The Shape of Time: A New Look at the Philosophy of History* (Middletown CN: Wesleyan University Press)

Needham, R. (1971) 'Remarks on the analysis of kinship and marriage' in Needham, R. (ed.) *Rethinking Kinship and Marriage* (London: Tavistock)

—— (1975) 'Polythetic Classification: Convergence and Consequences', *Man* Vol. 10, No. 3

Neustadt, R. and E. May (1986) *Thinking in Time: The Uses of History for Decision-Makers* (New York: Free Press)

New Times (1996) 'When the Guilty Have no Conscience', *New Times*, July

—— (1998a) 'Like the Phoenix let us rise from the ashes', *New Times*, 7–14 April

—— (1998b) 'United we stand, divided we fall', *New Times*, 17–24 April

—— (1998c) 'When Justice Tastes Bitter', *New Times*, 27 April–3 May

Newbury, C. (1974) 'Deux Lignages au Kinyaga', *Cahiers d'Études Africaines*, Vol. 14, No. 1

—— (1978) 'Ethnicity in Rwanda: The case of Kinyaga', *Africa*, Vol. 48, No. 1

—— (1980) 'Ubureetwa and Thangata: Catalysts to Peasant Political Consciousness in Rwanda and Malawi', *Canadian Journal of African Studies*, Vol. 14, No. 1

—— (1983) 'Colonialism, ethnicity, and rural political protest: Rwanda and Zanzibar in comparative perspective', *Comparative Politics*, Vol. 15. No. 3

—— (1988) *The Cohesion of Oppression: Clientship and Ethnicity in Rwanda, 1860–1960* (New York: Columbia University Press)

—— (1992) 'Rwanda: Recent Debates over Governance and Rural Development' in Hyden, G. and M. Bratton (eds) *Governance and Politics in Africa* (London: Lynne Rienner)

—— (1996) 'Rwanda: reconciliation or revenge?', *New Routes*, Vol. 1, No. 3. <www.life-peace.org/newroutes/newroutes1996/nr199603/rwanda.htm>

—— (1998) 'Ethnicity and the Politics of History in Rwanda', *Africa Today*, Vol. 45, No. 1

Newbury, C. and D. Newbury (1999) 'A Catholic mass in Kigali: Contested views of the genocide and ethnicity in Rwanda', *Canadian Journal of African Studies*, Vol. 45, No. 1

Newbury, D. (1974) 'Les campaignes de Rwabugiri: chronologie et bibliographie', *Cahiers d'Etudes Africaines*, Vol. 14, No. 1

—— (1980) 'The clans of Rwanda: An historical hypothesis', *Africa*, Vol. 50, No. 4

—— (1991) *Kings and Clans: Ijwi Island and the Lake Kivu Rift, 1780–1840* (Madison: University of Wisconsin Press)

—— (1997) 'Irredentist Rwanda: Ethnic and Territorial Frontiers in Central Africa', *Africa Today*, Vol. 44, No. 2

—— (1998) 'Understanding Genocide', *African Studies Review*, Vol. 41, No. 1

—— (1999) 'Ecology and the politics of genocide: Rwanda 1994', *Cultural Survival Quarterly*, Vol. 22, No. 4. <www.culturalsurvival.org>

Nicholas, H. (2003) 'Search for Justice Stalls in Rwanda', *Washington Times*, 2 January

Novick, P. (2001) *The Holocaust and Collective Memory: The American Experience* (London: Bloomsbury)

Nsengiyaremye, D. (1995) 'La transition démocratique au Rwanda (1989–1993)' in Guichaoua, A. (ed.) *Les crises politiques au Burundi et au Rwanda (1993–1994): Analyses, faits, et documents* (Paris: Éditions Karthala)

Overdulve, C. M. (1997) *Rwanda: un peuple avec une histoire* (Paris: Éditions L'Harmattan)

Pagès, A. (1933) *Au Ruanda: Un royaume hamite au centre de l'Afrique* (Brussels: IRCB)

Parkin, D. (1984) 'Political Language', *Annual Review of Anthropology*, Vol. 13

—— (1987) 'Comparison as the search for continuity' in Holy, L. (ed.) *Comparative Anthropology* (Oxford: Blackwell)

Passmore, J. (1974) 'The Objectivity of History' in Gardiner, P. (ed.) *The Philosophy of History* (Oxford: Oxford University Press)

Péan, P., C. Nick and X. Muntz (2000) 'Bruguière traque le président rwandais', *Le Vrai*, 12 October

Peaslee, A. J. (1965) *Constitutions of Nations. Vol.1, Africa* (The Hague: Nijhoff)

Pêcheux, M. (1982) *Language, Semantics and Ideology* (Basingstoke: Macmillan)

Peet, R. and M. Watts (1993) *Liberation Ecologies* (London: Routledge)

Perraudin, A. (1959) *Lettre Pastorale de Monseigneur Perraudin, Vicaire Apostolique de Kabgayi, pour le carême 1959*, 11 February

Petrie, J. (2000) 'The secular word HOLOCAUST: Scholarly myths, history, and 20th century meanings', *Journal of Genocide Research*, Vol. 2, No. 1

Physicians for Human Rights (PHR) (1997) *Investigations in Eastern Congo and Western Rwanda*. 16 July 1997. <www.phrusa.org/research/health_effects/humcongo.html> (Boston MA: Physicians for Human Rights)

Pomfret, J. (1997a) 'Evidence mounts of atrocities by Kabila's forces', *Washington Post*, 11 June

—— (1997b) 'Rwandans Led Revolt in Congo: Defense Minister Says Arms, Troops Supplied For Anti-Mobutu Drive', *Washington Post*, 9 July. <www.udayton.edu/~rwanda/articles/rpaledrevolt.html>

Pottier, J. (1995) 'Representations of Ethnicity in Post-Genocide Writings on Rwanda' in Igwara, O. (ed.) *Ethnic Hatred: Genocide in Rwanda* (London: ASEN Publication)

—— (1999) 'The "Self" in Self-repatriation: Closing Down Mugunga camp, Eastern Zaïre' in Black, R. and K. Koser (eds) *The End of the Refugee Cycle? Refugee Repatriation and Reconstruction* (Oxford: Berghahn Books)

—— (2002) *Re-Imagining Rwanda: Conflict, Survival and Disinformation in the Late 20th Century* (Cambridge: Cambridge University Press)

Power, S. (2002) *'A Problem from Hell': America and the Age of Genocide* (New York: Basic Books)

Prunier, G. (1993) 'Eléments pour une histoire du Front Patriotique Rwandais', *Politique Africaine*, Vol. 51

—— (1995) *The Rwanda Crisis: History of a Genocide (1959–1994)*. Expanded edn (London: C. Hurst & Co.)

Radcliffe-Brown, A. R. (1951) 'The comparative method in social anthropology', *Journal of the Royal Anthropological Institute*, Vol. 81, No. 1

Ramadhani, H. (1955) *Mapokeo ya Historia Wa-Iraqwa Mbulu*. Mimeo

Ranger, T. (1994[1983]) 'The Invention of Tradition in Colonial Africa' in Hobsbawm E. and T. Ranger (eds) *The Invention of Tradition* (Cambridge: Cambridge University Press)

—— (1996) 'Concluding reflections on cross-mandates' in Allen, T. (ed.) *In Search of Cool Ground: War, Flight and Homecoming in Northeast Africa* (Oxford: James Currey)

Rekdal, O. B. (1998) 'When hypothesis becomes myth: The Iraqi origin of the Iraqw', *Ethnology*, Vol. 37, No. 1

Reyntjens, F. (1985) *Pouvoir et Droit au Rwanda. Droit public et évolution politique 1916–1973* (Brussels: Musée Royal de l'Afrique Centrale)

—— (1994) *L'Afrique des Grands Lacs en Crise Rwanda-Burundi 1988–1994* (Paris: Karthala)

—— (1995a) *Rwanda. Trois jours qui ont fait basculer l'histoire* (Paris: Éditions L'Harmattan)

—— (1995b) *'Akazu*, "Escadrons de la mort" et autres "Réseau Zéro": Un historique des résistances au changement politiques depuis 1990' in Guichaoua, A. (ed.) *Les crises politiques au Burundi et au Rwanda (1993–1994): Analyses, faits, et documents* (Paris: Éditions Karthala)

Richards, P. (1996) *Fighting for the Rain Forest: War, Youth and Resources in Sierra Leone* (Oxford and Portsmouth: James Currey and Heinemann)

Ricouer, P. (1976) *Interpretation Theory: Discourse and the Surplus of Meaning* (Fort Worth: Texas Christian University Press)

Rogers, K. (1996) 'Froduard's Maiden Speech', *New Times*, October

Rosenberg, A. (1987) 'Was the Holocaust unique?: A peculiar question?' in Wallimann, I. and N. Dobkowski (eds) *Genocide and the Modern Age: Etiology and Case Studies of Mass Death* (New York: Greenwood)

Rosenfeld, G. (1999) 'The Politics of Uniqueness: Reflections of the Recent Polemical Turn in Holocaust and Genocide Scholarship', *Holocaust and Genocide Studies*, Vol. 13, No. 1

Ruhumuriza, E. (1996) 'How France Covered up Genocide in Rwanda', *New Times*, 16–25 December

Rutayisire, A. (1995) *Faith Under Fire: Testimonies of Christian Bravery* (Harpenden: African Enterprise)

Sahlins, M. (1985) *Islands of History* (Chicago: University of Chicago Press)

Saint-Jean, A. (1994) 'Rwanda: An activist reflects on her nation's trauma and recovery', *Ms Magazine*, Vol. 5, No. 3

Sanders, E. (1969) 'The Hamitic Hypothesis: Its Origin and Functions in Time Perspective', *The Journal of African History*, Vol. 10, No. 4

Santayana, G. (1905) *Life of Reason, Reason in Common Sense*, Vol. I (New York: Charles Scribner's Sons)

Santer, E. L. (1992) 'History beyond the Pleasure Principle: Some Thoughts on the Representation of Trauma' in Friedlander, S. (ed.) *Probing the Limits of Representation: Nazism and the 'Final Solution'* (Cambridge MA: Harvard University Press)

Sasserath, J. (1948) *Le Ruanda-Urundi, étrange royaume féodal* (Brussels)

Schabas, W. A. (2000) *Genocide in International Law* (Cambridge: Cambridge University Press)

Schabas, W. A. and M. Imbleau (eds) (1997) *Introduction to Rwandan Law* (Quebec: Éditions Yvon Blais)

Schafft, G. E. (2002) 'Scientific Racism in Service of the Reich: German Anthropologists in the Nazi Era' in Hinton, A. L. (ed.) *Annihilating Difference: The Anthropology of Genocide* (Berkeley: University of California Press)

Scherrer, C. P. (1999) *Genocide and Genocide Prevention: General Outlines Exemplified with the Cataclysm in Rwanda 1994*. <www.copri.dk/publications/WP/WP%201999/14–1999.doc>. COPRI Working Paper, No. 18 (Copenhagen: Copenhagen Peace Research Institute)

Scott, J. (1985) *Weapons of the Weak: Everyday Forms of Peasant Resistance* (New Haven: Yale University Press)

Service, E. R. (1962) *Primitive Social Organization: An Evolutionary Perspective* (New York: Random House)

—— (1975) *Origins of the State and Civilization: The Process of Cultural Evolution* (New York: W. W. Norton & Company)

Sibomana, A. (1999) *Hope for Rwanda: Conversations with Laure Gilbert and Hervé Deguine*. Trans. C. Tertsakian (London: Pluto)

Smis, S. (2000) 'The Legal Status of International Land Boundaries in Africa' in Doom, R. and J. Gorus (eds) *Politics of Identity and Economics of Conflict in the Great Lakes Region* (Brussels: VUB University Press)

Smith, R. W. (1987) 'Human destructiveness and politics: The twentieth century as an age of genocide' in Wallimann, I. and N. Dobkowski (eds) *Genocide and the Modern Age: Etiology and Case Studies of Mass Death* (New York: Greenwood)

—— (1998) 'State Power and Genocide Intent: On the Uses of Genocide in the Twentieth Century' in Chorbajian, L. and G. Shirinian (eds) *Studies in Comparative Genocide* (Basingstoke: Macmillan Press)

Southall, A. (1970) 'The illusion of tribe', *Journal of Asian and African Studies*, Vol. 5, No. 1

Soyinka, W. (1998) 'Hearts of Darkness', *New York Times Book Review*, 4 October

Stanford, M. (1994) *A Companion to the Study of History* (Oxford: Blackwell)

Stanton, G. (1989) 'Blue Scarves and Yellow Stars: Classification and Symbolisation in the Cambodian Genocide', Occasional Paper for the Montreal Institute of Genocide Studies, April 1989. <www.genocide watch.org/bluescarves.htm>

—— (1998) *Eight Stages of Genocide*. <www.genocidewatch.org/8stages.htm> (Washington DC: Genocide Watch)

Staub, E. (1989) *The Roots of Evil: The Origins of Genocide and Other Group Violence* (Cambridge: Cambridge University Press)

Stockton, N. (1996) *Rwanda: Rights and Racism*. Unpublished paper, released in December 1996

Storey, A. (2000) 'Story-Lines and Scapegoats: Discourse, the Rwandan Economy and Genocide', Unpublished ms (Dublin: Holy Ghost College)

Street, B. (1993) 'Culture as a Verb: Anthropological Aspects of Language and Cultural Processes' in Graddol, D., L. Thompson and M. Byram (eds) *Language and Culture* (London: BAAL and Multilingual Matters)

Struever, N. (1970) *The Language of History in the Renaissance: Rhetoric and Historical Consciousness in Florentine Humanism* (Princeton: Princeton University Press)

Swain, J. (1998) 'On the trail of the child killers: Colonel granted sanctuary in Britain denies genocide', *Sunday Times*, 6 December

Taussig, M. (2002) 'Culture of Terror: Torture and the Putumayo' in Hinton, A. L. (ed.) *Genocide: An Anthropological Reader* (Oxford: Blackwell)

Taylor, A. J. P. (1956) 'The Rise and Fall of "Pure" Diplomatic History', *Times Literary Supplement*, 6 January 1956

Taylor, C. (1999) *Sacrifice as Terror: The Rwandan Genocide of 1994* (Oxford: Berg)

Totten, S. and W. S. Parsons (1997) 'Introduction' in Totten, S., W. S. Parsons and W. S. Charny (eds) *Century of Genocide: Eyewitness Accounts and Critical Views* (London: Garland Publishing)

Tylor, E. B. (1871) *Primitive Culture: Researches into the Development of Mythology, Philosophy, Religion, Language, Art, and Custom* (London: J. Murray)

—— (1893) 'Anthropology' in *Encyclopaedia Britannica*

United Nations (1960) UN Visiting Mission to Trust Territories in East Africa: Report on Ruanda-Urundi. UN Doc. T/551

United Nations (UN) (1964) *Report of the Officer-in-Charge of the United Nations Operation in the Congo to the Secretary General*. 29 September 1964

—— (1985) *Revised and Updated Report on the Question of the Prevention and Punishment of the Crime of Genocide*. 2 July 1985. UN Doc. E/CN.4/ Sub.2/1985/6. <www.preventgenocide.org/prevent/UNdocs/whitaker>

—— (1993) Report by B. W. Ndiaye, Special Rapporteur, on his mission to Rwanda from 8 to 17 April 1993. 11 August 1993. UN Doc. E/CN.4/1994/ 7/Add.1. <www.preventgenocide.org/prevent/UNdocs/ndiaye1993.htm>

—— (1994a) Statement by the President of the Security Council. 7 April 1994. UN Doc. S/PRST/1994/16

—— (1994b) Special report of the Secretary General on UNAMIR. 20 April 1994. UN Doc. S/1994/470

—— (1994c) Security Council resolution adjusting UNAMIR's mandate and authorising a reduction in its strength. 21 April 1994. UN Doc. S/RES/912(1994)

—— (1994d) Letter from the Secretary-General to the President of the Security Council requesting that the Council re-examine the revised mandate given to UNAMIR in resolution 912(1994) and consider what action it could take in order to restore law and order in Rwanda and end the massacres. 29 April 1994. UN Doc. S/1994/518

—— (1994e) Statement by the President of the Security Council. 30 April 1994. UN Doc. S/PRST/1994/21

—— (1994f) Security Council resolution expanding UNAMIR to 5,500 troops and mandating UNAMIR II to provide security to displaced persons, refugees and civilians at risk and to support relief efforts and imposing an arms embargo on Rwanda. 17 May 1994. UN Doc. S/RES/918

—— (1994g) Report of the United Nations High Commissioner for Human Rights on his Mission to Rwanda of 11–12 May 1994. 19 May 1994. UN Doc. E/CN.4/S-3/3

—— (1994h) Resolution adopted by the UN Commission on Human Rights at its Third Special Session: The situation of Human Rights in Rwanda. 25 May 1994. UN Doc. E/CN.4/S-3/4

—— (1994i) Report of the Secretary-General on the situation in Rwanda. 31 May 1994. UN Doc. S/1994/640

—— (1994j) Security Council Resolution extending the mandate of UNAMIR until 9 December 1994 and authorising the deployment of two additional battalions. 8 June 1994. UN Doc. S/RES/925

—— (1994k) Report on the situation of human rights in Rwanda submitted by Mr. R. Degni-Ségui, Special Rapporteur of the Commission on Human Rights. 28 June 1994. UN Doc. E/CN.4/1995/7

—— (1994l) Security Council Resolution 935 (1994). 1 July 1994. UN Doc. S/RES/935 (1994)

—— (1994m) Report of the Secretary-General on the Establishment of the Commission of Experts Pursuant to Paragraph 1 of Security Council Resolution 935 (1994) of 1 July 1994. 26 July 1994. UN Doc. S/1994/879

—— (1994n) Letter dated 28 September 1994 from the Permanent Representative of Rwanda to the United Nations addressed to the President of the Security Council, transmitting a statement of the Government of Rwanda on the establishment of an International Tribunal for the prosecution of persons responsible for genocide and other serious violations of international humanitarian law in relation to Rwanda. 29 September 1994. UN Doc. S/1994/1115

—— (1994o) Letter dated 1 October 1994 from the Secretary General to the President of the Security Council transmitting the interim report of Commission of Experts on the evidence of grave violations of international humanitarian law in Rwanda, including possible acts of genocide (Annex: Preliminary Report of the Independent Commission of Experts established in accordance with Security Council resolution 935 (1994)). 4 October 1994. UN Doc. S/1994/1125

—— (1994p) Verbatim record of the 3453rd meeting of the Security Council, 8 November 1994. UN Doc. S/PV.3453

—— (1994q) Security Council Resolution Establishing the ICTR. 8 November 1994. UN Doc. S/RES/955. <www.ictr.org/wwwroot/ENGLISH/Resolutions/955e.htm>

—— (1994r) Report on the situation of human rights in Rwanda submitted by Mr. R. Degni-Ségui, Special Rapporteur of the Commission on Human Rights, under paragraph 20 of Commission resolution E/CN.4/S-3/1 of 25 May 1994. 14 November 1994. UN Doc S/1994/1157/Add.1

—— (1994s) Letter from the Secretary-General to the President of the Security Council transmitting the final report of the Commission of Experts (Annex: Final Report of the Commission of Experts established pursuant to Security Council resolution 935 (1994)). 9 December 1994. UN Doc. S/1994//1405

—— (1994t) Report on the situation of human rights in Zaïre, prepared by the Special Rapporteur, Mr. Roberto Garretón, in accordance with Commission resolution 1994/87. 23 December 1994. UN Doc. E/CN.4/1995/67. <www1.umn.edu/humanrts/commission/country51/67.htm>

—— (1996a) Report on the situation of human rights in Zaïre, prepared by the Special Rapporteur, Mr. Roberto Garretón, in accordance with Commission resolution 1995/69. 29 January 1996. UN Doc. E/CN.4/1996/66. <www1.umn.edu/humanrts/commission/country52/66-zre.htm>

—— (1996b) Report of the International Commission of Inquiry [into arms trade to the ex-FAR]. UN doc. S/1996/195 annex. March 1996

—— (1996c) Situation of human rights in Rwanda. Sub-Commission on Prevention of Discrimination and Protection of Minorities. Resolution 1996/3. 19 August 1996

—— (1996d) Report on the situation of human rights in Zaïre, prepared by the Special Rapporteur, Mr. Robert Garretón, in accordance with Commission resolution 1996/77. 16 September 1996. UN Doc. E/CN.4/1997/6/Add.1. <www1.umn.edu/humanrts/commission/thematic53/97ZAIRE.htm>

—— (1996e) Letter dated 25 July 1996 from the Secretary General to the President of the Security Council transmitting the report of the International Commission of Inquiry on the 21 October 1993 assassination of the President of Burundi, Melchior Ndadaye, and the massacres that followed (Annex: report of the International Commission of Inquiry on the 21 October 1993 assassination of the President of Burundi, Melchior Ndadaye, and the massacres that followed). UN Doc S/1996/682

—— (1997a) Report on the situation of human rights in Zaïre, prepared by the Special Rapporteur, Mr. Roberto Garretón, in accordance with Commission resolution 1996/77. 28 January 1997. UN Doc. E/CN.4/1997/6. <www.hri.ca/fortherecord1997/documentation/commission/e-cn4–1997–6.htm>

—— (1997b) Report on the situation of human rights in Zaïre, prepared by the Special Rapporteur, Mr. Robert Garretón, in accordance with Commission resolution 1996/77 Addendum Report on the mission carried out at the request of the High Commissioner for Human Rights between

25 and 29 March 1997 to the area occupied by rebels in eastern Zaïre. 2 April 1997. UN Doc. E/CN.4/1997/6/Add.2. <www.hri.ca/fortherecord1997/documentation/commission/e-cn4-1997-6-add2.htm>

—— (1997c) Report of the joint mission charged with investigating allegations of massacres and other human rights violations occurring in eastern Zaïre (now Democratic Republic of the Congo) since September 1996. 2 July 1997. UN Doc. A/51/942

—— (1998a) Letter dated 29 June 1998 from the Secretary General addressed to the President of the Security Council with the Annex 'Report of the Secretary General's Investigative Team charged with investigating serious violations of human rights and international humanitarian law in the Democratic Republic of Congo'. 29 June 1998. UN Doc S/1998/581

—— (1998b) Letter dated 25 June 1998 from the Permanent Representative of the Democratic Republic of the Congo to the United Nations Addressed to the Secretary-General. 25 June 1998. UN Doc. S/1998/582. <www.hri.ca/fortherecord1998/documentation/security/s-1998-582.htm>

—— (1998c) Letter dated 25 June 1998 from the Permanent Representative of Rwanda to the United Nations addressed to the Secretary-General. 29 June 1998. UN Doc. S/1998/583. <www.hri.ca/fortherecord1998/documentation/security/s-1998-583.htm>

—— (1998d) Statement by the President of the Security Council. 13 July 1998. UN Doc. S/PRST/1998/20. <www.hri.ca/fortherecord1998/documentation/security/s-prst-1998-20.htm>

United Nations High Commissioner for Refugees (UNHCR) (1996) UNHCR worries over fate of refugees in Zaïre. Press Release, 6 December 1996. (Geneva: UNHCR)

United Nations Wire (2002) 'Del Ponte Protests to Security Council that Rwanda is not Co-operating', *UN Wire/United Nations Foundation*, 25 July 2002. <www.unfoundation.org/unwire/2002/07/25/current.asp>

US Committee for Refugees (USCR) (1996) 'How many refugees are in eastern Zaïre? Why estimates Vary'. 26 November 1996. <www.refugees.org/news/press_releases/1996/112696.htm>. (Washington DC: USCR)

—— (1997) Site visit to Eastern Congo-Zaire. Analysis of Humanitarian and Political Issues. April 16 to May 10 1997. June 1997 (Washington DC: USCR)

US Congress (1996) *Refugees in Eastern Zaïre and Rwanda*. Hearing before the Subcommittee on International Operations and Human Rights of the Committee on International Relations, House of Representatives, 4 December 1996. <commdocs.house.gov/committees/intlrel/hfa43123.000/hfa43123_0f.htm>

US State Department (1996i) Daily Press Briefing. 3 December 1996. <www.hri.org/news/usa/std/96-12-03.std.html>

—— (1996ii) Daily Press Briefing. 4 December 1996. <www.hri.org/news/usa/std/96-12-04.std.html>

Uvin, P. (1997) 'Prejudice, Crisis, and Genocide in Rwanda', *African Studies Review*, Vol. 40, No. 2

—— (1998) *Aiding Violence: The Development Enterprise in Rwanda* (West Hartford CN: Kumarian Press)

Vail, L. (1989) 'Introduction: Ethnicity in Southern African History' in Vail, L. (ed.) *The Creation of Tribalism in Southern Africa* (London: James Currey)

Van der Kelen, L. (1997) 'Genocide in Oost-Zaïre: Concrete bewijzen nieuwe massamoorden', *Het Laatste Nieuws*, 22 February

Van Hoyweghen, S. (1996) 'The Disintegration of the Catholic Church in Rwanda: A Study of the Fragmentation of Political and Religious Authority', *African Affairs*, Vol. 95, No. 308

Vansina, J. (1998) 'The Politics of History and the Crisis in the Great Lakes', *Africa Today*, Vol. 45, No. 1

Verwimp, P. (2000) 'Development ideology, the peasantry and genocide: Rwanda represented in Habyarimana's speeches', *Journal of Genocide Research*, Vol. 2, No. 3

Victor, K. (1998) 'Bisesero: a symbol of resistance', *New Times*, 17–24 April

Vidal, C. (1974) 'Economie de la Société Feodale Rwandaise', *Cahiers d'Etudes Africaines*, Vol. 14, No. 1

—— (1991) *Sociologie des Passions: Côte d'Ivoire, Rwanda* (Paris: Khartala)

Visathan, V. (1996) 'Hutuland Tutsiland?', *New Times*, January–February

Vlassenroot, K. (2000) 'Identity and Insecurity: The Building of Ethnic Agendas in South Kivu' in Doom, R. and J. Gorus (eds) *Politics of Identity and Economics of Conflict in the Great Lakes Region* (Brussels: VUB University Press)

Wagner, M. D. (1998) 'All the bourgmestre's men: making sense of genocide in Rwanda', *Africa Today*, Vol. 45, No. 25

Watson, C. (1991) *Exile from Rwanda: Background to an Invasion* (Washington DC: USCR)

Watson, P. (1994) 'Tribal Feuds Throw Rwanda in Crisis', *Toronto Star*, 23 February

Weber, M. (1949) '"Objectivity" in Social Science and Social Policy' in Shils, E. A. and H. A. Finch (eds) *The Methodology of the Social Sciences* (New York: Free Press)

Weissman, S. (1997) 'Living with Genocide: The U.S. could play a significant role in stopping African genocide – but it doesn't', *Tikkun*, Vol. 12, No. 4

Whitaker, B. (1985) Revised and Updated Report on the Question of the Prevention and Punishment of the Crime of Genocide. 2 July 1985. UN Doc. E/CN.4/Sub.2/1985/6. www.preventgenocide.org/prevent/UNdocs/whitaker

White, H. (1973) *Metahistory: The Historical Imagination in Nineteenth Century Europe* (Baltimore: Johns Hopkins University Press)

—— (1987) 'The value of narrativity in the representation of reality' in White, H. *The Content of the Form* (Baltimore: Johns Hopkins University Press)

—— (1992) 'Historical Emplotment and the Problem of Truth' in Friedlander, S. (ed.) *Probing the Limits of Representation: Nazism and the 'Final Solution'* (Cambridge MA: Harvard University Press)

Whitehead, A. N. (1967) Science and the Modern World (New York: Free Press)

Wiesel, E. (1968) *Legends of Our Time* (New York: Holt, Rinehart & Winston)

Willum, B. (2000) 'ICTR Prosecutor rejects allegations of Kagame arrest warrant', *Rwanda Newsline*, 30 October. <www.willum.com/articles/rwanda30oct2000/indexright.htm>

Wilson, R. (1997) 'Representing Human Rights Violations: Social Contexts and Subjectivities' in Wilson, R. (ed.) *Human Rights, Culture and Context, Anthropological Perspectives* (London: Pluto Press)

—— (2001) *The Politics of Truth and Reconciliation in South Africa: Legitimizing the Post-Apartheid State* (Cambridge: Cambridge University Press)

Winter, R. (1994) 'Power, not tribalism, stokes Rwanda's slaughter', *Toronto Globe*, 14 April

Wurzburger, W. S. (1980) 'The Holocaust Meaning or Impact', *Shoah*, Vol. 2, No. 1

Xinhua (1998) 'Extradite Criminals says the Government', *New Times* 11–18 May

Yinger, J. M. (1994) *Ethnicity: Source of strength? Source of conflict?* (Albany: State University of New York Press)

INTEGRATED REGIONAL INFORMATION NETWORK (IRIN) FOR
CENTRAL AND EASTERN AFRICA (UNITED NATIONS: OFFICE
FOR THE CO-ORDINATION OF HUMANITARIAN AFFAIRS)

IRIN (1996i) The Conflict in South Kivu, Zaïre and its Regional Implications. 7 October 1996

—— (1996ii) Update on the Conflict in South Kivu. 11 October 1996

—— (1996iii) Weekly Roundup of Main Events in the Great Lakes Region 7–13 October 1996. 13 October 1996

—— (1996iv) Weekly Roundup of Main Events in the Great Lakes Region 14–21 October 1996. 22 October 1996

—— (1996v) Weekly Roundup of Main Events in the Great Lakes Region 22–7 October 1996. 27 October 1996

—— (1996vi) Update on South Kivu. 26 October 1996

—— (1996vii) Emergency Update (EU) #1 on Kivu, Zaïre. 30 October 1996

—— (1996viii) EU #2 on Eastern Zaïre. 31 October 1996

—— (1996ix) EU #3 on Eastern Zaïre. 1 November 1996

—— (1996x) EU #4 on Eastern Zaïre. 2 November 1996

—— (1996xi) EU #5 on Eastern Zaïre. 4 November 1996

—— (1996xii) EU #6 on Eastern Zaïre. 4 November 1996

—— (1996xiii) EU #7 on Eastern Zaïre. 5 November 1996

—— (1996xiv) EU #8 on Eastern Zaïre. 5 November 1996

—— (1996xv) EU #9 on Eastern Zaïre. 6 November 1996

—— (1996xvi) EU #10 on Eastern Zaïre. 6 November 1996

—— (1996xvii) EU #11 on Eastern Zaïre. 7 November 1996

—— (1996xviii) EU #12 on Eastern Zaïre. 7 November 1996

—— (1996xix) EU #13 on Eastern Zaïre. 8 November 1996

—— (1996xx) EU #14 on Eastern Zaïre. 8 November 1996

—— (1996xxi) EU #16 on Eastern Zaïre. 11 November 1996

—— (1996xxii) EU #17 on Eastern Zaïre. 11 November 1996

—— (1996xxiii) EU #18 on Eastern Zaïre. 12 November 1996

—— (1996xxiv) EU #19 on Eastern Zaïre. 12 November 1996

—— (1996xxv) EU #20 on Eastern Zaïre. 13 November 1996

—— (1996xxvi) EU #21 on Eastern Zaïre. 13 November 1996

—— (1996xxvii) EU #22 on Eastern Zaïre. 14 November 1996
—— (1996xxviii) EU #23 on Eastern Zaïre. 14 November 1996
—— (1996xxix) EU #24 on Eastern Zaïre. 15 November 1996
—— (1996xxx) EU #25 on Eastern Zaïre. 15 November 1996
—— (1996xxxi) Bulletin. 15 November 1996
—— (1996xxxii) EU #26 on Eastern Zaïre. 16 November 1996
—— (1996xxxiii) EU #27 on Eastern Zaïre. 17 November 1996
—— (1996xxxiv) EU #28 on Eastern Zaïre. 18 November 1996
—— (1996xxxv) EU #29 on Eastern Zaïre. 18 November 1996
—— (1996xxxvi) EU #30 on Eastern Zaïre. 19 November 1996
—— (1996xxxvii) EU #31 on Eastern Zaïre. 19 November 1996
—— (1996xxxviii) EU #32 on Eastern Zaïre. 20 November 1996
—— (1996xxxix) EU #33 on Eastern Zaïre. 20 November 1996
—— (1996xl) EU #34 on Eastern Zaïre. 21 November 1996
—— (1996xli) EU #36 on Eastern Zaïre. 22 November 1996
—— (1996xlii) EU #38 on Eastern Zaïre. 25 November 1996
—— (1996xliii) EU #58 on Eastern Zaïre. 16 December 1996
—— (1997i) EU #75 on the Great Lakes. 9 January 1997
—— (1997ii) EU #84 on the Great Lakes. 22 January 1997
—— (1997iii) EU #88 on the Great Lakes. 28 January 1997
—— (1997iv) EU #89 on the Great Lakes. 29 January 1997
—— (1997v) EU #92 on the Great Lakes. 3 February 1997
—— (1997vi) EU #95 on the Great Lakes. 6 February 1997
—— (1997vii) EU #97 on the Great Lakes. 8–10 February 1997
—— (1997viii) EU #98 on the Great Lakes. 11 February 1997
—— (1997ix) EU #104 on the Great Lakes. 18 February 1997
—— (1997x) EU #106 on the Great Lakes. 21 February 1997
—— (1997xi) EU #109 on the Great Lakes. 26 February 1997
—— (1997xii) EU #111 on the Great Lakes. 28 February 1997
—— (1997xiii) EU #113 on the Great Lakes. 3 March 1997
—— (1997xiv) EU #245 on the Great Lakes. 10 September 1997
—— (1997xv) EU #257 on the Great Lakes. 26 September 1997
—— (1997xvi) EU #279 on the Great Lakes. 26 October 1997
—— (1997xvii) EU #280 on the Great Lakes. 29 October 1997
—— (1998i) Update No. 335 for Central and Eastern Africa. 17–19 January 1998
—— (1998ii) Rwanda executes 22 people convicted of genocide. 24 April 1998
—— (1998iii) Update No. 435 for Central and Eastern Africa. 11 June 1998
—— (1998iv) Update No. 503 for Central and Eastern Africa. 16 September 1998
—— (1998v) Update No. 517 for Central and Eastern Africa. 6 October 1998
—— (1998vi) Update No. 528 Central and Eastern Africa. 21 October 1998
—— (2000i) Amnesty concerned over arrested soldiers. 25 February 2000
—— (2000ii) Murder Of Presidential Adviser 'Political Killing'. 7 March 2000
—— (2000iii) Genocide 'revisionists' out to discredit government. 20 March 2000
—— (2000iv) UN memorandum on 1994 plane crash found. 29 March 2000
—— (2000v) UN memo on Habyarimana plane crash 'under seal'. 10 April 2000

—— (2000vi) Genocide suspect to be interviewed on Habyarimana crash. 8 May 2000

—— (2000vii) French judge interviews genocide suspects. 17 May 2000

—— (2000viii) Genocide suspects request plane crash report. 26 May 2000

—— (2000ix) Tribunal rejects request to order plane crash inquiry. 2 June 2000

—— (2000x) Tribunal orders release of internal UN memo. 9 June 2000

—— (2000xi) Tribunal denies French judge plane crash report. 22 June 2000

—— (2000xii) Update No. 1038 for the Great Lakes. 24 October 2000

—— (2000xiii) Del Ponte addresses alleged RPF massacres with Kagame. 14 December 2000

—— (2000xiv) Government denies links with Habyarimana's death. 19 December 2000

—— (2001i) Former mayor goes on trial. 14 March 2001

—— (2001ii) Update No. 1153 for the Great Lakes. 10 April 2001

—— (2001iii) Government welcomes arrest of genocide suspects. 13 July 2001

—— (2001iv) Government puts genocide victims at 1.07 million. 19 December 2001

—— (2002i) ICJ rejects Belgium's arrest warrant of Ndombasi. 15 February 2002

—— (2002ii) ICTR preparing to indict first Tutsis. 12 April 2002

Index